eenagers

A Natural History

Teenagers

DAVID BAINBRIDGE

GREYSTONE BOOKS

D&M PUBLISHERS INC.

Vancouver/Toronto/Berkeley

Greystone Books
A division of D&M Publishers Inc.
2323 Quebec Street, Suite 201
Vancouver BC Canada V5T 4S7
www.greystonebooks.com

Published simultaneously in Great Britain in 2009
by Portobello Books, London.

Library and Archives Canada Cataloguing in Publication
Bainbridge, David–
Teenagers : a natural history / David Bainbridge.—Canadian ed.

ISBN 978-1-55365-437-7

1. Adolescence. 2. Teenagers. 3. Adolescent psychology. I. Title.

HQ796.B257 2009   305.235   C2008-906636-7

Text design by Lindsay Nash
Cover design and illustration by James Nunn
Printed and bound in Canada by Friesens
Printed on acid-free paper that is forest friendly (100% post-
consumer recycled paper) and has been processed chlorine free
Distributed in the U.S. by Publishers Group West.

This book is dedicated to everyone I knew back then. Hmm.

Contents

Introduction
A Silver Lining

Being a teenager is a positive and understandable experience. I realize that it is rarely described in those terms, but I aim to convince you that this statement is true.

Everyone reading this book will either have experienced adolescence or be experiencing it right now. And we all feel its effects for ever. The teenage years are in fact the most interesting of your life. Science says so. These years can also be the most positive – it all depends on what you make of them.

Between ten and twenty, many things can happen for the first time, some of them good, some of them not, and some of them somewhere in between. You will decide for yourself which is which over the course of this book: acne, adult relationships, alcohol, big exams, breasts, depression, driving, drugs, empathy, growth spurts, independence from parents, masturbation, new and alarming hair, orgasm, pornography, puberty, responsibility, self-control, sex, smelliness, smoking, work. That alphabetical list is certainly not complete, but it does give you a taste of how much has to be packed into a decade.

However, the sheer number of new things that have to be

done is not the only problem. None of us goes through adolescence in isolation. When you are a teenager, there seems to be a bewildering number of experts around. Everyone wants to give you advice on what you should and should not do, how you should do it and with whom you should do it. There soon arises in the young mind a suspicion that adults cannot really remember their own teenage years clearly enough to be able to give good advice. This suspicion feeds into a growing mistrust of authority, which gets even worse when teenagers discover that adults cherish such distrust in themselves, but dislike it in anyone under twenty years old. Surely this is the time when people are meant to grow up enough to stop believing everything they are told?

So an inescapable conflict is built into adolescence. Just when we become mature enough to want to make our own decisions, everyone starts telling us to work hard, plan ahead, not to drink, not to take drugs and not to sleep with anyone. When teenagers then press their elders for the reasons for their advice, those reasons are rarely forthcoming. A good example of this is the taking of illegal drugs. We all know that many people take drugs and seem to enjoy them, yet at the same time teenagers are continually told that drugs are 'bad'. All the sensible teenage mind can conclude is that someone out there is either wrong or lying. This is not being difficult, it is simply being logical. But why does advice to teenagers so often come without evidence to back it up? If adults are completely truthful, do they usually know what the evidence actually is?

This brings me on to the approach of this book. Where can the evidence be found? The good, and perhaps surprising, news is that the evidence is already in existence – although much of it has only appeared in the past five years. We now know a great deal about drugs, sex, puberty and the teenage brain; this knowledge just needs to be presented in a sensible, clear way so that we can all see how we function as teenagers, and what lessons we can learn. The efforts of scientists, doctors and therapists in the past few decades have revolutionized our understanding of every part of the growing-up process. We know how most of human adolescence works and we also have some good ideas about why it evolved in that way. It can seem messy, unpredictable and even perverse at times, but there is an undeniable pattern at work underneath all that teenage tumult. In writing this book, as I have distilled the developmental biology, the palaeoanthropology, the neuroscience, the physiology, the psychology, the therapy and the politics, I have become ever more convinced that adolescence is the most crucial time of our lives.

As you can see, I believe that adolescence is eminently 'understandable', but you may remember that I also recklessly used the word 'positive'.

The teenage years are potentially a very good time in your life. Unfortunately, people often talk about them as if they were no more than an unpleasant hurdle between blissful childhood and mature adulthood. Admittedly, there are many things to be done in our second decade of existence, and I have already listed a few of them, but they are best seen as a positive opportunity. Indeed, our understanding of human evolution and the history of human society supports this more upbeat view. Instead of a painful and uncertain transition between two stages in life, being a teenager should be seen as a time when we can have the best of both worlds – the charming wonder of a child and the reassuring independence of an adult.

Compared to other animals, human beings have an unusually long pre-adult existence, and it would be perverse to claim that this is simply to extend a period of suffering. Instead, much of the evidence suggests that evolution has given us our teenage years for a very good reason – in the long run they help us to succeed as individuals (that is what evolution tends to do). It is a time when we can play a little, live a little and grow up a little. Sometimes we are given the impression that adolescence is a time fraught with extreme danger and stress. Obviously nothing comes without risk, but we should never lose sight of the fact that being a teenager is a unique opportunity to experiment with the world, ourselves and other people. Things may seem very serious at the time, but few of our teenage actions have long term consequences for when we are older. I sometime worry that we make teenagers too frightened to try new things – after all, life is for living. Everyone should have been just a little bit irresponsible before they get to twenty.

So why should I be the one to write this book, and why did I want to?

Perhaps I should tell you a little bit about my life, to reassure you that I can approach the subject of being a teenager from an unusual and unbiased angle. Obviously, I can do the usual glib adult thing of saying, 'I was a teenager once,' and this is of course true. More specifically, I can tell you that I was born nine months before the first moon landing and was brought up in the south of England. I was a happy little kid and ended up doing most of the usual teenager things: trying to get served in pubs under age and trying to go out with people who could drive cars. I argued a bit but had a lot of fun and then I went to university, where I had even more fun. I happen to have a good memory, so I was able to get on a course to train to be a vet. Because of this, I am already adept at dealing with aggressive furry animals. I also developed an interest in how evolution has shaped us humans over the last billion years, and this fascination has stayed with me – right into the writing of this book.

I then worked as a vet for a year, which often meant spending my time explaining biology to sensible and interested members of the public who happened not to have any scientific training – something I now do in my books. I then went to do scientific research at the Institute of Zoology in London, a maternity hospital in Oxford and a vet school in London, and I also started to teach university students as well as advising school students thinking about their future careers. Gradually this started to take over, and my main job at Cambridge is now teaching and advising students full-time.

While all this was going on, I somehow fell into writing books about biology for the general public. The first one was about pregnancy, the second was about sexuality and the third about the brain. I worked hard on my old veterinary ability to explain biology to people, and I hope that shows in this fourth book. Writing the books has taught me that just about anything in biology can be made fun and comprehensible if you cut out all the long words and simply try and tell a story. Crucially, the books also made me realize what a pivotal time the teenage years are, but how little of this is common knowledge.

These became my main motives to write this book, and also the reasons why I thought I was the person to write it. I am interested in growth, sex and the mind, and why evolution has left us growing, copulating and thinking the way that we do. I think the story of being a teenager is worth telling, and that it might help some people understand themselves and their foibles a little better. Much of my work involves older teenagers, and I am constantly horrified by how many young people who seem attractive, intelligent and confident on the outside are torn apart inside by insecurity, anxiety and self-doubt. My aim in this book is to explain why these things happen, and why there are ways to help.

One enemy of the enjoyment of being a teenager is that adolescence can sometimes be rather over-analysed – too vulnerable to the reductionist's knife. That may seem a strange thing for someone to say when they have written a book about how teenagers work, but let me tell you what I mean. There have been many books written about puberty, and many about sex education. There are also lots about drugs and addiction and even more about teenage relationships. There are even a few which specifically explain the 'teenage brain'. Many of these books are extremely good, but I do worry that they create a sense that these different topics are entirely separate from each other. Yet so far as I recall, being a teenager was more of a mish-mash of all these things – trying to form relationships while my body did weird things and my brain started to work in a different way (at least when it wasn't infused with alcohol or other things), all the time being aware that my whole being was becoming sexualized. It was all much vaguer and mixed up than the books suggest, and perhaps it is that chaotic unpredictability that can lift being a teenager to a higher, more intense level of experience than any other phase in our lives.

So it is important not to think of adolescence as involving several discrete, unconnected changes. Instead, they all overlap – your sex affects the way you work, your relationships affect your reactions to having sex, drugs affect your moods, and so on. However, I needed to chop this book into manageable sections, so the five parts are (in order) about: growing; thinking; drugs; relationships, and sex.

But they will blur together to some extent. Everything is going on at the same time, and each aspect of teenage life affects every other. And the reason why being a teenager can seem more confusing than any other 'life stage' is that there are simply more things happening than at any other time – a teenager is neither a child nor an adult, but a complex mixture of both. These years are not a gap – rather they are a wonderfully exciting collision when all the different strands of our life get tangled together in a way that will never happen again.

And out of that beautiful tangle will come the strands that make up an adult, much better prepared because of their teenage years. As we will see in this book, evolution created teenagers because they are the best way to become adults. We cannot live for ever, so we must replace ourselves with new people – in other words, our offspring are our way of cheating death. Could adolescence be any more positive than that?

Adolescence can be a wonderful, valuable time. Being young is a gift, not an ordeal.

1. Aches and Gripes and Lumps and Bumps

Why growing up is hard to do

Conversation by the pool:
My three-year-old nephew: 'Where's your willy?'
My three-year-old daughter: 'I haven't got a willy.'
My three-year-old nephew: 'Then how do you wee?'

The only time in my life when I have kept a diary was between the ages of fourteen and eighteen.
Although this is not an age usually associated with diligence in boys, I wrote an entry every day for three and a half years, almost always within twenty-four hours of the happenings. Disasters and hangovers permitting, I would sit down and write honestly and frankly about what had happened to me every day and every night.

I soon developed the ability to write in a script and style that would be completely incomprehensible to anyone else, and this gave me great confidence. It is amazing what you will admit to yourself on paper, especially when you know your writing is entirely secret. Of course, on many days nothing much happened, but scattered throughout those hundreds of pages are moments of crucial importance in my life – new experiences, new perspectives and new feelings – more in those few years than at any other time before or since. The humdrum mixed with the bizarre mixed with the delicious. I liked to refer back once in a while just to see how much I had changed in such a short time, and how things I had recently thought impossible and exotic had become accepted and commonplace. The growing narrative of the diary gave me a real sense that I was *going* somewhere.

As I wrote and wrote and kept reading back I noticed that, almost without realizing it, something had happened to me. Very gradually my experiences, perspectives and feelings seemed to mount up into something quite dramatic. Without realizing it, I was not the same sort of person any more. All those accumulated changes now looked like a barrier, a mountain range between me at eighteen and me as a child. I still clung to my belief that boys do not have to grow up – I still do sometimes – but the evidence was stacking up against that idea. I had enjoyed being a child and I was enjoying being eighteen, but the two enjoyments were not the same. There was no going back.

That is why I included the quote above – because I thought it might make you think about how you too changed (or maybe are changing) as a teenager. No doubt that little conversation will seem like the sort of thing you could only have said many years ago. It may even be hard to imagine that you were once a person like that, but the fact is that you *were* and you can never be that person again. Those three lines of infantile jabber say so much about childhood – the sexual naïvety; the honest inquisitiveness about the lives of others; the assumption that everyone is like you. You too probably think that there are many mountains of change between you now and you then. Maybe we all spend our teenage years as mental, emotional and sexual mountaineers.

The other reason I used that quote is that it makes an important point about growing up. On the surface, that little pool-side conversation was about the basic differences between male and female sexuality, and how children are less sexual than teenagers and adults. But at the same time, it shows that children also think and act in fundamentally different ways from us. Contrary to what you might think from most discussions about teenagers, adolescence is not entirely about the start of sex. Admittedly, sex is an important part of life, and adolescence is when many people begin to do it, but the second decade of our lives is far more than a crude training course in copulation. In this book, an important point I will return to again and again is that as teenagers we all have to grow up in many different ways – sexually, physically, intellectually, emotionally, spiritually – and all these processes are mixed up together. You may become 'sexualized' when you are a teenager, but you also become 'intellectualized', 'emotionalized' and 'spiritualized' too. Oh, and you have to get bigger as well.

As you will soon see, I believe that there is so much that is unusual about the second decade of life that it deserves to be seen as an important life-stage in its own right, and not just as a transitional stage between childhood and adulthood. Indeed, I will show you that it is actually even more important than that – that it is a fundamental biological difference between humans and other animals. That said, it is worth mentioning the often-quoted idea that the 'teenager' is nothing more than a modern social construct. According to this theory, until the Second World War (or some other arbitrary date), people exited childhood and entered adulthood without passing through what we now think of as a 'teenage' stage. However, while it is true that society's attitudes to teenagers have certainly changed over the years, and that teenage activities have often been ignored or suppressed, this does not mean that teenagers did not exist before the late twentieth century. There are many literary examples which show that the concept of the teenager as a thing apart has existed for centuries, albeit in forms modified to fit the times. The ancient Greeks and Romans made great play of the status of youths and maids in their societies, for example – Homer and Virgil both wrote sub-plots which are defined by their edgy teenage protagonists. Also, can you imagine Shakespeare writing *Romeo and Juliet*, with all its overpowering, impulsive, contrary passion, about adults? No: teenagers are not a social idea – they are quite simply different from everyone else.

This first part of the book is an attempt to answer the mysterious question: 'where do teenagers come from?' The complexity of the teenage experience means that there are several, linked ways to answer that question. First of all, we will look back into our fossil history to see when teenagers first appeared, and what actually constitutes the advent of the 'true teenager'. Then we will examine the processes that herald the onset of puberty and adolescence in today's teenagers – when the body finally decides to finish the job of making us men or women. Then we will consider the effects of all this change on the parts of us not directly involved in having sex with other people. We do not want to leap forward to actual sex too soon – so instead we will think about growing taller, thinner, fatter, smellier, hairier and so on. After all, most teenagers spend more time wanting sex, avoiding sex, worrying about wanting it and avoiding it, than actually doing it. We are going to take the same approach, and do the equivalent of sitting in our room and worrying about things like why our armpits become smelly, and only get back to the nitty-gritty of sex in Part Five. Finally, we will blend the fossil and biological signs of the coming of human adolescence into a theory of why teenagers appeared, and what they are here for.

So Part One will look at the bodily changes that teenagers must endure, tolerate or enjoy – some of the humdrum, bizarre and delicious things I scribbled about in my journal. And if you want to amaze yourself by how many things change when we are teenagers, I suggest that you hunt through your personal possessions to see if you can find your own teenage diaries, doodles or letters. All I can advise is, do not mysteriously lose that written record like I did. Writing my diary seemed a good idea at the time, but I must admit that I heave a slight sigh of relief that it is lost. I have no idea where that diary is now, nor whether its current owner is getting close to cracking my code.

Where did the teenagers come from?

It may seem strange to ask where teenagers come from. After all, any animal that lives twenty years must go through being a teenager. Yet being a human teenager is a far more distinctive experience than simply having a numerical age between thirteen and nineteen. There is something very different about adolescence. It is a remarkable, some would say unique, feature of human life. It has its own role to play and its own controversial evolutionary history. Indeed, there is now good evidence that it is the essential characteristic of the human race on which our success is built.

To find the origins of adolescence, we must take a very broad view of human life. First of all, if adolescence is what made humans so different, we must start by thinking about what is actually different about our species. Then we will see how understanding the ten-million-year chronology of the acquisition of our distinctively human suite of characteristics is our first step in making sense of all those characteristics. We now think that adolescence is one of those typically human features, and throughout this book we will keep a keen eye on how it relates to all the others.

I must emphasize that, as a veterinary surgeon with a zoological training, it is philosophically pleasing for me to view humans as 'just another species'. After all, they are animals like any other, subject to the same rules of biology as any other, and amenable to study like any other. Also, I naturally object to the idea of human superiority because it has led to much of our species' cruelty and overconfidence. However, the more I study human biology, the more I realize what weird and unusual things we are. Although I hate to admit it, there really do seem to be several characteristics that make human beings special in comparison to other animals. And adolescence has a role to play in most of them. Let us look at what they are, dividing them into four groups.

Locomotion	Brain	Reproduction	Life-plan
Bipedal walking	Increased cognitive abilities	Menstruation	Longevity
		No period of 'heat'	Paternal provision of food/resources
	Language	Sex for non-procreative reasons	Long post-reproduction survival
		Menopause	Prolonged period of dependence by offspring

The first human characteristic is the way we walk. Unlike most primates, and indeed most mammals, humans walk around on two legs, and this ability may have evolved around six million years ago. Bipedalism, as it is called, is not unknown in other mammals but most bipedal marsupials and rodents use their erect stance to jump, not walk. Of course many primates can walk on two legs if they want to, but they actually spend very little of their time doing so. In contrast, mature humans walk on two legs all the time, and they are very efficient bipeds too – one does not usually think of humans as being a physically superior species, but their ability to run long distances is matched by few others. The story of human bipedalism is an interesting one but we will not say much about it in this book, as its link to adolescence is indirect at best – after all, children can walk and run very well by the age of ten. However, as you will see, our two-legged way of getting about does have some relevance here because it allows us to carry food to our fellow humans, and frees our hands for manipulation and tool use. And it also allows us to lug our demanding offspring around, even before they are developed enough to cling on to us.

The second set of characteristically human features relates to the brain, and they are often claimed to represent the definitive difference between us and other animals. Surely our brain is what has made us so successful? For reasons we will investigate in Part Two, the human brain is by any measure (and there are many mathematical ways to compare brains) exceptionally large, and this presumably explains our tremendous 'cognitive' abilities. Cognition is a general term which means our ability to process information from our senses, understand it, create mental symbols and images relating to it, plan, and act on it to solve problems. Yet no matter how clever we seem, it is possible that human cognition is not fundamentally different from that in other mammals, but is simply more extensive. The same cannot be said of the other great triumph of the human brain: language. Many other animals communicate with sound, and some of them do it in a complex way, but only humans have a full system of spoken language, in which a small set of letters or syllables are strung together in ever-changing sequences to create syntax, grammar and the ability to articulate abstract concepts. Evidence from animal behaviour, linguistics, language decipherment and cryptography all strongly suggest that language is unique to humans.

The third group of human traits is to do with reproduction. For now this third group will probably seem like an unrelated bunch, but by the end of the book I aim to have woven them into the whole story of humanness. First of all, women menstruate, which is a process which occurs in only a few primate species. Also, women do not exhibit signs of sexual receptivity when they ovulate – they do not go 'on heat' like most other female animals, so neither they nor men knew when they were fertile until modern science told them (the ancient Greeks thought women were most likely to conceive when they were menstruating). Related to this is the fact that, as we all know, humans have sex for lots of reasons other than to produce babies – something almost unheard of outside we randy primates. Finally, human female fertility 'switches off' over a relatively brief period called the menopause – a phenomenon possibly unique to humans, although it has been claimed also to occur in gorillas and some whales. All in all, reproduction is the most important thing we do – indeed Darwinian natural selection works because some animals manage to breed while others do not. Therefore it should not come as a surprise to learn that a weird species like ours has some weird features of its reproduction.

The fourth and final group of human features is those relating to the chronology of our life. These are sometimes called our 'life history', but I will use the term 'life-plan', as it implies that there are reasons we live our lives this way. Although the human life-plan may seem the least tangible way in which we differ from other animals, I believe it is the most interesting because it is the everyday, common-sense demonstration of the evolutionary and biological trends that make us human. The human life-plan is also interesting because we worry about it so much – we take for granted that we can walk, talk, think and breed, but we never tire of discussing the demands of our children, our negotiations with our sexual partners and what we feel about getting older. And those discussions sum up the unusual features of the human life-plan. We are an extremely long-lived species, our seventy-or-so years clocking up at least twice the age of our primate cousins. Although we live so long, in human hunter-gatherer societies food is gathered mainly by individuals between twenty and fifty years of age, usually men, who thus are nutritionally supporting the other activities of their society – another unusual human feature. One of those supported activities is the survival of both men and women for many years after they have ceased to produce children, a phenomenon rare in other species. The other activity which requires this nutritional support is the one which interests us most in this book – the care and rearing of our incredibly slow-developing progeny. In no other species are offspring so dependent on others for twenty years (or almost one-third of the lifespan, if you choose to look at it that way). Clearly, human lives are exceptionally long and unusual – with one group of individuals 'in their prime' supporting both a large cohort of old individuals and a demanding swarm of infants, children, juveniles and adolescents edging their way slowly and painfully towards maturity. We are social and we are strange.

All in all, humans are an unusual lot. It is difficult to think of a species that differs so much from all the others. We will return to most of these features of our species in this book, but in this first chapter the obvious way to attack the question of where teenagers came from is to ask what is known about the evolution of the human life-plan, and especially that twenty-year period of the human offspring's dependence on its parents. A life-plan may not seem like the sort of thing that would fossilize well, but it is remarkable how much modern palaeoanthropology has told us about the evolution of human adolescence.

Much has changed in the last two centuries – everyone with a modicum of sense now believes that humans evolved from other primates. The anatomical and molecular similarities are staring us in the face, and the fossil record tells us a story of ape-like things turning into human-like things that is difficult to ignore. However, like any good theory, scientists are only too keen to point out the gaps in our story of human evolution. We probably acquired most of the exciting features typical of humans in the last ten million years, but there are frustrating gaps in the fossil record – at the stage when the human line was splitting from the chimps, and also when the genus *Homo* appeared, for example. Also, anyone who works with fossils is aware that we only get to see the fossils that nature allows us to see. Just as there are gaps in time, there are also geographical gaps in the human fossil record: regions of Africa where the elements simply pulverized our fallen ancestors into unrecognizable dust. Add this to the fact that most early hominid populations were thinly spread over vast areas, and that they probably varied a great deal over those ranges, and you can see why we get a very selective view of our own history.

These problems aside, it is generally agreed that our ancestors went through a series of transitions as they struggled to survive in the changing African climate. Until six million years ago, the common ancestors of chimpanzees and humans lived in forest environments and had brain volumes of approximately 400 millilitres – roughly as large as a good-sized orange, and similar in size to modern chimp brains. After that time, something important happened and while the chimps stayed in their sylvan idyll, their sister species moved out to inhabit the less densely vegetated tree savannah at the forest margins. An important group of these is gathered together in the genus *Australopithecus* and they spread to inhabit much of the African continent between four and two million years ago. Although climbing was probably still very important to them, they had developed the distinctive bipedal walking we enjoy today.

Anthropologists sometimes speak of something unspeakably traumatic happening next – the evolutionary equivalent to the fall from Eden. The African climate became considerably drier, the forests shrank and the deserts expanded. In a transition that led to the existence of our species, our ancestors moved into drier, sparser bush savannah habitats around two million years ago. This move obviously required them to keep their wits about them and their brains grew to 800 millilitres (two oranges) and tool use probably became more prevalent and complex than in chimps. They are now dignified by the name *Homo* to make clear their similarity to ourselves. One species, *Homo erectus*, was to be a fixture of the landscape of Africa, and even Europe and Asia, for almost two million years.

Thereafter, human evolution was a rapid affair, with good old *Homo sapiens* appearing just 250,000 years ago with an impressive three-orange (1,200 millilitre) brain and a knack with tools. And intriguingly, our brains have not changed much in the last 150,000 years, so we are all walking about with Stone Age brains. Maybe the original design of the three-orange *sapiens* brain was so good that there was no need to modify it. Our rather 'retro' brain has proved to be astoundingly adaptable and gave us enough nous to develop agriculture 12,000 years ago and writing and towns perhaps 6,000 years ago. And the rest is, literally, history.

But where does adolescence fit in to this story? When did the first teenagers giggle and mope their way across the majestic sweep of the dark continent? It may seem over-optimistic to look for the story of teenagers among the shattered bones and teeth of our distant ancestors, but it has indeed proved possible to do so.

One of the reasons adolescent palaeoanthropology answers our questions is that the history of our species has been a tough one, so some of our ancestors died before reaching adulthood, bequeathing us a few scattered adolescent hominid fossils. Understandably, these fossils are the subject of intense scrutiny, but there is much debate about whether we can draw conclusions about age and development from an isolated fossil from a dispersed, varied population. However, we know that characteristic changes take place in the skeletons of growing children – especially in the teeth, skull bones and growing regions of the long bones – that allow forensic pathologists to estimate the age of young skeletons. We also know that the same is possible for our closest living relative, the chimpanzee, although the timings of all the changes are different, because chimps grow differently to us.

So when an immature fossil hominid is discovered, it is immensely tempting to apply the same calculations to its bones. This is exactly what has been done with the 'Turkana boy', an immature *Homo erectus* from 1.6 million years ago discovered in Kenya in 1984. Turkana boy was hoped to be the key to understanding the evolution of the human life-plan, but was instead the start of an anthropological argument that rages to this day. By forensic standards, he looked like the first human teenager. What an amazing find that would have been; clear evidence that *Homo erectus* was still immature in its teens. However, the criteria on which that claim was based did not agree with each other very well – his teeth, skull and long bones all gave different estimates for his age: ten, thirteen, fifteen. At best this suggested that the boy's age could be only ten years old. At worst it implied that variations in growth between different individuals make forensic ageing of fossil bones a very inaccurate science.

There is another big problem with applying our systems of ageing modern humans to fossil ones. Using the growth characteristics of modern humans only works if we can assume that our ancestors grew in the same way as us. But if *Homo erectus* retained a more chimpanzee-like pattern of growth, which only became more like ours as they later evolved into *sapiens*, then the system will not work. Indeed, if we compare Turkana boy's skeleton to a chimp, most of the calculations suggest that he was roughly nine years old when he died. This of course assumes that he grew like a chimp, which may also be untrue, but at least it delivers a more consistent answer. So Turkana boy may still have been in his first decade – our first candidate for a fossil teenage human has slipped through our fingers.

You may now be wondering whether there can ever be a

way of knowing how old a fossil hominid was when it died. We need to be able to age a child whose remains have been lying in the ground for a million years, and be able to age it absolutely, rather than relative to its assumed similarities to humans or chimps. This may seem like a tall order, but remarkably it can now be done to a high degree of accuracy – and we do not even need juvenile fossils to be able to do it.

The solution to our problem lies in those most easily fossilized parts of the body, the teeth. The outer, shiny enamel layer of the teeth is the hardest stuff in the body. It may seem like a dead, inert tissue, but it is laid down before the tooth emerges from the gum by a single layer of cells called ameloblasts. The ameloblasts do not produce enamel at a constant rate, however, but secrete different amounts at different times of day. This variation creates a repeating pattern of layers of enamel, akin to the tree rings that result from varying rates of wood growth throughout the year. Of course these enamel layers are extremely thin, but if a tooth is ground into slivers and illuminated with polarized light, the layers may be viewed under a microscope. Counting these dental 'growth rings' effectively allows us to time how long the tooth took to form.

We now have a great deal of faith in this 'dental stopwatch' because the results it gives for tooth growth in living primates tie in very neatly with several features of their life-plan, including longevity and age at puberty. So what does it tell us about how quickly our relatives and ancestors grew up? We used to think that *Homo erectus* grew up as slowly as modern *sapiens* because we both have thick enamel, whereas faster-growing chimps have thin enamel. However, the dental stopwatch has now shown us that *erectus* laid down their thick enamel much more rapidly than us, but over a shorter time. We may both be *Homo*, but only we *sapiens* grow up slowly.

This elegant age-determining system has shown us that our modern pattern of dental development and slow growth evolved surprisingly late – the current estimates are that the age of onset of human adulthood crept over ten years some time between 800,000 and 300,000 years ago. The first teenagers. So the characteristically sluggish development of young humans evolved long after we started to walk on two legs, and long after we stopped climbing trees, but still some time before our brain made the final leap to three-orange size 250,000 years ago. So if the advent of teenage life is linked to any obvious physical change, it is linked to the final increase in the size of our brain. Indeed, it *preceded* that change by a fascinatingly short period. Adolescence could not be the result of increased brain size, because adolescence came first, but instead we can now entertain the appealing idea that adolescence was what allowed our brain to make its great leap forward. Teenagers as the cause of increased mental ability may seem like a contradiction in terms, but maybe that is indeed what the ancient teeth are telling us. We will return to this idea in Part Two.

So, in the past few years, the ancient teeth and bones have shown us that the first 'numerical teenagers' – the first humans older than twelve yet still immature – appeared around the time of the transition from *Homo erectus* to *sapiens*. But were they really teenagers in the true sense? We have discovered when humans first evolved their characteristically slow development, but adolescents are not simply big children who happen to be older than twelve. They have an essentially different quality to children, and we have not yet defined what that is, nor discussed how it evolved. The 'differentness' of teenagers is obvious to us all but as we will see, it is difficult to define. It involves a gawky spurt of growth, increasing social, language and intellectual skills as well as the sexual upheaval of puberty. How many disparate changes will we have to combine to define adolescence? So far we have discovered the time in our past when human development finally slowed down enough for there to be time for adolescence. How adolescence then took on its distinctive qualities is another story altogether. We are by no means finished with the evolution of the teenager.

What flips our sexy switch?

I was once sitting on a Tokyo underground train when a local girl sat down opposite me. She looked like one of those trendy young things so common in the capital and she bore a carrier bag from a chichi boutique. This was a time when Japanese businesses would often use little snippets of colloquial English as a badge of their cosmopolitan style. This often had humorous results as these phrases were obviously chosen with little care as to what they actually meant. I am sure that non-Japanese are guilty of precisely the same crassness when we wear clothes emblazoned with Japanese *kanji*, but it still raised a smile when I ate a 'Love Burger' or drank a refreshing can of 'Sweat'. Yet nothing could match the effect on a native English speaker of noticing that this girl had been selecting her couture from a shop called 'Early Puberty'.

Puberty is a sensible place to continue our quest for the nature and origins of adolescence, because it seems such an essential part of being a teenager. However, we will now have to use a different approach than we did for finding the origins of 'numerical' teenagers, because puberty really does not leave fossils. Despite this lack of fossil evidence, it seems certain that something akin to puberty must have existed from the time animals first appeared. All animals have two stages to their lives – an infancy during which they are not able to procreate, and an adulthood when they are.

Animals must be mature before they breed, and the original reason for this was that they simply needed to grow big enough to produce offspring – otherwise animals would have got smaller and smaller as the generations went on. Since those ancient days, this deliberate delaying of fertility until maturity has become much more elaborate in many animal species – to avoid inter-sibling incest for example, or to first breed at an optimal time, or even to prevent sexual conflict with mature competitors – but it remains a consistent feature of animal life. The attainment of reproductive maturity at puberty (*pubes* is Latin for adult) occurs in all animals, and in humans it usually takes place during the teenage years.

Along with most of our backboned kin, puberty in mammals is a chance to coordinate our breeding with the environment. We observe the world around us – the time of year, the availability of potential mates, our degree of physical development – and based on this information our body makes a decision to become reproductively active. The body system that is good at observation and making decisions is the brain, so it should come as no surprise that it is the brain that controls puberty. As we will see several times in this book, in many ways the brain is our primary reproductive organ.

If we look at the closest living relatives of vertebrates (backboned animals), we see evidence that the very first section of our brain to evolve was probably the part involved in controlling reproduction. The close relatives in question are lancelets, which at first sight look rather like fish fry. However, closer examination reveals that although they have a fishy body and tail, unlike fish they do not have a head with eyes, jaws and brain. Although apparently headless, they have a nerve cord running along their back that is probably equivalent to our spinal cord. Intriguingly, under the front end of this cord is a region of cells which use environmental cues to influence the lancelet's inner biology. And on the underside of the human brain lies a corresponding region which controls of many of our internal processes, and puberty in particular. This ancient breeding controller is the hypothalamus: it is roughly the size of a small grape and it lies dead-centre in your head.

Studies in fish have shown that the hypothalamic cells destined to control reproduction first appear at the very front of the developing embryo. They form as a 'placode', a slab of cells on the embryonic snout which subsequently invades into the centre of the head. Placodes also help to form the major sense organs – eyes, ears and nose – and the cells later involved in puberty appear right next to the placode destined to form the smell-sensitive lining of the nose. This is an interesting juxtaposition, as we will later see that smell plays an important role in teenage amorous adventures. Also, there are medical consequences of the close link between the origins of smell and reproduction: children with 'Kallman syndrome' can neither smell nor undergo puberty, due to the lack of smell-sensitive cells in the nose and puberty-controlling cells in the hypothalamus.

Once separated from their smelly counterparts, and ensconced within the hypothalamus at the base of the brain, these few immigrant cells soon develop into nerve cells, or 'neurons', and start to secrete the hormone which they will use to control the entire reproductive system. This hormone is 'gonadotrophin-releasing hormone', or GnRH. It is a small 'peptide' molecule made by stringing just ten amino acids together (most peptide chains are longer, and are often called 'proteins'). Small it may be, but GnRH has enormous effects on animals, and it is the activity of these hypothalamic GnRH neurons which controls puberty.

GnRH is not only small, but it does not even act directly on the reproductive organs. Like all hormones, it is released into the bloodstream and exerts its effects when it is detected by cells some distance away. In the case of GnRH those cells are only millimetres away from the hypothalamus – in the pituitary gland which dangles from the underside of the brain. The hypothalamic neurons secrete their GnRH into a unique mesh of tiny blood vessels which convey it directly to special cells in the pituitary. When stimulated by GnRH these pituitary cells secrete 'gonadotrophin' hormones ('gonad nourishers') into the bloodstream to act directly on the ovaries or testicles. The gonadotrophins are much longer peptides than GnRH, each containing approximately two hundred amino acids.

The hormonal control of reproduction does not stop there. Being a teenage boy or girl means much more than just having active ovaries or testicles. As we will see, young male and female bodies are built very differently, and almost every part must function differently in the two sexes. To allow this, most parts of our bodies are under the control of hormones released by our gonads in response to gonadotrophins from the pituitary. And when you consider that the pituitary is, in turn, controlled by the GnRH neurons in the brain, you can see that there is a clearly defined chain of command controlling our sexy selves.

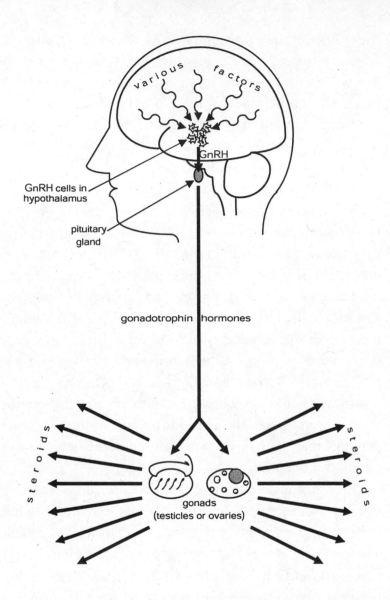

This control system is crucially important: scientists now agree that after a period of relative quiescence in childhood, it becomes fully activated during puberty. Indeed, it is the activation of the hypothalamic GnRH neurons in the brain that actually *causes* puberty. That little cluster of snout cells that invaded the brain is the key to one of the most dramatic transformations in our life.

With the hypothalamus waiting impatiently to start puberty, I should perhaps pause to say something about the difference between girls and boys. The brain may initiate the process of puberty common to both sexes, but it does not control whether we are boys or girls in the first place. The story of the process by which we are allocated our sex is a rich one and I told it in my previous book, *The X in Sex*. Although some animals use more complex methods, humans use a simple binary genetic switch to determine their sex. The biological implications of this system are immense and affect almost every aspect of our life, but the actual mechanism itself is simple. Most of us inherit twenty-three chromosomes from each of our parents, yielding a total of forty-six little libraries containing our twenty-thousand-or-so genetic instructions. These forty-six include twenty-two pairs of ordinary chromosomes as well as two sex chromosomes. Those sex chromosomes come in two varieties named, for historical reasons, X and Y. Women have two Xs and men have an X and a Y. Mothers can only bequeath an X chromosome to their babies whereas fathers may pass on either an X or a Y, thus determining their child's sex. The Y dictates the sex of a developing baby because it carries a single genetic instruction which causes the embryonic gonads to become testicles. If there is no Y present, those gonads become ovaries. Everything else springs from that one instruction – testicles make hormones that turn fetuses into boys but if testicles are absent, fetuses become girls. This is how the developing baby establishes the basic sexual template on which the brain can act a decade later.

The most remarkable feature of puberty is that it is a new beginning. For the first decade of life children, although obviously male or female, appear distinctly sexless and immature. Then a predictable series of changes takes place which converts them into sexual adults. The time when puberty starts varies a great deal between individuals, but once started the course of events varies little. For centuries scientists have wondered how the body knows when to start puberty after being sexually dormant for so long, but only in the last few decades have we started to understand the spur to this miraculous reproductive awakening. Our new model of how puberty starts is based on maturation of the brain itself, and it places the little hypothalamic GnRH neurons right at the centre of things. It suggests that children are sexually immature because the GnRH neurons are inactive, and that puberty takes place when they become active. So to find out what starts puberty, all we have to do is find out what switches the GnRH neurons on.

It now appears that the activity of GnRH neurons is controlled by other parts of the brain. The hypothalamus is awash with incoming signals telling it how to control the body: usually direct inputs from nerves plugging in from elsewhere in the brain. All this incoming 'advice' is not surprising when you consider that the main function of the hypothalamus is to integrate information from outside and inside the body. Certainly it is fiddly work to discern exactly which parts of the brain feed into the all-important GnRH cells, but the technical difficulties should not overwhelm us. They also raise the possibility that not only can we find out what pathways trigger puberty, but more importantly we may also be able to discover how puberty is attuned to external influences and internal well-being. We may be able to progress from the 'when' and the 'what' of puberty to the 'why'.

The incoming nerves converging on the GnRH neurons can be distinguished by the different chemicals they release. Those chemicals may be divided into two groups – the chemicals that suppress the GnRH neurons (perhaps during childhood?) and those that stimulate them (perhaps during puberty?). However, it is likely that these two families of chemicals do not act in a clear-cut 'on or off' fashion, but that a gradual shift in their balance of power is what causes puberty.

There are several suppressive substances ladled onto GnRH neurons. For example, gamma-aminobutyric acid (GABA) is a chemical which acts to damp down activity throughout the hypothalamus (a waning of its effects at puberty may explain why schizophrenia and epilepsy often start in adolescence). A second suppressive factor is melatonin – a hormone secreted by the pineal gland on top of the brain. Melatonin is secreted when it is dark and as we will see, production of sex hormones is synchronized with the day-night cycle at the start of puberty. A third group of inhibitory chemicals are opioids, morphine-like chemicals produced in many parts of the brain. Their role in puberty is unclear at present, but we will revisit the question of why the brain makes something like morphine in Part Three. The final substance on this list could turn out to be the most interesting, despite being cryptically named 'neuropeptide Y'. The effects of neuropeptide Y on the reproductive system are complex, but this may be because this substance could turn out to be the way in which reproduction is attuned to nutrition. When we look at the many factors controlling the shifting timing of puberty in Chapter 5, we will see that stores of body fat could be the most important. Neuropeptide Y may be the crucial link between body fat and fertility.

Just as we have discovered substances that inhibit the all-important GnRH neurons, further delving into the hypothalamus has also identified the chemicals that may activate them at puberty. For example, glutamate is a substance which activates many hypothalamic cells, has a strong effect on GnRH neurons, and could be viewed as a counterbalance to the inhibitory effects of GABA. Second on the list, the blood-borne hormone insulin is a particularly exciting positive influence on GnRH neurons, as we already know a great deal about what it does. Famous for its role in diabetes, insulin is the most important hormone controlling metabolism – so to find it so directly linked to the process of puberty is a strong hint that we are only allowed to enter puberty when our body believes we are metabolically ready. Finally comes the cutely named kisspeptin, which has been attracting increasing interest because of its very specific effects on reproduction – injecting it causes levels of reproductive hormones to increase, and blocking its effects causes them to decrease. Yet even here there is overlap with other body systems – kisspeptin also seems to prevent the spread of tumours.

Our understanding of the sexual awakening of puberty is very much a work in progress. We have a list of anti-puberty brain chemicals and a list of pro-puberty chemicals, and all are the subject of intense research. Yet we have learned one central fact about human puberty – boys and girls get sexy because of activation of GnRH neurons, a small group of cells that invaded into the centre of their heads when they were embryos. These cells take the final decision to start puberty, and most of the rest of the brain seems to want to advise them. Discovering all this was a great achievement, and it takes us very close to a true understanding of puberty. Puberty is a critical change in our lives – perhaps the most critical and most ancient of all – and our evolutionary history has ensured that our brain makes it occur at the right time. Studying the inner workings of the hypothalamus will eventually show us not just what happens at puberty, but *why* things happen when they do.

Why all the bodily unpleasantness?

We may only now be discovering the causes of puberty, but we all know its effects. Many of us have a mental image of hormones tearing around the adolescent body creating untold havoc, wresting us from the smooth-skinned innocence of childhood. The teenage years are all sweat, hair and grease, and most of the time it seems as if nature is deliberately trying to shock us by its ability to forcibly eject us from infancy.

The bodily changes that puberty causes can seem strange or even callous, but we are gradually making sense of them. In the last few decades we have pieced together an understanding of the process of pubertal change, and we also began to comprehend how those changes drove the evolution of modern humans. Puberty is certainly not all bad – by the time it is complete, men and women are delightfully different in many subtle ways. Our sexuality is enjoyable because it is indirect – the strong masculine hand, the graceful feminine neck, the mental revelling in the body of our partner. Human sex is so much more than the brief genital connection seen in other animals, and we are obsessed by its complexity and how we think about it. All this complexity and subtlety is rooted in our teenage years. This is one of the best reasons why adolescence is the zenith of human achievement, even if the changes we undergo at puberty do not always seem so positive at the time.

We now like to think of puberty as a 'reactivation' of sexual activity. This is because, although we may find it unsettling, the reproductive system is not entirely inactive before puberty. In fact, it is perhaps most active immediately after birth. There are large quantities of reproductive hormones sloshing about a newborn baby's system, and these can lead to outward signs in girls that resemble menstruation and lactation, a phenomenon once thought spooky enough to be called 'witch's milk'. Although there is less external evidence in baby boys, they are probably in greater hormonal tumult than girls. Boys' pituitary glands secrete more gonadotrophin hormones in the first few months of life than girls' do, and it seems likely that these are important in sexual development – perhaps driving testicular growth, or pushing the male brain along its bumpy developmental road (we will wander down *that* in Part Two).

After this neonatal reproductive flurry, things calm down for a few years, physically at least. Children's bodies are relatively sexually dormant, although their brains are constantly trying to find their place in the world. This means that children can use these years to acquire some understanding of their future sexual status and also, in their naïvely experimental way, get an idea of what their bodies are for. This book is not about children, but it is worth pointing out that our years of sexless childhood may be an unusual human phenomenon: most animals transit seamlessly from a high-hormone infancy to an even-higher-hormone puberty, without stopping on the way.

The next stage in our development is a strange one and

seems, too, to be a characteristically human thing; it occurs during what we think of as childhood; and it involves an organ we do not usually think of as reproductive – the adrenal gland. The process is called 'adrenarche' (rhymes with 'oligarchy'). We do not know why, but around the age of seven in girls or nine in boys, the adrenal glands – two small glands, one above each kidney – become more active. Adrenarche causes production of a sex hormone called dehydroepiandrosterone, often mercifully abbreviated to DHEA. This phenomenon continues into our twenties but unfortunately we are not even sure what it does. DHEA is not a very potent hormone. It does not seem to drive the small transient growth spurt that occurs in childhood, for example. Tellingly, if adrenarche fails to occur, a child will still subsequently go through puberty as expected. However, adrenarche is probably responsible for increased skin gland secretion and growth of sparse pubic hair ('pubarche'), and thus may explain why these are often the first sign of impending puberty. DHEA may also make children deposit fat stores which can later be used as a cue to start puberty proper. In the next chapter, we will also see that some scientists claim that human adrenarche was pivotal in driving the evolution of the fast-growing human child's brain. So, all in all, adrenarche is connected to puberty, but perhaps only loosely.

As we enter our second decade, our pituitary gland becomes more insistent, showering more gonadotrophin hormones on our eager gonads (a process called 'gonadarche'). This occurs because of the awakening of the GnRH nerve cells in the brain. For some reason, gonadotrophins are initially secreted only at night – a phenomenon not seen in adults. Also, the increase in gonadotrophin levels occurs later in boys than girls, possibly due to a rewiring of the brain induced a decade earlier by all those baby boy hormones. Whatever the reason, this 'boy lag' probably explains why delayed puberty is commoner in boys and premature puberty is commoner in girls.

Gonadotrophins do not act directly on most tissues of the body, but instead exert their effects by making the ovaries or testicles produce sex steroid hormones. Sex steroids are evolutionarily very ancient, are made by many animals all across the animal kingdom, and certainly have profound effects on many tissues in the teenage body. Chemically, steroids are a similar bunch because they are all made from the same ubiquitous raw material, cholesterol – so they are fatty molecules, unlike GnRH and gonadotrophins. Also, they are the most famous of all hormones, so you will already have heard of most of them.

The cells in the ovary or testicle take cholesterol and use enzymes (large proteins) to chemically modify it – chopping bits off, adding new bits on – and the first sex steroid they make is progesterone. There is a stick-diagram of its chemical structure on the next page. Like most life molecules, progesterone is based on a framework of carbon atoms (at the corners of the polygons in the diagram) with hydrogen atoms clustered all around (so many, that I have left them out). Progesterone is made up of four rings of carbon atoms stuck together, with some extra carbon ('C') and oxygen ('O') atoms hanging off the sides. The two-dimensional picture makes it look like a flat structure, but each hexagon and pentagon is actually flexed and distorted so that the whole molecule has a complex three-dimensional shape. We now know that the upper-left edge of the molecule is the important bit, as it is this part which activates 'receptor' molecules in the target cells which respond to steroids.

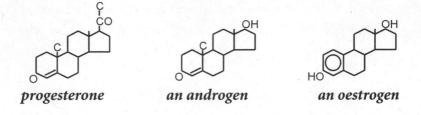

progesterone　　　　*an androgen*　　　　*an oestrogen*

Sometimes ovarian and testicular cells go a little further – they lop off some carbons to turn the progesterone into an androgen molecule, such as testosterone or DHEA. You may not think that the androgen looks very different from progesterone, but the tiny differences make androgens exert completely different effects. Finally, the androgen molecule may be further modified to make an oestrogen. Oestrogens differ more from androgens than they might look in the picture: their 'left-most' carbon ring is 'aromatic' – it has a flat, undistorted shape that gives oestrogens unique properties. You may be worried to hear that there are aromatic compounds with similar oestrogenic properties in beer.

All this jiggery-pokery with fatty steroid molecules may seem arcane until you realize that it is the interplay of these hormones that causes almost all of the changes of puberty, and a great deal more besides. However, we are often presented with an oversimplified view of how steroids work – progesterone and oestrogen being 'feminine' and androgens being 'masculine'. But life is more complicated than that. For a start, teenage girls and teenage boys all make progesterone, oestrogens *and* androgens, so there is nothing exclusive about any of them. Rather, it is the relative quantities of the hormones, the potency of the molecules produced, and the presence of cells ready to respond to them, which cause the differences between men and women. To blur the boundaries further, steroids are made not only by the ovaries or testicles, but by the adrenal glands as well.

Boys are, as in so many things, simpler. Almost all the 'masculinization' that occurs in teenage boys is due to the effects of androgens steadily secreted by the testicles, but even here there is complexity. There are several different androgens at work, each helping to drive a different aspect of the development of the male body. Also, counter-intuitively, there are some cells in teenage boys that only respond to androgens if they have been converted to oestrogens first. And teenage girls are a yet more complex hormonal soup. Oestrogens do indeed trigger some of the sexual maturation of the female body, but girls' ovaries and adrenals also produce considerable amounts of androgens which are essential for some aspects of puberty. And eventually progesterone also plays a role – although there is not a great deal of it around until girls start their menstrual cycles. From that point onward, girls are subject to a roller-coaster of cyclically alternating oestrogen and progesterone production for the rest of their fertile lives.

Despite the tangled interplay of the sex steroids, once the hormonal choreography of puberty has started it progresses in a remarkably consistent manner. Even though puberty may start at very different ages in different girls and boys, the stages and changes of normal puberty are played out with remarkable predictability. Boys start the different stages in the following sequence: testicle enlargement, penis growth, pubic hair growth, motile sperm production ('spermarche'), facial and armpit hair, growth spurt, body hair, muscle and heart growth. In girls the chronology is: breast tip swelling ('thelarche'), pubic hair, maturation of genitals, female pattern of fat deposition, growth spurt, more generalized breast growth and body hair, menstrual cycles ('menarche'), fully fertile cycles. And these sequences are played out so consistently that any significant departure from the sequence can be taken as a sign of abnormality. Also, viewing the changes of puberty as a chronological sequence emphasizes just how long the whole process takes. Girls often start breast growth at the age of eight, but many are not fully fertile until they are eighteen. Even more dramatic is the slow pace of change in boys – deposition of large manly muscles may not occur until well into the twenties, and patterns of male body hair often continue to change throughout adulthood. Puberty is not a sudden event, but a slow, gradual change.

So the sequence of pubertal change seems fixed, but of course it is the actual bodily modifications that fascinate us. We will now look at these changes and consider why each of them occurs. You will see that even the most unpleasant changes confer some practical benefit on us, or at least they did at some point in our past. When you start to view puberty as a product of evolution, much of what happens to teenagers begins to make sense. Also, an assumption we must challenge is that puberty is the only thing that makes boys' and girls' bodies so different, when in fact their non-reproductive tissues are already very different by the time puberty starts. Admittedly the differences induced by puberty are more spectacular than those that existed beforehand, but boys and girls are not starting puberty from the same place. Finally, the story of puberty will tell us a great deal about what men and women find attractive, because sexual attraction has been a driving force in the evolution of teenagers.

Why do teenage girls and boys look different?

Puberty changes some aspects of the teenage body more than others. Obviously the reproductive organs mature dramatically, but even more startling is the way puberty changes our outward appearance – our skin and our body shape.

Skin, especially, dominates our view of puberty. As the part of us that the outside world, including our lovers, will see and touch, it undergoes more than its fair share of teenage change. Also, many skin changes, or at least their disordered early stages, occur early in puberty before we are sexually or emotionally able to make sense of them. This unfortunate timing, and the fact that you cannot easily hide your skin, means that adolescent skin can be a distressing and depressing thing.

With that in mind, it is unfortunate that the first hair to appear at puberty grows around the genitals. In girls pubic hair first grows on the labia, and in boys it grows on the upper surface of the penis. Growth then gradually spreads to fill the pubic triangle above the genitals and then spills over onto the thighs. In boys it will also spread in a line up towards the navel, and of course the pubic hair boundaries will eventually merge into general body hair. Pubic hair has a characteristic appearance best described by the colloquial phrase 'short and curly'. Its growth driven by androgens in both sexes, its texture is unlike other hair and this has led biologists to speculate about its function. Although we still have more theories than real evidence, one thing seems clear – humans have lost almost all their fur, so we need good reasons to explain why they have retained what little remains.

It has long been suggested that we have pubic hair to disperse sexual scents produced by the sweat glands in our genital regions, acting as a 'wick' up which these oily secretions can seep before they are wafted away by the wind. Initially this seems a good explanation as it explains why both the hair and the glands are there. However, our primate relatives do not have such genital scent wicks, and certainly not curly ones – and many animals actually have relatively sparse hair over their scent glands (think of cats' temples). Also, similar scent-wicking arguments are used to explain the presence of armpit, 'axillary', hair in humans. Armpit hair is sparse, fine and straight, and it is much easier to imagine scents being spread by gentle breezes through this stuff. Perhaps armpit hair disperses our scents far and wide whereas pubic hair traps it for those who get up close and personal.

Another utilitarian explanation is that pubic hair keeps us warm, but why the triangle above our genitals is in such need of insulation is unclear. It has also been claimed to prevent dirt entering the female genitals, although this theory renders male pubic hair functionless even though it is more profuse. Some have suggested that pubic hair retains a layer of air to promote the health of the underlying skin, and this strange theory makes some sense – the armpits and groin are indeed common sites of skin-cleft infections. A nineteenth-century source even proposes the eye-watering hypothesis that pubic hair is a vestige of the hair to which our ancestors' infants clung. A variation on these rather mechanical justifications for pubic hair is the idea that it prevents chafing between the genitals and thighs when walking. I personally think this idea is a good one, because it explains why teenagers grow pubic hair *in advance* of their genital development. Alternatively, does pubic hair prevent chafing between partners during the unusually human practice of face-to-face copulation? Of course, some couples now remove their pubic hair expressly to improve the tactile experience of sex, but it is claimed that this works best if both partners participate in the pre-coital depilation. One can almost imagine a prehistoric pubic arms race in which women evolved pubic hair to prevent abrasion by their partners' hair, leading to corresponding evolutionary countermeasures by men.

Other theories of pubic hair relate not to its use to the bearer, but to the signals it sends to other people. First of all, it is unlikely that pubic hair is itself a sexual lure, mainly because it does not differ much between the sexes – and it tends to be the differences between the sexes that excite us. However, it is reasonable to suggest that pubic hair is a general badge of maturity, a kind of sexual 'open for business' sign. Another hypothesis is the delightfully titled 'vulvo-cryptic' theory, which suggests that pubic hair is the cause of just about everything we cherish as human. The story goes like this. When humans started to walk upright, female genitals were suddenly hidden from men as never before. This increased women's control over who mated with them and when. Adding pubic hair made their genital concealment yet more complete and allowed them to use their sexual control to actively manipulate men. As a result, human sex became a complex process based on communication, emotional interaction and thought. And this is why humans have language, emotion and great cerebral powers. Admittedly, this may not be an entirely watertight theory, but it is certainly thought-provoking.

Pubic hair has an interesting cultural history which says a great deal about our attitudes towards it. We do not know when people first started removing pubic hair, but the practice was probably carried out in ancient Greece and Rome. The contexts in which pubic hair was considered acceptable have certainly changed between then and now, and today they vary in different cultures around the world. For much of the known history of Western art, pubic hair has traditionally been omitted from 'high art' representations of the nude, female at least. In contrast, pubic hair was depicted in pornography from the ancient world to the mid-twentieth century. Since the late eighteenth century, however, pubic hair has appeared more frequently in art. And the inversion of classical customs has become complete now that pubic hair is almost entirely absent from modern pornography. These changes do have considerable bearing on teenagers, as the first naked people many of us see beyond our own family are in pictures. Certainly, the ebb and flow of cultural etiquette suggests that we are not entirely at peace with our pubic hair. Yet this is probably not because we see it as something sexual, as this would fail to explain our reversal in attitudes in the last two thousand years. Perhaps instead it is due to teenagers' reactions to girls' and women's pubic hair. Do they see female body hair as a masculine characteristic best hidden or removed?

But general body and facial hair are fundamentally different from pubic hair. Body and facial hair are different in texture, they develop later in puberty and they also look different in the two sexes. Body and facial hair actually have a very similar pattern of distribution in women and men, but in women they are so fine and grow for so little time before being shed that they are usually almost invisible, probably due to differences in quantity and type of circulating androgens. Still, why men need more body hair than women is unknown and, as only some women find it attractive, it is unlikely that it is a general sexual lure. Perhaps body hair makes men seem very slightly larger to those they are trying to intimidate, like a cat raising its hackles. Alternatively, a fine coating of hair gives the skin a surprising amount of protection against abrasion, and if we are to believe traditional ideas about gender roles, prehistoric men had a physically rougher life than women. Men have bushier eyebrows too, and along with the shape of their brow this may divert sweat from falling in their eyes. The male beard is also difficult to explain, although many have tried – if it is an overt sign of maleness, then it is difficult to explain why it is so often shaved off. Our attitudes to our fur are indeed strange. As we leave hair behind, bear in mind that the word 'horrid' is derived from the Latin word for 'bristly' and that the word 'bizarre' may come from the Basque for 'bearded'.

The glands in the skin also change at puberty, often in concert with changes in the hair. We have three main types of gland in our skin – eccrine sweat, apocrine sweat and sebaceous glands – and they all change in different ways. Eccrine glands secrete watery salty sweat through their own discrete openings on to the skin surface. In most animals, eccrine glands are concentrated in the paws where they increase grip on smooth surfaces, but in we naked humans the evaporation of eccrine sweat has proved to be a good way to dissipate heat. However, foot odour results from the bacterial digestion of eccrine sweat by bacteria to produce methanediol and iso-valeric acid, two chemicals also found in some pungent cheeses. The eccrine glands do not change much at puberty, and it is for this reason that both children and adults can suffer from smelly feet.

The apocrine sweat system is different, and changes more at puberty. Apocrine glands secrete a more oily sweat, in this case into hair follicles, which then emerges to coat the hair. In humans, apocrine sweat probably acts to emulsify eccrine sweat into a thin evaporating film, instead of it dripping off uselessly. Apocrine sweat also carries scents attractive to the opposite sex – folklore abounds with stories of young lovers devising ways to waft their apocrine sweat towards the object of their affections. (In Part Five we will look in more detail at how smell guides our sexual choices.) However, the conscious part of the human brain is not actually aware that fresh apocrine sweat smells of very much. At puberty, androgens increase the production of apocrine sweat in both sexes and also change the recipe of fatty acids within them, and this is why body odour often starts at this time – sometimes as the very first sign of puberty. Body odour is the result of bacterial breakdown of apocrine sweat to yield chemicals that the conscious brain *does* perceive as smelly. However, this distinction between fresh and digested apocrine sweat is an important one because it means that body odour can often be managed by washing and antisepsis.

Also discharging into the hair follicles are the sebaceous glands, which produce sebum, an even more greasy secretion which coats the hair, retains moisture in the skin, and in humans probably also acts as a water repellent. This last function may explain why these glands are mostly present on the surfaces of the body exposed to rain – the chest, upper back, face and scalp. The surge in activity of sebaceous glands at puberty is driven by androgens in both sexes, and it is important because it causes two unpleasant features of adolescent life. The first is that most of us have greasier hair after puberty. This is part of adulthood that humans have been keen to change yet loath to lose – the hair care industry makes its money by selling us detergent shampoos to strip off our hair oils, conditioners to repair the disruption caused by the shampoo, and sprays and gels to set our hair in a fixed position, just as our own oils would have done had we left them there. Considering that sebaceous secretion is driven by androgens, it is perhaps not surprising that the more glutinous gels are directed at the male half of the market.

The second effect of androgen-driven sebaceous secretion is that traditional scourge of the teenager: acne, or 'acne vulgaris' to give it its even more revolting full name. Acne is blockage and inflammation of sebaceous glands, which explains why acne affects androgen-fuelled boys more often than girls, and also why it affects skin areas with lots of sebaceous glands. Acne may be less common or severe in teenage girls, but premenstrual acne can occur into adult life. One problem with acne is that although its hormonal basis is known, the exact skin changes involved are uncertain and may vary between individuals. This is probably why so much unhelpful folklore has grown up around the condition; so what actually happens in acne?

The first part of the acne puzzle is over-production of sebum caused by androgens, mainly testosterone. However, this 'seborrhoea' is probably not sufficient on its own to cause acne. The second factor is that the duct through which hair and sebum are extruded to the outside world can become blocked with dead skin cells. Dead skin cells themselves are not abnormal – we shed billions of them from our hair follicles all the time – but sometimes their sheer quantity is enough to jam up the hair follicle with a yellow plug of skin cells and sebum which slowly oxidizes to the characteristic black colour of the comedo or 'blackhead'. A third piece of the jigsaw is that some people have more of a bacterium called *Propionibacterium acnes* on their skin, and this is instrumental in setting up infections in blocked follicles. The acne puzzle is completed by the fact that in some teenagers the follicle is more likely to rupture and spill its noxious contents into the surrounding skin. This sets up a dramatic local inflammation which eventually removes all the debris, but can lead to scarring. This scarring is why people tell teenagers not to squeeze their spots, even though those teenagers know very well that the spot will be gone sooner if they do.

So the science of acne is complex, with at least four factors controlling whether a teenager suffers it or not. This lack of a single cause means that treatment is often only partially successful. Antibiotics are good for managing severe bacterial acne, but they do not address the original problem of excess sebum damming up in blocked follicles, although benzoyl peroxide may help with that. We do have drugs that suppress the effects of androgens, but obviously these must be used with care in developing teenagers. As well as frustration at the inadequacies of medical treatment of acne, it is difficult to give an acne sufferer a positive view of the disease. Acne is not a phenomenon that achieves anything – instead, it is a temporary effect of the inept development of the gland system which moistens the skin and deflects rain. There is no magic 'reason' for acne that will assuage the concerns of teenagers, and those concerns can be profound. As we will see later, acne is a major cause of depression and even suicide in teenagers.

Teenage skin is important in one more respect, although you may not have thought of it as related to the skin. Breasts are extremely elaborate skin glands – probably evolved from ancient apocrine sweat glands – so we will consider breast development along with the rest of the skin. Breast development in girls is driven by oestrogens, mainly from the ovaries, and also prolactin, yet another peptide hormone from the pituitary gland. Like much of puberty, breast development follows a reliable pattern, often starting before the age of ten with a small conical swelling beneath the nipple, which can occasionally become slightly sore. This is later augmented by a more general growth of the breast which lifts the conical nipple away from the chest, often to the extent that it points slightly to the side and the whole breast starts to hang down somewhat. Frequently, the nipple cone then flattens out and merges with the rest of the swelling breast. All this time a branching system of milk-conveying tubes has been spreading throughout the globe of the breast, although it will not develop fully until progesterone levels increase in pregnancy. And as with body hair, the differences between girls' and boys' breasts are mainly those of degree – boys do form a small duct system, and later in life can even suffer from breast cancer.

Breasts are fascinating for all sorts of reasons. The most striking feature of human breasts is that they consist mainly of fat, which makes them far more pendulous than the mammary glands of any other animal. Crucially, not only do most female animals have small mammary glands when they are not producing milk, but they also have even smaller glands before their first pregnancy. The size and shape of breasts varies dramatically between women for reasons that we do not understand, but their prominence is perhaps most inexplicable during adolescence – teenage girls' breasts are not usually pregnant or lactating, and they are often not even fertile enough to get pregnant. Teenage girls are our biggest clue that human breasts may be uniquely prominent for a reason unrelated to producing milk.

There has been much speculation about why human breasts are so prominent. The suggested reasons fall into two groups – those related to child care, which are often championed by women, and those relating to sexual attractiveness, often proposed by men. The oldest child-related suggestion is that humans have very short chins, and that this makes it difficult for our babies to suckle from a teat on a flat mammary gland. This idea seems unlikely to me, partly because there are some fairly chinless baby monkeys around and they seem to cope perfectly well. However, there is certainly something strange about human breast-feeding – unlike most infants, babies are supposed to fill their mouth with breast when feeding, although for some reason they do not seem to do this instinctively, as many sore mothers will attest. Another suggestion is that the breast evolved so that the nipple is conveniently close to infants being carried either in the arms, or slung on the hips of their bipedal mothers. Before the invention of the bra, breasts presumably sagged early in life, so did this lower them to the same level as a carried child's mouth? Finally, some anthropologists believe that humans went though a semi-aquatic stage in our evolution, living along an ancient African coastline. They use this theory to explain several distinctive features of human biology, one of which is that the breast evolved as something for the bobbing infant to grab on to. However, this theory does not explain why no other aquatic species has pendulous mammary glands throughout their adult life, nor why lactating women tend to dislike their breasts being seized.

These child-oriented theories of breast size have two major problems. The first is that they do not explain why human breasts are so large when women are not breast-feeding. Also, they do not explain why the breast is such a sexually sensitive area. These flaws suggest that attractiveness to men is, after all, an important factor in the evolution of breasts. This idea depends on a process called sexual selection, which we think has been important in many aspects of human evolution. Whereas *natural* selection means that animal species change when certain individuals produce more offspring because they possess characteristics which help them thrive in their environment, *sexual* selection means that some individuals produce more offspring simply because they possess traits which the opposite sex finds attractive. This means that animals can pass on their genes to the next generation because they attract mates, rather than because they are actually any better at surviving – sexual selection explains the peacock's tail for example. In the natural world there are many examples where sexual selection seems to have taken place, so it is not unreasonable to suggest that women evolved pendulous breasts because men liked them. Indeed some scientists claim that almost every difference between boys and girls that appears at puberty evolved because it was attractive to the opposite sex. However, the problem with sexual selection is that it is often difficult to explain why one sex (in this case men) started to like a certain trait (in this case breasts) in the first place.

It has been suggested that breasts are a straightforward

sexual lure – there to attract men. This idea is supported by the fact that girls grow breasts in advance of becoming fertile, and the fact that in many human societies breasts are covered until marriage, but not afterwards. However, it does not explain why men originally started to like breasts. Perhaps they first developed a general appreciation of the distinctive curves of the female form, and breasts subsequently swelled to appeal to that preference. A more radical idea is that rounded breasts evolved to mimic buttocks at a delicate stage in human evolution when men were adapting to the new face-to-face sexual position. Yet there is little evidence to support this idea that breasts are a surrogate for buttock-deprived men, especially considering that we do not really know whether humans evolved rounded buttocks or breasts first. More sensibly, it has been proposed that a man is attracted to pendulous breasts because they are a sign of high potential milk production for his future babies. Yet even here there are problems – the link between breast size and milk production is far from clear, and this theory also cannot explain the wide variation in size of women's breasts. After all, many men and teenage boys like small breasts, as long as they are obviously attached to the female of the species.

A final sexual selection theory of human breast evolution is appealing because it works both ways – men are selecting women and women are selecting men. It also has its roots in other unusual features of human life – long-term coopera-tion by couples, and fathers' provision for their partner and children. According to this theory, men became interested in breasts for one of the previously mentioned reasons, or perhaps because breast swelling was one of the few external signs of ovulation in women. The next stage was that women started to select breast-appreciating men, because these men were more likely to stay with them and support them while they were pregnant or lactating – when their breasts would of course be even more voluptuous. And then the whole thing snowballed – men loving breasts more and more, and women evolving more prominent breasts and loving the men who loved them. So perhaps teenage girls really do grow breasts in anticipation of attracting the right man, although they are not doing this out of some sort of evolutionary generosity – they still have their own interests at heart.

It certainly seems as if a major function of puberty is to change the way teenagers look. If skin is one aspect of the body which is dramatically altered by puberty, then body shape is another. Before puberty, boys and girls have similar body shapes, but afterwards they are obviously feminized or masculinized. And although none of these changes to adolescent body shape is necessary for making babies, they go a long way towards making us physically attractive to the opposite sex. In Part Five we will see that teenagers have specific brain circuits that allow them to appreciate each other's body shapes. Of course, like all things in human sexuality, the appreciation of body shape is a subtle thing. Boys do not have to be muscle-bound lumps to be attractive and girls do not need to be buxom wide-hipped earth goddesses – we can respond to very subtle cues, but the cues must be there.

Also, many of the differences between girls' and boys' body shapes are present before puberty, albeit in lesser form. A good example of this is the upper body and arms. Under the influence of androgens, boys develop larger chest cavities to increase their ability to draw in oxygen and pump blood with their larger heart. The male chest probably also serves as a display of masculinity to females and threat to other males –

and jackets further emphasize the top-heaviness of men. The large male chest pushes the shoulders apart, an effect enhanced by the wearing of epaulettes in the armed forces. I admit that I still remember the 1980s fashion for women to wear shoulder pads, presumably as a mimic of the body shape of the 'dominant' male – a trend that extended to spindly teenage girls in what now seems a hilariously dated way. Female self-image must have changed since those years, and many teenage girls now wear clothes which emphasize the small chest – small, fitted tops of light material emphasize rounded shoulders and longer, finer necks. A small rib cage also means that girl's abdomens are very long, which leaves more space for later pregnancies. And crop tops and low-rise jeans allow this long female belly to be shown off to greatest effect.

A further difference between the sexes is that men possess much more muscle than women – another effect caused by androgens. Indeed, the anabolic steroids that unscrupulous athletes inject into themselves are merely artificial forms of male sex steroids. Unsurprisingly, the anabolic effects of androgens mean that boys, already stronger than girls before puberty, are *much* stronger after puberty – a man can grip with twice the force of a woman. The increased muscle mass also makes men look different, with massive shoulders, flat bellies (so I am told) and muscular thighs and buttocks – among the features that women find most sexually attractive about men. Unfortunately, this is where teenage boys lose out, because the growth spurt of muscle often occurs at a late stage of puberty, sometimes as late as the early twenties. Apart from making teenage boys look wimpy, the real tragedy of this delay is that male metabolism often seems to change when the muscle growth ceases – I have noticed that my male university students can easily get into the habit of consuming huge numbers of calories (i.e. beer) because they simply do not seem to be able to put on weight, but that these habits come to haunt their midriff after the age of twenty-two or so. Another effect of increased muscle mass in boys is that it makes them less flexible than girls – so girls walk with a more flowing gait than the boys who stomp along beside them. Reduced male flexibility also exacerbates the clumsiness of adolescence. And we can explain these differences if we accept that gender roles in surviving hunter-gatherer societies reflect the mainstream of past human evolution. Perhaps girls really do deftly pluck the fruit from the tree while boys kill the beast and beat the stuffing out of their enemies.

In some ways, the other side of adolescent muscle is fat. From puberty onwards, oestrogen makes girls preferentially lay down fat over their buttocks and thighs. Also, they usually carry around 50 per cent more fat than boys and much of this is stored in a layer beneath the skin. This is why teenage girls appear smoother and curvier, because the fat hides their muscle definition. So whether or not fat is a feminist issue, it is certainly a female characteristic. And as we will see, in some of its forms fat is extremely attractive to the male senses, but the downside to this is that the changing shape of the teenage female body could be a major cause of eating disorders in girls. One reason why women carry more fat may be that they have not had to run around so much over the last few million years – and it has been claimed that the weight of all this fat is more important in causing the discrepancy between women's and men's athletic abilities than women having less muscle or smaller lungs. Another reason for the existence of girls' fat stores is that they are an energy reserve for pregnancy and lactation, because it is these, rather than everyday physical exertion, which probably placed the greatest strains on our female ancestors. This tendency to store for the future is apparent in my female students, who find it all too easy to put on weight as soon as they arrive at university and start consuming more calories (i.e. more beer). An intriguing final explanation proposed for girls' thigh and buttock fat stores is that they reduce the female centre of gravity, which makes women more stable when carrying children – but I must admit that I have not yet conducted any experiments to see which young parents are the easiest to trip.

There are already differences between the male and female limbs before puberty, but once again these are further emphasized by the hormonal flux. Boys have relatively larger hands and feet than girls, and this may be an indirect effect of androgens, which increase secretion of growth hormone from the pituitary gland. Of course, this difference makes sense if we believe that men are built to run, wrestle and stab, but some of the other differences in our arms are harder to explain. If you hold your arm straight with your palm uppermost and look along its length, what you will see depends on your sex. Men's arms follow a fairly straight line, whereas women's bow out dramatically at the elbow – if you have never examined this in a member of the opposite sex, you may be surprised how great the difference is. We do not know why this difference exists, but it means that men tend to carry heavy bags with their palms facing backwards and women hold them with their palms forwards. There is a similar angulation at the female knee, and my nine-year-old daughter has already developed a 'girly' gait as a result. Another difference that has received a great deal of recent attention is finger length, although this is mainly a pre-puberty effect. Boys tend to have ring fingers longer than their index fingers due to prenatal androgen exposure, whereas girls' fingers are usually the other way round. Strikingly, parents who believe that their sons are more disruptive and aggressive are usually bad-mouthing boys with unusually long ring fingers. And as if to make this issue even more contentious, it seems that homo-sexual women tend to have a more male-like hand shape, with longer ring fingers, than heterosexual women.

Perhaps unsurprisingly, the greatest skeletal differences between the sexes occur in the pelvis and legs. Girls and boys have been shown to walk differently from as young as eight-een months, but puberty greatly exaggerates these childhood differences. Among primates, the human pelvis takes an exceptionally long time to mature, and the differences between the male and female pelvis become very dramatic in teenagers. While boys are growing large robust hip joints, girls are widening their birth canal. There has been a great deal of debate about how these distinctively human features evolved, because the human pelvis is exceptional in two ways – we all walk upright, and women deliver large-headed babies. These two demands presumably put different, and perhaps conflicting, pressures on our pelvis. Australo-pithecines seem to have already developed many of our modern adaptations for bipedal walking, but big brains and wider pelvises probably came later, during the *Homo erectus* and *sapiens* eras. Certainly, the pelvic measurements which increase most markedly in modern teenage girls are the very dimensions that are crucial for successful childbirth. Also, the human birth canal is not only wide but also bends around a corner, making the human baby's passage to the outside world unusually tortuous.

All this affects how girls walk, or at least we assume it does.

The width of the birth canal has pushed the female hip joints further apart and this alters the movements of the hip and redistributes the forces which stress the pelvis and thighbone – making girls and women more prone to certain injuries. However, while teenage girls do appear to walk differently from boys, there is surprisingly little agreement about how they differ. Although we assume that women 'wiggle their hips' when they walk, it has been difficult to measure exactly what that entails. The only thing that biomechanics experts seem to agree on is that girls take shorter steps and walk more slowly than boys, and perhaps combining this with protuberant buttocks is enough to make their gait look very different. Equally contentious is the effect that high heeled shoes have on 'enhancing' the female gait. Again, we assume that high heels make women rotate their hips more and arch their backs to make them stick out their bottoms, but both of these effects have been difficult to demonstrate. High heels certainly reduce the range of movement at the ankle and also place dramatically increased strain on the knee joints, but these are not usually thought of as alluring feminine characteristics. So, perhaps surprisingly, teenage girls tottering along in stilettos may be doing no more than shortening their paces, slowing their gait and making their legs look longer (which, confusingly, is a male characteristic).

A final set of skeletal differences between girls and boys is established in the teenage face. Androgens (and the hormones they control) make the skeleton of male faces more robust, with prominent 'scowling' brow ridges and jutting, macho chins. Also, boy's teeth are larger, not because they contain more hard-wearing enamel, but because they have more dentine bulking them out. Androgens also make the voice box cavity larger, the laryngeal cords thicker, and the whole larynx hang lower, creating the distinctive knobbly Adam's apple prominent in the already short male neck. In contrast, teenage girls retain many child-like features – rounded 'open' faces, small teeth and long smooth necks.

This retention of juvenile characteristics into adulthood is called 'paedomorphosis', and it sometimes fools people into making unjustified value judgements. The crudest assumption is that women are not only inherently 'childlike', but also 'childish'. However, we now believe the whole human race evolved largely by paedomorphosis – many of the characteristics we think of as human are actually retained features of infant apes, such as domed heads, weak chins, prominent brows and thin fur. So, from this perspective, teenage girls could be seen as 'leading the way' in retaining more and more juvenile features, while boys partially revert to their ape ancestry. (A rather more disturbing perspective on female paedomorphosis is the effect it might have on male sexual desire. If men's brains are hard-wired to be attracted to fine-limbed, smooth-skinned, high-voiced, round-faced people, does this explain paedophilia? Are male paedophiles simply men who are more attracted to the characteristics women retain from childhood than those women acquire during puberty?)

As we will see in the last chapter of Part One, perceptions of female maturity will be central to our ideas of what teenagers are. So far, we have discovered when human teenagers evolved, what hormonal forces drive them through puberty, and how the changes of puberty relate to their future roles. But puberty is not the same thing as maturity, and even a combination of puberty *and* maturity are not sufficient to make a teenager – there is more to it than that. So why did humans evolve adolescence, and what are teenagers for?

Why are girls more mature?

So far, you may have noticed two things about adolescence. One is that it is a surprisingly long process, and the other is that boys are slow developers – their adrenals and gonads start up later, and even then the male body develops at a fairly leisurely pace. I remember as a teenager that girls of my age seemed very grown up, and that I was growing so slowly that it looked like it would take some years before I caught up. As it turns out, this was not just teenage angst, but a very real phenomenon – teenage change occurs a couple of years later in boys than in girls. However, standing in contrast to this boyish slowness is one important exception: fertility. This law of teenage male sluggishness in everything except fertility is central to understanding teenagers and why we evolved them. Boys are slow for a good reason.

When scientists wish to understand any of nature's apparent 'rules', they always find it helpful to study the exceptions to that rule. And as it happens, we do understand why boys often become fertile before girls, even though the male hormonal system is less mature. The answer is based on the simplicity of male reproduction and the complexity of female reproduction. The function of the male genitalia is simply to make sperm. By mid-adolescence this is a well established, continual process, smoothly generating tens of millions of sperm a day. As you might expect, it is driven by androgens, and it does not vary much throughout adult life. The testicles are there, and they just get on with their job.

Girls are very different creatures, because there is more to female reproduction. Just as boys have to make sperm, girls have to make eggs. However, girls' reproductive organs also have to play a second role, which is that they must be able to make hormones to support pregnancy. The female reproductive system is a dual arena for sex and pregnancy, and it must be able to switch efficiently between the two activities. This dual functionality is built into girls' menstrual cycles, with two weeks of oestrogen dominance leading to the ovulation of a fertile egg, followed by two weeks of progesterone dominance when the system is suspecting that it might be pregnant – if no baby is detected, then menstruation takes place and the whole cycle starts up again. Indeed, this constant flipping between fertility and possible pregnancy is the very reason why women have cycles. Unlike boys who just plug away continually making sperm, girls are in a constant state of reproductive indecision.

The fact that girls cycle when boys do not, explains why teenage girls take longer to become fertile. Not only do they have to develop the hormonal interactions that boys use to maintain their steady state, they also have to develop an extra interaction between the ovary and pituitary gland that boys simply do not need. Just before ovulation, the ovary and the pituitary enter a uniquely unstable state in which they both stimulate each other – a state called 'positive feedback'. This causes a huge, almost uncontrolled release of hormones

which climaxes in ovulation and the start of the proges-
terone-dominated phase of the cycle. Thus positive feedback
is a very special phenomenon, which only occurs in females
and is essential for female fertility. Girls usually become
fertile later than boys simply because they need time to
develop this additional, dramatic interaction. Many teenage
girls may seem reproductively mature when they are in fact
not yet fertile, often undergoing years of erratic, incomplete
cycles, in which they either do not ovulate, or do not yet
possess the hormonal machinery to become pregnant.

If fertility is the criterion by which boys seem more
mature, then the criterion by which girls seem demonstrably
more mature is height. If there is one thing that embarrasses
teenage boys, it is the few years in which they are frustratingly
shorter than girls of the same age. It is bad enough that most
other things are conspiring to make boys look immature, but
being surrounded by unattainable leggy females is the last
straw. However, we will now see that teenage growth is what
has crystallized our understanding of the relative immaturity
of boys – why they are less mature when they are actually
more fertile, and why thinking about the relative maturity of
the two sexes will explain the phenomenon that is the
teenager.

Young animals can grow incredibly rapidly – the cham-
pion growers of the animal kingdom include giant dog
breeds, birds of prey, large flightless birds and whales.
These infants grow so fast that they are on a real knife-edge
of growth, in which any change in their diet can lead to
deformity or failure. Although children often seem to grow
'like weeds', humans are in fact a relatively slow growing
species. We have to get quite big in the end, but we take an
unprecedented two decades to do it. Many mammals of

similar size are fully grown and have their own offspring by the time they are three years old. This slow maturation of our species will crop up several times in this book, but for now you can just accept that we are not in any hurry to grow up.

Once we are born, almost all of our increase in height is caused by structures called growth plates. Most of the long bones in our limbs have a growth plate near either end, and the vertebrae in our backs contain them too. The two growth plates in a long bone are sheets of cartilage interposed between the knobbles of bone at each end, and the tubular shaft in the middle. They have a very ordered internal structure and they spend two decades neatly stacking new bone onto the end of the shaft. As a result, they slowly lengthen the shaft, ratcheting the two ends of the bone further and further apart. And so the child or teenager grows. The process is driven by growth hormone from the pituitary, and androgens and oestrogens play a supporting role as well. But then, at eighteen in girls or twenty-one in boys, the growth plates simply stop working and are replaced by a bony scar – so we cannot grow any longer. We think that oestrogens cause the growth plates to shut up shop (a few rare individuals cannot respond to oestrogen and never stop growing), and this is presumably why growth stops earlier in girls than boys.

Yet knowing the mechanics of how bones lengthen is only the start of the strange story of human teenage growth. Things really get weird when we look at how fast we grow at different ages. The following diagram is just that – a graph of the millimetres grown each month by boys and girls in the first two decades of life:

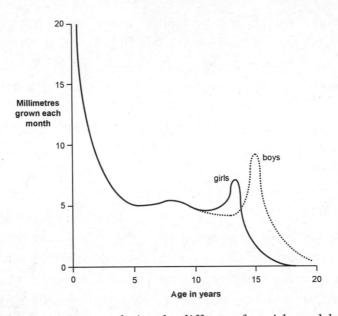

These curves are obviously different for girls and boys. They are also unlike the growth curves for any other animal – most mammals simply grow rapidly after birth and then slow down as they approach adult size. In fact, the human curves are unusual in four different ways. First of all, babies undergo a dramatic deceleration in growth as soon as they are born, and this continues throughout infancy – typical human sluggishness. Second, growth rates pick up very slightly at around eight or nine years of age – the childhood growth spurt. Third, and most dramatically of all, there is a sudden acceleration of growth in the teenage years – the spectacular and controversial adolescent growth spurt. Fourth and finally, the graph is visible evidence of girls maturing more quickly than boys, as their adolescent growth spurt occurs a couple of years earlier. Picking apart these strange features of human growth will explain a great deal about teenagers.

The graph highlights the differences between the heights of teenage girls and boys. Girls are clearly 'spurting' earlier, but of course boys end up taller. However, compared to many primate species the human sexes are not really very dissimilar in height – an average woman is 93 per cent of the height of an average man. We humans are not what biologists call very 'sexually dimorphic'. Similarity in size between the sexes is usually a sign of an animal society where males are not especially dominant, so maybe this says something about us. Of course it also helps for human females to be a reasonable size because their pelvises must allow the passage of such large-headed babies. And scientists have now dissected the male–female difference in height into four causes. The first is that boys are very slightly taller by the end of childhood – maybe 1.5cm – a difference so small that it does not show up on my graph. Also, boys then have a couple of extra years in which to grow *before* their spurt starts, and in those years they grow by roughly 6cm. Next, their growth spurt is bigger than girls', so they gain an extra 6cm during it. Finally, they continue growing a few years longer than girls *after* the spurt because their growth plates arrest later, adding an extra 1.5cm or so.

So it is not just the difference between the sizes of the adolescent growth spurt in the two sexes that makes them interesting. What is fascinating is the difference in timing between the sexes, and indeed the fact that the spurt occurs at all. Scientists argue about human growth a great deal, but most of them agree that the pattern of human growth is very unusual. Furthermore, some suggest that the adolescent growth spurt is absolutely unique to humans, and is in fact the defining feature of our species' life-plan. And I have to say that I agree with them.

Other primate species undergo transient increases in growth rate when they are juveniles, but the sheer magnitude of the human spurt and the way it affects every long bone in the body is truly spectacular. Teenage boys' growth rates can double within a year – imagine growing a centimetre a month! The adolescent growth spurt, and to a lesser extent the childhood spurt, have even led biologists to suggest that humans have added two novel stages to their life-plan. Most animals have infant (breastfeeding), juvenile (weaned, before puberty) and adult (after a sudden puberty) phases of their lives. Humans seem to have added a long childhood (after breastfeeding, but still very dependent) and adolescence – a strange stage of staggered growth spurts and ludicrously protracted puberty.

But why undergo this bizarre growth spurt in adolescence? What is it about humans that has led us to evolve this unusual system? Some have suggested that the adolescent growth spurt occurs so our bipedal abilities can be optimized before adulthood, but I cannot really see why that would be the case. First of all, twelve-year-old children are perfectly good at running about, and surely a sudden growth spurt can only unbalance an adolescent teenager's coordination? In fact, we suspect that children undergo their smaller, childhood growth spurt to help them walk and run. During that spurt it is the legs that preferentially lengthen – I can see it happening almost by the day in my daughter. It has been sensibly suggested that the childhood spurt occurs once children are too large to be carried, and have to 'keep up with the rest of the tribe'. This would also explain why there is no significant difference between the childhood growth spurt in boys and girls.

Another explanation for the adolescent growth spurt is that it is a 'catch-up' stage after the slow growth of childhood. This theory presupposes that we know why humans evolved childhood, and most theories about childhood relate to the brain. Most humans survive not by their strength or speed, but by their wits. It is the three oranges-worth of buff jelly in your heads which will decide your fate. As we will see in Part Two, that jelly takes two decades to mature fully – a slow-growing brain is the price we have paid for being so darn clever. And we now think that we evolved children to be little brain incubators – charming, unthreatening people whose brains are not finished, but who do not eat much of our valuable food because they are small. It makes sense to keep them small for as long as possible, because all they have to do is talk all the time, break things and manipulate adults. But eventually they must grow up, and this is where the adolescent growth spurt is claimed to come in. Children are by their very nature small, and when the decision is made for them to grow up, they might as well do it as quickly as possible. So is the adolescent growth spurt just a crude, inelegantly rapid way to stretch children into adults?

There may be some truth to this catch-up idea, but it seems unsatisfying to suggest that adolescence is just a side-effect of childhood. Also, there are some tangible objections to the idea of adolescence as catch-up. First of all, the brain is by no means 'finished' by the start of adolescence – the process of childhood brain maturation simply merges imperceptibly into a process of adolescent brain maturation no less intense. So there is no sudden cessation of brain development after which we humans have to 'catch up'. Second, if the spurt is for catching up after a slow childhood, why do girls spurt two years earlier than boys? And finally, perhaps the most telling thing about the adolescent growth spurt is that it does not actually have to happen for humans to reach adult height. Children born without gonads, or who have had them removed for medical reasons, do not undergo an adolescent growth spurt. Yet they grow to perfectly normal heights. So, paradoxically, the growth spurt does not seem to exist to help us grow. How can that make any sense?

Perhaps we have been thinking about teenage growth in the wrong way. Maybe the adolescent growth spurt is not important because it makes us grow – maybe it is important *only* because it occurs at different times in the two sexes. One theory is that girls undergo an early growth spurt so that adults can assess their 'potential' as soon as possible. A teenage girl's height is quite closely related to the internal diameter of her pelvis, which is of course very closely linked to her ability to bear children successfully. This theory maintains that in ancient human societies, teenage girls were traded between clans, but that they could only be traded equitably once they had neared their adult height, thus allowing a valid assessment of their pelvic size. And the early growth spurt hastens the time at which this trading can be done. While I cannot find any awful flaws in this theory, it does sound rather cumbersome, and it makes quite a few assumptions. Also, it does not explain why boys undergo a growth spurt – no one cares what their internal pelvic dimensions are.

There is one hypothesis which I believe fits the evidence best. It is a bold idea, and it explains why both boys and girls undergo the adolescent growth spurt, and why girls do it first. It claims that the lag between the sexes is the actual reason for the existence of the spurt. And if it is correct, the spurt occurs expressly to make adolescent girls seem mature and adolescent boys seem immature. It also implies that the period of prolonged puberty and the difference in maturity between the sexes is the very essence of adolescence.

According to this theory, girls undergo an early growth spurt for a good reason – it makes them look mature. Mid-teenage girls are tall, slightly curvy, and have breasts. They look grown up, and are accepted into the adult social world early, where they often start practising their future roles. We will see in Part Two that the female brain may also feign maturity a little earlier as well, but whether or not that is true, we all know about the difficult few years when girls are simply more of a social asset than boys. And we also know that girls often date older boys (oh, the recalled torment). But the irony of all this is that these girls are usually infertile – the complexity of female reproduction means that they are playing at being mature, without actually being able to become pregnant.

Boys do things the other way round. The average mid-teenage boy is short, weedy and has a light dusting of unimpressive body hair (sorry to be so direct). He may also be less socially adept. He is, however, usually fertile, although his unprepossessing appearance means that his fertility is unlikely to be put to the test. He has to wait. He will one day grow into a man with all the sexual weaponry to make women swoon, but not yet. However, one thing that can be said in favour of teenage boys is that they are not threatening – on their own at least – and maybe this explains their slow development. And being unthreatening is a very good idea in a world where alpha males are swaggering around. This theory maintains that the teenage boy has evolved to avoid conflict and survive until he is mature – he is living to fight another day.

It took us a while to get there, but we seem to have found something approaching a definition of adolescence. It is longer than a sudden event, and more complex than a simple gradual shift. It is the time in our lives when a cluster of pivotal processes are arranged in a neat sequence in time. The process of puberty is stretched over a decade at least, and superimposed upon that decade is the unique story of human adolescent growth. Adolescence is the time when the staggered growth spurts of boys and girls conspire to make them as dissimilar as possible at the very same time as their sexuality is lurching clumsily into action. No wonder it hurts sometimes.

Already we can see that being a teenager is a complicated thing. If it can be defined at all, it is only in relation to many different simultaneous processes. However, it does seem to be a good way of linking together the disparate elements of our list of unusual features of the human species. But even now, we have only looked at the physical changes of adolescence. Getting taller and undergoing puberty do not an adult make. What about socializing outside the family, risk taking, self-analysis and conflict? In the next section of this book we will move from the physical to the mental world, and see how there are yet more changes that must occur if we are to reach adulthood. And those changes must mesh seamlessly with each other, and with our bodily changes. If all this intermeshing goes awry, then teenage life can get very difficult.

2. Thinking, Risk and Rock 'n' Roll
Why teenage brains are different

Now old desire doth in his death-bed lie,
And young affection gapes to be his heir;
William Shakespeare, *Romeo and Juliet*

Two recent news stories.

The first story reported the sentencing of a group of young men from Suffolk. All in their twenties, they had been convicted of a serious attack on two other men as they left a nightclub late at night. Sadly, this is not a rare occurrence, but this case had some unusual features. First, the entire incident was recorded on closed-circuit television cameras, and the footage of the defendants kicking the crumpled victims had made the prosecution's case considerably more compelling, as well as filling a few seconds on local news programmes. But a different aspect of the case caught my attention as I was sketching out my plan for this book: the presiding judge justified the sentence he meted out by stating that the men 'acted not as humans, but as unthinking teenagers'.

Another news story described the predicament of a young man from Surrey whose life has been in turmoil since the age of seventeen. Watching the television news one night, he saw an item about an old woman who had been viciously attacked. The teenager was struck by the horror of the attack – so much so that he could not erase from his mind the idea of how terrible it must feel to have done such a thing. He had never been violent, but now the idea that he was potentially able to maim an elderly woman horrified him. He started to go out of his way to avoid old women, especially small, frail ones. He did not want to hurt them; he simply feared that he might. He started to experience panic attacks at the sight of old women, sometimes falling unconscious, until he eventually admitted himself to a psychiatric ward – which he was alarmed to find was itself largely populated by old women. Since that time, he has spent several stints in prison, which he has found to be a reliable way of avoiding his elderly tormentors. He is now a father, but is unable to take his children to the local park to play, for fear of what he might do to elderly female passers-by.

How did the teenage mind get into this mess? How can it be vilified by adults as brutally callous, yet so internally cautious that it renders itself socially impotent? To the outside world, the adolescent brain appears as a tangle of contradictions: stubborn and inconsistent; thoughtless and introspective; exuberant and depressed. Yet to teenagers the problem is often simpler: they simply cannot get their mind to do what they want it to do. Children's and adults' brains often appear well suited to pilot children and adults through their respective worlds, but teenagers' brains seem mysterious, counter-intuitive and frustrating. In this part of the book I will explain why.

Adults make their own decisions, and children have most of their decisions made for them. Teenagers, of course, are stuck somewhere in the middle. As they gradually gain more freedom, they must learn to plan what to do with that freedom. To equip them for this, they are poised at the most exciting point in the story of human cerebral change – the human brain changes throughout life, but that change is most complex in the second decade. Recent scientific discoveries go a long way towards showing that adolescence is, perhaps surprisingly, the high point of the human brain – when the brain is at its largest, most flexible and most mutable. The teenage years are when our greatest asset – our mind – is most forged. Change in the teenage body is important, but for humans, change in the brain is more important still.

However, while there has been a great deal written about the teenage brain in recent years, many of the claims made are not yet justified by the data. In original published papers, neuroscientists are usually careful to explain whether they have reported an anecdote, a statistical similarity or a causal link. Yet much of this clarity is lost when books or articles are written. Often, scientists' speculative suggestions are converted into popular belief. Within the last decade we have learned a tremendous amount about how the teenage brain changes, but only slowly is that change being linked to how teenagers behave. And surely it is that end-product, human adolescent behaviour, which is important. Most of the strange and irresponsible things we do as teenagers will not return to haunt us in later life, but a few of them do. And throughout the rest of this book, I will argue that the behaviours and responses we learn as flexible, malleable teenagers often dictate the course of the rest of our lives.

But remember that teenagers are not just a transitional phase between protected childhood and independent adulthood – they are active, sensitive people whose minds work in a strikingly different way. Teenagers' attitudes to risk, convention and pleasure are entirely different to adults', and we now think we know why. My teenage memories happen to be of lying on the white lines in the middle of the road, or listening to *Led Zeppelin III* for the first time, or standing underwear-clad in the middle of a field watching the July sun rise – teenage life can be uniquely vivid and immediate. All adults have similar memories of adolescence, distorted, distanced and rationalised by the lens of age. But that distortion is not due to nostalgia or simple failure of memory; instead it occurs because our brain has changed since we were teenagers. Those memories come from a time when our mind was different.

Why are teenagers brainier than everyone else?

If we are to understand the central role that adolescence has played in the human brain's struggle for supremacy, we must first consider what is so special about that brain. Sometimes, we humans seem unique, chosen creatures, possessing mental powers denied to all other animals. At other times, animals behave – plan a solution to a problem, or throw us a knowing glance – in a way that makes us wonder if our intellect differs from the beasts in quantity, rather than quality. So: is there a physical basis of human intellectual superiority?

The first thing to emphasize is that there is no structure present in the human brain that is not also present in the brains of other primates. Primates do have some special cell types in their brains, but these are but subtle variations on cells present in other mammals' brains. In fact, the brains of all backboned animals – fish, amphibians, reptiles, birds and mammals – are all laid out on the same plan. I described the evolutionary narrative of this common scheme in my previous book, *Beyond the Zonules of Zinn*, but for now what is most important is that the human brain is the uppermost part of the central nervous system (the lower part being the spinal cord) and is divided into sections which get progressively larger from bottom to top: hindbrain, midbrain, interbrain and side-brains. The side-brains are better known as the cerebral hemispheres – the huge paired corrugated globes which dominate the external appearance of the human brain.

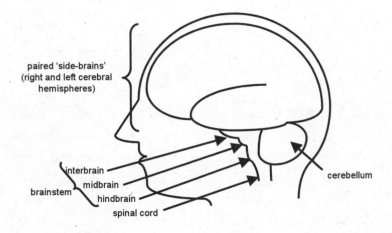

Some parts of the brain are relatively larger in certain species – the smelling part in dogs, the seeing part in falcons, and the tasting part in catfish – but all the parts are present in all the vertebrates. You may be surprised to learn that all the different segments of the human brain are present in modified form in carp, toads, snakes, ostriches and whales. This apparent lack of obvious human difference clearly irritated early anthropocentric anatomists. They spent a great deal of time describing spurious defining features of the human brain, yet it remains an intriguing fact of life that there is nothing structurally unusual about our minds.

Structure is not everything, of course, so we often assume humans are more intelligent because we have big brains –

you may remember Chapter 1's story of the one-orange-size *Australopithecus* brain changing into the two-orange *Homo erectus* brain and the three-orange *Homo sapiens* brain. Yet the human brain is not the largest brain in existence – a bottlenose dolphin's brain is the size of four oranges, and a sperm whale's is a veritable shopping bag of twenty. Of course we do think of dolphins and whales as being bright and chatty, but maybe not *that* bright and chatty. Probably, these cetacean brains are big partly because cetaceans are big. In general, there is a tendency for larger animals to have larger brains – if you know the weight of a mammal, then there is a formula that allows you to predict the weight of its brain with considerable accuracy. We do not know why large animals need larger brains – one might have expected seeing, hearing and thinking to require the same amount of computation whatever size you are – but the link between the weight of body and brain remains extremely clear.

Having said that, there are a few animals that do not fit the mould. For example, primates have unexpectedly large brains for their size, so the predictive formula does not work for them. We have always assumed that the disproportionately large primate brain has something to do with the complex world in which primates find themselves – a three-dimensional, visual, arboreal, diverse, socially complex environment from which a monkey must learn to extract its varied diet and establish its social status, while avoiding death by snake bite or falling from a great height. The big-brain trend becomes more dramatic in the great apes, with the even more outsized orang-utan, chimp and gorilla brains, but it is the human brain that is completely 'off the scale' – far, far larger than would be expected for a mammal of our size. We are the über-primate.

With a large brain comes convolution. Ever since the first known writings about the human brain five thousand years ago, savants have marvelled at the corrugated surface of the human brain. The surface of our cerebral hemispheres is thrown into a tangle of contorted, sinuous ridges, separated by deep clefts – and our ridges and clefts are much more pronounced than those in the brains of the farm animals, horses, cats, dogs and small furry animals dissected throughout history – mice hardly have them at all. For much of the last few thousand years we thought that brain convolutions were indicators of intelligence. However, we now know that brains simply get more corrugated as they get bigger. This is because our brains are internally subdivided into two tissues: grey and white matter. Grey matter is the nerve cells themselves, whereas white matter is the bundles of fibres running wire-like from cell to cell. We do not really know why the cell clusters and the connecting fibres are partitioned into separate grey and white regions in this way – it just seems to have been how mammal brains evolved. This white/grey distinction will be important, however, when we start to look at teenagers' brains.

In the mammalian cerebral hemispheres, most of the grey matter is concentrated into a thin sheet of nerve cells on the outer surface – the cerebral cortex – overlying a complex tangle of white matter fibres beneath. As humans evolved more massive brains, our grey matter sheet had to enlarge: it had to increase its surface area. However, as the volume of a brain increases, its surface area does not keep up: this is just a mathematical fact (if a brain gets twice as large in height, length and width, its volume increases eightfold, while its surface area increases only fourfold). To keep up with the increase in brain volume, the cerebral cortex became folded and corrugated to increase its surface area. The human cortex has now become so folded that two-thirds of the grey matter is hidden in the clefts and only one-third is visible on the surface. Yet this is just a side-effect of having a voluminous brain; it is not in itself a sign of intelligence. Because of this, cetacean cortices are often more convoluted than ours.

So human brains have the same structure as many other animals', although they are unexpectedly large. But if different species emphasize particular parts of the shared brain plan, which parts have we humans emphasized? First of all, we have tended to push a great deal of our inner workings as high up in the brain as possible, an extreme form of a trend seen throughout the vertebrates called 'cephalization'. Functions that would be carried out in the brain stem of most mammals are now carried out higher up in humans: in the cerebral hemispheres. For example, domestic animals walk with their brain stem, whereas we use our hemispheres to do it – although in a cute evolutionary throwback, crawling babies use the old quadrupedal brain stem regions. Because of this increased emphasis on the cerebral hemispheres, our entire system of moving our bodies is different from most mammals, with bundles of grey matter ('basal nuclei') buried deep within the hemispheres helping to control our bipedal strides and fine manipulations.

The human cortex has also enlarged for reasons unrelated to movement. We will soon see how brain regions which process language and interpret social cues have come to dominate our cortex. Even more spectacular is our brain's emphasis on cognition – complex perception, interpretation, emotion, planning and action. Cognition is probably widely dispersed throughout the human brain, and indeed has started to take over several previously 'not-very-cognitive' regions. However, there are certain areas of the cortex which seem especially important for our higher thought processes. One of these, right at the front of the cerebral hemispheres, is called the 'prefrontal cortex'. The prefrontal cortex is exceptionally large in humans and as a result the human brain looks comparatively front-heavy, an evolutionary trend called 'frontalization'. As we will see, the prefrontal cortex is a crucial part of the adolescent story, as it is the seat of much of what is unique at that time – it is 'teenager-central'.

In the scheme of things, the human brain has obviously been driven to the extreme, becoming an oversized, cephalized, frontalized, cognitive powerhouse. And in Part One we saw how the last phase of this evolutionary story was preceded, tantalizingly, by the emergence of the first human teenagers. We were tempted to speculate that it was the appearance of teenagers that actually allowed the final stages of human brain evolution to occur, but is this what really happened? To find out we need to look not only at how the human brain evolved over millions of years, but also at the strange story of how the human brain is repeatedly made anew in each of us as we develop.

Animals and people go though several stages of development. The first is the embryonic stage, in which a single fertilized egg plays out an elaborate series of genetically organized duplications, migrations and contortions to become something that looks remarkably like a little animal. Humans are embryos for roughly nine weeks, by the end of which they are an inch and a half long and have all their major organs in the right shape, in the right place, and ready to grow. The rest of gestation is taken up by the fetal stage, during which most of those preformed organs simply grow until they reach the correct size at birth.

It is beyond the scope of this book to tell the entire story of prenatal development, but there is an important point worth making about the formation of the brain and the rest of the body. For most of the body, this division of intrauterine life into two phases – a rapid, organizing, shaping, embryonic phase and a slower, growing, fetal phase – is quite distinct. Babies have to arrange their body plan when they are very small simply because the chemicals which coordinate that arranging can only travel a few millimetres. In compete contrast, the developing brain does not fit into this neat embryonic-then-fetal scheme. The brain is structurally very incomplete by nine weeks of gestation, so it must continue to develop its internal architecture throughout pregnancy. The brain is a tardy organ, and it could be argued that it is still in an 'embryonic' phase when every other organ in the body is in the 'fetal' phase. This prolonged period of delicate construction makes the brain especially vulnerable to poisons and deficiencies; as a result, the brain is the organ most often affected by congenital abnormalities

This relative tardiness of the brain is a feature of all mammals, but in humans things become even stranger after birth. Whereas the rate of brain growth declines rapidly after birth in other animals, the human brain continues its frenetic pace of development throughout the first two years of life. This is, in fact, the main reason why the human brain is so large – not because of its size as it squeezes through the enlarged birth canal. This uniquely lengthy postnatal period of brain growth has led some scientists to claim that the human infant is really a fetus wrenched into the outside world simply so that its brain can expand, free from the restrictions of its mother's pelvis. The human infant's brain is remarkably demanding: the brain of a resting newborn has been estimated to use a staggering 87 per cent of the child's energy, compared to 20 per cent in adults. Many of the statistics are impressive: the developing human brain may be five times more metabolically active than a chimp brain; the one-orange-sized human neonatal brain grows twenty thousand new nerve cells *per second*; and the number of new connections between those cells must be far greater.

This screaming pace of infant brain growth means that the brain has almost attained its final size before childhood is over. In fact, the brain reaches 95 per cent of its adult size by the age of six. That is why children are little people with big heads. Of course, it is superficially obvious to say that children are little, but in Part One we saw that evolutionary biologists have argued that children are just that: small, energy-efficient repositories for the slow-growing human brain.

All this leaves teenagers in a strange situation. We know that teenagers evolved immediately before the evolution of the large *Homo sapiens* brain, yet it seems that the modern *sapiens* brain almost stops growing before adolescence. This suggests that the evolution of the teenage stage in the human life-plan did not *directly* cause the increase in brain size that has made our species so successful. In short, you do not need teenagers just to grow a big brain. Instead, the role of adolescence in brain evolution will prove to be more subtle. We do not have teenagers so we can grow a big brain; we have teenagers so we can configure and perfect the huge sprawling brain we develop when we are children. This subtle, honing role for adolescence makes sense when you consider that, in the context of the human life-plan, there is much more to a brain than its size – does a six-year-old child seem 95 per cent adult to you?

So development of the human brain is uniquely slow and full of contradictions – the embryo's brain that lags behind the other organs; the fetus's brain that is actually 'embryonic'; the infant's brain that is actually 'fetal'; the six-year-old's brain that is nearly full size, though still clearly infantile in functioning. And then there is late childhood and adolescence during which the brain must whittle itself into adult form, without being allowed to get much bigger. Size-wise, adolescence is a period of relative cerebral stasis, which is surprising, considering the dramatic mental changes which are taking place. From now on we must see the adolescence of the brain as a period of change without growth.

However, one striking fact that emerges from studying the growing human brain is that teenagers have the largest brains of all. After the age of six, the brain continues to grow very slowly – adding those final 5 per cent by early adolescence. Brain size peaks at around twelve years in girls, fourteen in boys (the 'boy lag' occurs here too) and then starts a slow shrinkage that continues through adult life. Adult readers may find it strange that teenagers have larger brains than them, but teenage readers will probably smile and feel that they knew it all along.

The causes of these unique human patterns of brain development are hotly debated. I have already mentioned that we assume that primates needed big brains to cope with their complex environments and social machinations. Why humans' brains became even larger is more contentious. One popular theory centres around the idea that the evolution of the human body and life-plan was linked to our diet. At some point in our past we opted to eat high-quality foodstuffs which were difficult to acquire. These foods may have been quite varied, and rather than specialize our bodies for acquiring just one type of food, we became generalists. Our bodies were not strong or fast or ferocious, but they could be used in many different ways. And to control them we evolved a large brain that was inherently flexible – able to learn and train to do new things over periods of weeks, months and years. The downside of this is that humans are not innately good at anything; the upside is that our adaptable brains can learn to be good at *everything*. Studies in modern hunter-gatherer societies suggest that it takes decades for men to learn how to hunt, decades for women to acquire their skills at food acquisition and childcare. And with a little cooperation we got to the moon.

The biological mechanisms by which humans reached this high level of cerebral adaptability are now becoming apparent. The genetic basis of the triumphant human brain is now becoming clear. Every human cell contains roughly twenty thousand genes – twenty thousand digital instructions coded in a long molecule called DNA. This is impressive when you consider that some cars contain more parts than that, yet are capable of rather less impressive feats. We share almost all of those twenty thousand genes with chimps, and so our brain was probably formed by genes which were modified during the course of human evolution, rather than created anew. By looking line-by-line at the changes in our genes since the era when the common ancestor of chimps and humans walked the earth, we can see that there has been particular pressure for change in some of the genes used in the human brain. Frustratingly, we do not know what most of these much-changed brain-used genes actually do, but no doubt further research will soon tell us. Once we crack the code, the story of human brain evolution is there to be read, fossilized, as it were, into our DNA.

To take one example of the genes implicated in forging the human brain, let us look at those involved in a rare congenital condition called 'microcephaly'. These genes have changed far more in the lineage leading to humans than in the lineage leading to chimps, and they are used mainly in the developing cerebral cortex. When children inherit damaged forms of these genes, they are born with small, slow-growing brains, and experience learning difficulties. Intriguingly, their adult brain is approximately the size of an *Australopithecus* brain: one orange. These few genes that have changed dramatically in human evolution, which are used in the cortex, and whose dysfunction leads to a pre-*Homo* brain size, are too good evidence to ignore. It is a tour de force of human evolution that the spectacular, species-defining increase in human brain size could be the result of just a handful of genes already present in other primates.

But a large brain is no use if it is not organized, and this is where adolescence comes in. We now know that there is nothing structurally unique about the human brain – we simply have much more brain relative to our body size than other animals. We are gradually approaching the philosophical realization that the difference between humans and other animals is an unsatisfying mixture of quality and quantity – we have so much cerebral cortex that it has reached a 'critical mass' which permits our advanced intellectual processes. However, we possess this exuberant mass of cortex by the age of six, and it does not function as an adult brain until we are much older. This unwieldy mass of writhing chaotic cortex must be trimmed and pruned and ordered and streamlined until it has the potential to think like a Newton, a Picasso or a Presley. The brain is built too large, but it is flexible and plastic. It is the plasticity of the human brain that makes us so adaptable – an adaptability that allowed us to survive the unspeakably traumatic changes in human life that were forced on us as we evolved in the changing African landscape. Simply to cope with the world, we had to have mutable, mouldable brains.

That is what teenagers are for…

Are teenagers driven by their hormones?

Before we soar in the rarefied air of human cognition, let us bring ourselves back down to the earthiness of lust and flirting. There are many books about the differences between the male and female brain – some of them making challenging claims about the role of sex in human mental misery, some claiming that nature outweighs nurture or vice versa, and some even suggesting that we come from different planets. Rather than rehash what has gone before, I would like to start this new look at the changing adolescent brain with three suggestions.

First of all, it is obvious to any casual observer that the brains of teenage boys and teenage girls often work in different ways. Of course, I use the word 'often' because there is always overlap between two groups of individuals. That said, it is hardly surprising that there is a difference between girls' and boys' brains and behaviour; it would be frankly weird if the most complex organ in the body did not differ at all between the sexes.

My second suggestion is that the differences between the sexes result from a mixture of intrinsic, hard-wired, sex-defined differences in the structure of the brain, and alterations in brain function in response to the different ways society treats girls and boys. This is the 'nature and nurture' debate, and when considering which of these two shapes the brain, it seems impossible to reach any answer other than 'a bit of both'. An entirely hard-wired brain would be inflexible and unresponsive, while an entirely nurture-defined mind would be vulnerable, inconsistent and directionless. The power of nurture was confirmed to me this morning as I put my children on the school bus, only to hear another parent shout at her five-year-old son, 'Stop whinging like a *girl!*'

My third suggestion – and I am sure you knew this was coming – is that the most interesting time to study the differences between the sexes is the teenage years, when they are exposed in their most unrefined, visceral form.

For the rest of this second part of the book, I am going to assume that all these three suggestions are correct.

Adolescence is sex differences stripped bare. As children we are already amused by the differences between the minds of boys and girls, but as teenagers these differences take on an alarming immediacy. Teenagers are told that they are at the whim of their hormones, but we will see that teenage mood is probably not just an outward indication of hormonal fluctuations. Other factors could influence adolescent behaviour. For example, it is unlikely that the teenage mind is oblivious to the newly sexualized body in which it finds itself – surely a brain develops differently if it is housed in a male body than in a female body? To further enhance this adolescent cerebral divergence of boys and girls, teenagers start to become sexually attracted to people for the first time. I still remember a time in my early adolescence when girls were *painfully* attractive, and I am sure I am not the only one who felt that way. However, although teenagers can become overwhelmed by the mental differences between the sexes, we need not be. We will certainly examine the differences between teenage boy-brain and girl-brain, but we must realize that the adolescent brain has contributed more than just sex to our species' unprecedented success. Most animals do sex, but only we humans do supremacy.

So, how early does the brain know its sex? The answer to this question is that brain cells in male and female embryos behave differently very early on. For many years we thought an embryo's sex was conferred entirely by a simple genetic switch on one of the sex chromosomes. This switch turns the gonads in male embryos into testicles, with the result that those testicles then produce the hormones that masculinize the rest of the body (or not, in female embryos). Apart from a slight difference in the speed of growth of male and female embryos at the few-cell stage of development – perhaps due to a slight rearrangement of the sex chromosomes – we thought that the presence or absence of the genetic sex-determining switch was the first sign that an embryo 'knew' what sex it was. However, more recent studies have shown that even before that early stage, nerve cells in the brain respond differently to sex steroid hormones depending on whether they come from a female or a male embryo. This remarkable discovery suggests that there is a special process by which sex is ingrained in the brain even before it is built into the rest of the body – providing yet more evidence that the brain is our primary sexual organ.

After that early stage, most scientists agree that androgens and other hormones from the testicles are instrumental in causing many of the biological differences between infant boys and girls. For example, a surge of hormones in fetal boys directs the conversion of the indeterminate embryonic genitals into penises, prostates and so on, while the absence of such a surge allows girls to progress along their preordained path of clitorises and uteruses.

It is widely believed that the controlling role of androgens also helps to make boys' brains different from girls'. However, there is much uncertainty about how this happens, and there are several reasons for this. First, much of our understanding of what is now known as 'brain sex' comes from experiments in other species – especially primates and rodents – and it is unlikely that these species develop in exactly the same way as humans. As we will see, this has led to confusion about when the brain responds to masculinizing hormones – it could be before birth, around birth, in the first few months of life, or any combination of those. Another problem is that there are conflicting claims about structural differences between the male and female brain: for example, certain regions of the rodent brain differ very markedly between the sexes, while corresponding differences in humans are less dramatic. Compounding these problems is the fact that it is inherently difficult to study human behaviour, especially in secretive teenagers who are all too aware when they are being observed. As a result, some of the best information we have about sexual behaviour comes from observing copulation behaviour in other species – a very crude measure to compare with a species like ours in which copulation is just one small facet of sexual behaviour. Indeed, we also face the problem that there is no single sexual behaviour which defines men, nor one which defines women – humans like to swap roles for the sake of it. Finally, as we have already seen, young humans are easily influenced by the people, culture and environment around them, making simple controlled studies of teenage sexual behaviour almost impossible.

It may be difficult to study, but the 'hard-wiring' of sexual behaviour is hugely important for understanding teenagers. It would be simplistic to think of them as slaves to their hormones when, in fact, far more important may be the behaviours etched into their brains before they were six months old. Studies in other species certainly support this view. In rodents, the presence of androgens in the first few days of life is critical, dramatically masculinizing and 'defeminizing' later, adult copulation behaviour. In monkeys, the effects of androgens are similar but less clear-cut. Androgen exposure before birth once again masculinises and defeminises later sexual behaviour, although androgens do not stop fetal female monkeys having sexual cycles when they reach adulthood – evidence for a complex system in which different aspects of sexuality may be hard-wired by different doses of hormones, types of hormones, or hormones present at different times.

Of course we cannot carry out such experiments in humans, and anyway, it is harder to methodically assess the complexities of masculinzation and defeminization in flirty, shy human teenagers. However, there is now evidence that the large amounts of androgens made by boy babies in the first few months of life (see Part One) may have an actively masculinizing function. Also, doctors sometimes create experiments for us (for example when sex hormones are administered to pregnant women to manage abnormalities of pregnancy) which show that the sex steroids often thought of as 'female' may also play a role – exposure to oestrogens and progesterone during gestation feminizes subsequent sexual behaviour. Despite the difficulties inherent in studying humans, it is increasingly clear that teenage sexual behaviour is built upon a brain already sexualized around the time of birth.

Much of this perinatal sexualization is invisible – it leaves no structural change in the anatomy of the brain. But there are some tangible anatomical differences between the male and female brain, and all of them are established by the start of adolescence. Famously, the average man's brain is larger than an average woman's brain, by roughly 9 per cent. This is probably an effect of the 'whale phenomenon' I mentioned earlier: that larger animals have larger brains. The same is true of the increased convolution of the male brain, which is a necessary mathematical consequence of its greater volume. But to balance the size discrepancy, there is clear evidence that in places the female cerebral cortex is thicker than the male.

Probably more important are the specific differences between the sizes of particular brain regions, although in only a few cases do we know why these occur. For example, two of the basal nuclei (grey matter clumps important in human movement and cognition) show 'sexual dimorphism' – one called the 'caudate nucleus' is larger in girls and another called the 'globus pallidus' is larger in boys. Also, the large white matter bundle connecting the right and left cerebral hemispheres and allowing them to communicate with each other – the corpus callosum – is often said to be larger in girls. Hormones seem to be at work here: the indisputably larger corpus callosum of the female rat has been shown to be induced by oestrogens during the period of young adulthood. But, as if to confirm our idea of a 'perinatal template' for later sexual behaviour, the juvenile rat's brain can only respond to oestrogen if it has already been 'forewarned' by exposure to oestrogens around the time of birth.

The differences between the sexes that make most sense are those in the hypothalamus – the ancient region on the underside of the brain which controls the body's biological functions. For example, there are differences between the male and female 'paraventricular nucleus', which secretes the hormone 'oxytocin' involved in birth contractions, lactation, orgasm, affection and trust – at least some of which phenomena are of considerable importance to teenagers. Yet what those structural differences mean is still unknown. Also, the 'suprachiasmatic nucleus' differs between the sexes, and this is thought to be the location of the brain's main twenty-four-hour clock – more about that later. Most intriguing of all are the differences in a patch of grey matter in the hypothalamus known to be involved in sexual behaviour in many animals: the 'preoptic nucleus'. The preoptic nucleus exhibits more sexual dimorphism than any other part of the brain – one region is five times larger in male rats than in female rats, and this discrepancy is caused by differences in steroid hormone levels around the time of birth. The differences are less spectacular in humans – perhaps our sexuality is less hard-wired than a rat's – but they are present all the same. A further,

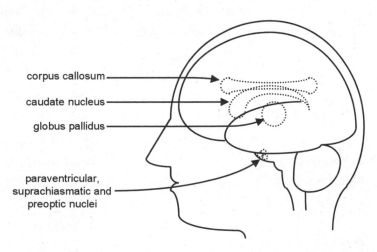

corpus callosum

caudate nucleus

globus pallidus

paraventricular,
suprachiasmatic and
preoptic nuclei

more controversial claim is that in homosexual men, some parts of the preoptic nuclei are more like those of women than those of heterosexual men. The story of the preoptic nucleus is set to run and run.

So assigning a sex to the brain is a process that occurs very early in life, and one which affects many brain regions. Teenagers inherit a brain that already knows what sex it is, and for all we know, it may have its future sexual preferences built in too. Of course much of that sexuality was hidden during childhood, but it now starts to express itself. So how much of teenage sexual behaviour is built in at the start, how much is controlled by hormones, and how much is socially learned?

Of course, hormones are the usual suspects. Yet it has been surprisingly difficult to demonstrate hormonal effects on teenage behaviour. Circulating levels of androgens often correlate with the age at which boys first have sex – this means that in a large cohort of boys, those with higher androgen levels tend to start having sex earlier. However, this does not imply a cause. The high androgen levels could be encouraging boys to have sex, or alternatively some brain process more active in certain boys may cause increased androgen levels and, independently, sexual activity. And when sexual behaviours not directly related to copulation were studied, no link at all was found between androgens and behaviour. Teenage boys do report more sexual frustration than girls, and report that this adversely affects their concentration. However, this may be because boys, relatively immature in other ways, are able to experience orgasm from an earlier age – maybe they are frustrated because they know what they are not getting.

So there is no spectacular direct causal link between hormones and sexual behaviour in teenage boys, although androgens presumably act indirectly by making the body mature and capable of being stimulated and aroused. In fact, we are not at all sure that androgens have much direct effect on sexual desire in adult men either. Paradoxically, this may be because male behaviour is so sensitive to androgen concentrations – very low levels of androgens may cause reduced sexual activity in adult men, but most men are way above the range within which the level of androgens actually makes much difference. Most men's brains are already 'fully dosed' with androgens. As we will see later, psychological factors are a more common cause of sexual dysfunction in adult men, and the same is probably true of teenage boys. That said, teenage boys may spend a few months with their androgen levels slowly climbing through the range within which dose matters, but studies so far may not be sufficiently detailed to detect those few months. We could work all this out much more quickly by castrating some teenage boys and dosing them with testosterone, but there are not many volunteers for that sort of study.

Girls are even more mysterious. Once again, concentrations of androgens correlate with the age at which girls start to have sex, but what is causing what is as uncertain as it was in boys. There are several published studies about sexual behaviour in monkeys, but measuring the effects of hormones on frequency of copulation does not tell us whether the hormones make females more interested in sex or whether they simply make them more attractive to males. Once again, human sexuality seems just too complex to draw direct parallels with other primates. Several questionnaire-based studies have asked when during the menstrual cycle women most like to have sex, but they might prefer sex at certain times because their varying hormones alter the sexual responsiveness of their bodies, rather than because these hormones directly affect their brains. However, some studies have attempted to study aspects of sexuality not dependent on the body's responses – for example, the regions of women's brains activated by erotic images do seem to change over the course of the menstrual cycle. Of course, it could be argued that we cannot have an entirely cerebral sexual response, divorced from bodily arousal – no doubt how sexy you feel is bound to be partly dependent on how you feel about your body.

The lack of a direct link between hormone levels and female sexual behaviour has led to explanations similar to those made for men. For example, women may respond to androgens, but only at a level higher than that usually present in their system – an argument which implies that women are not usually dependent on androgens for their sexual behaviour. And teenage girls, with their lower hormone levels, are presumably even less driven by their hormones.

Some primatologists have suggested that there is a very good reason why we cannot discern much of a link between hormones and teenage sexual behaviour: the link has been extinguished as our species evolved. According to this theory, a distinctive feature of humans is that sexual behaviour has been 'disconnected' from the hormones that used to drive it millions of years ago. This disconnection makes the links between hormones and sex very remote. We have already seen that hormones are responsible for building a body that can respond sexually, and this is of course necessary for sexual activity, but those hormones no longer drive our day-to-day sexual behaviour. Freeing sex from hormonal control is probably what freed human sexuality to become more complex, social and subtle. Hard-wired teenage brains may need only the tiniest hormonal nudge to set them thinking about the pleasure of the company of the opposite sex (apologies to those who want to know about homosexuality – we will discuss it in Part Five – but here again there is little evidence of hormonal control of homosexual behaviour). Once in the presence of the object of their desires, the brain takes over and the rest of sex is a very mental affair – talking, toying with social relationships, testing others' sexual interest. In humans, even the act of copulation is all about thought – practising, experimenting, teasing and communing.

This theory that humans have separated sex from hormones explains a great deal. It explains the subjective mental intensity of love; it explains why most sexual problems are psychological; and it explains why we cannot find clear links between hormones and teenage sexual behaviour – maybe they are not there to be found. Of course it runs counter to the popular perception that teenagers are controlled by their hormones, so we will have to find different reasons for their distinctive behaviour. Yet the theory also liberates us to see the differences between the sexes for what they are – a template of 'mental sexuality' laid down around birth, and subsequently overlaid by the social influences of adolescence.

Looking at romantic and sexual behaviour in teenage boys and girls, we can now start to dissect out hard-wired and socially induced phenomena. For example, falling in love seems to have little hormonal basis – children often develop crushes before puberty, and premature puberty does not hasten the age at which children first fall in love. Also, a major factor determining whether teenage girls exhibit 'masculine' interests and behaviour is their own perception of whether their parents consider those things 'acceptable' – a clear example of social influences at work. Sexual hard-wiring is also very evident – visual sexual imagery activates different parts of boys' and girls' brains, with boy's brains showing a higher level of activation. It has even been claimed that the female and male brain are wired up to yield entirely different responses to most situations in life – girls hard-wired to empathize, and boys hard-wired to systematize and abstract. We are still not certain how fundamental are the differences between the sexes, but we will see later that these theories can help to explain why girls and boys suffer different psychological problems in adolescence.

We have been forced to discard our idea that teenagers are controlled by their hormones. Instead, they are playing sexual roles programmed into them around the time of birth, and this leaves our traditional view of adolescence in disarray. Somehow it was reassuring to dismiss teenage behaviour as the direct result of a hormonal maelstrom. Our new view of the teenage brain is more alarming: a sexual organ emerging from the slumber of infancy, suddenly exposed to the teenage social and sexual whirl. In this new light, the adolescent mind now appears obstinately independent yet frighteningly fragile. But there is yet more change to come: at the same time all this is happening, the brain must also completely redesign itself.

Why are teenagers' brains different?

We all know the teenage mind. It differs in so many ways – it experiences overwhelming sensations, strong, sudden emotions and dramatic, unpredictable moods. It flits between intense sociability, complete introversion and apparent thoughtlessness. Always searching for its place in the world and honing its intellect, it is untrammelled and uninhibited, reaching peaks of creativity unmatched in adults. It is almost as if there is too much mind inside a teenager's head.

The adolescent brain differs from the adult in almost every conceivable way. It is not just a brain that has recently discovered sex and hormones, and it is certainly not a simple transitional stage between child and adult. The most frustrating and the most rewarding aspects of the adolescent mind are not obviously related to sex, and some of them seem diametrically opposed to sociability, too. The teenage mind is so distinctive that we must look to some fundamental biology to explain it. And the teenage brain cannot be explained easily – it behaves in a uniquely complicated way, it is larger than at any other age, and its appearance in our evolutionary history

directly preceded our species' attainment of incredible intellectual powers. I believe that the teenage brain is the central
phenomenon of the human race.

That is all very well, but what real, tangible evidence do we
have of what is going on inside the adolescent cranium? Until
ten years ago, the evidence was very thin and was based on
dissection of the occasional dead teenager's brain which
found its way onto the neuroanatomist's slab. The brains
available for comparison were few, and obviously only gave a
'snapshot' of brain anatomy at a single, fatal moment in time.
What was needed was a way to follow the brain development
of many healthy people throughout their first few decades of
life – without having to kill them. And the ability to do this
came in the form of a huge magnet and some radio antennas.

Magnetic resonance imaging (MRI) is a technique that
sounds so unlikely that I still find it hard to believe that it
actually works. I once underwent a two-hour MRI scan for
an experiment conducted by one of my friends, and I can
report that I was entirely unaware of having my mind
probed. I was slid into the centre of an enormous dough-
nut-shaped magnet, which was then switched on. This had
the effect of aligning the protons in my head – water and fat
are full of protons, mainly at the centre of hydrogen atoms,
and protons spin about an axis which can be aligned along
a magnetic field. An antenna then fired a short burst of
radio waves into my head, which temporarily knocked my
protons out of alignment. Within a tiny fraction of a
second, my head protons then fell back into the thrall of
the magnet, and in the process emitted a radio signal which
was picked up by a second antenna. This was repeated at
millions of points arranged in a three dimensional grid
throughout my head, and the return signals were combined

into a picture – many pictures in fact, each one a cross section though my brain.

Early MRI studies yielded low resolution images, but technology gradually improved. Resolution increased, and the full force of modern computing power was brought to bear on the radio signals spewing from people's magnetized heads. The growth and distortion of cerebral convolutions could be tracked over the years, thicknesses and volumes of the living cortical sheet were measured, and subtle differences in individuals' anatomy were followed in real time. Then a new technique, functional MRI, allowed scientists to measure blood flow and cellular processes in different regions of the brain – this was the procedure applied to me. Suddenly we can look in detail inside a living human brain. Within the last ten years we have finally gained the near-magical ability to follow the course of brain development from childhood through adolescence to adulthood. And during adolescence, something exciting is happening to the cerebral cortex's corrugated sheet of grey-matter nerve cells and the dense tangle of white-matter nerve fibres beneath it.

For some time it had been suspected that the amount of cortical grey matter was at its highest at some point in childhood or adolescence. Rather than reflecting sheer numbers of neurons, it was thought that that this is due to an exuberance of connections, or 'synapses', between nerve cells. The number of synapses in a two-year-old's brain is already probably greater than that in an adult's brain. This proliferation of synapses seems to continue throughout childhood, and has recently been confirmed by MRI studies which show the cortical grey thickening at this time. Intriguingly, more recent studies have shown that the profusion of grey actually reaches its zenith during adolescence, after which the grey matter thins and wanes.

The rise and fall of the cortical grey is not a simple issue, however: the amount of grey matter reaches a peak at different times in different individuals and in different regions of the brain. Although these variations mean that MRI studies must be interpreted with caution, some findings are now generally accepted. First of all, the average age of peak grey-matter thickness occurs two years earlier in girls than boys – yet another example of 'boy lag'. Secondly, different regions of the cortex follow different developmental paths. For centuries anatomists have arbitrarily divided each human cerebral hemisphere into four regions – 'occipital', 'temporal', 'parietal' and 'frontal', and by good fortune these have turned out to be the site of fairly discrete brain functions.

At the back of the brain are the occipital lobes, involved in the processing of vision. These behave unlike the other lobes in that their grey matter steadily grows throughout adolescence and into our twenties. Protruding from the lower flanks of the brain are the temporal lobes, with roles in memory and processing of sound information – including the especially human skill of understanding language, which has been localized to a region called Wernicke's area. The temporal lobes have also been implicated in some strange phenomena, such as religious experiences. The grey matter in the temporal cortex reaches its greatest thickness around sixteen years of age and then recedes. The upper flanks of the brain are made up by the parietal cortex, a region which analyses touch and taste sensations, but also synthesizes and interprets the evidence of all the senses to a very high level of understanding. The parietal grey peaks at eleven years old, although some studies suggest that this occurs even earlier.

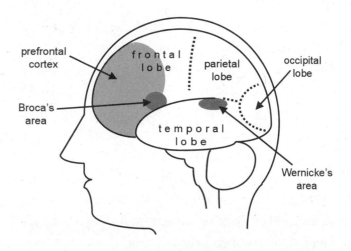

The regions of the teenage brain which have attracted most attention are the frontal lobes – which form the front half of each cerebral hemisphere. This is because the frontal lobes are unusually well developed in humans, and they probably carry out many of the functions which we do better than other animals. They are also claimed to be the site of many of the differences between adolescents and adults. The back parts of these lobes play a role in controlling movement, including Broca's region, specialized for the articulation of speech. The front parts of the frontal lobes are even more exciting as they probably carry out many processes required for cognition: for example concentration, attention, and transient storage of multiple concepts in a conscious 'work area' where they can be analysed and compared. The pre-frontal cortex is also where we 'think about what we want': organizing sequences of actions or communication aimed at achieving our goals. We humans are an inherently social species, so it makes sense that as part of this planning process, the prefrontal cortex also plays a role in controlling our impulses and instincts, allowing us to think ahead and take account of the thoughts of others. Considering what the prefrontal cortex does, and how we change as we leave child-hood, it is not surprising that we sometimes think of it as the 'teenage cortex'. The amount of prefrontal grey matter peaks at around twelve years of age, but even within the prefrontal cortex there are variations – the part controlling impulsive, instinctive behaviour peaks some years before the part we use to plan methodically towards our goals.

And the new MRI studies have shown us that human cortical grey matter is by no means fully developed by the start of adolescence. Far from it: some regions have not even finished their first, synapse-proliferating, connection-forming phase. So the story of the cortical grey is another example of the painfully slow development of the human brain. Of course, all this leads to the question of what makes the cortical grey shrink once it has reached its peak during adolescence. It seems unlikely that this is a crude degenerative process, because adults are better at many mental tasks than teenagers. Instead, we think the shrinkage of the grey is due to a very specific and well-organized adolescent restructuring of the exuberant child's brain.

By the time the cortical grey reaches its maximum volume, it is an absolute tangle of nerve connections. There are more synapses in the brain now than at any other time, and we believe that there are simply too many for the brain to work efficiently. Adolescent grey matter shrinkage is probably due to selective loss of synaptic connections between cells, a process called 'pruning'. Put simply, synaptic pruning clears away the connections which are not needed in adulthood. There appear to be rules underlying pruning, and certain synapses are especially liable to be clipped off: synapses which are not used much; synapses which stimulate rather than inhibit neurons; synapses which affect nearby neurons more than those which cover large distances; synapses in some cortical regions more than others. Throughout the teenage years, the overgrown brambles of the childhood cortex are savagely nipped and hewn to leave a beautifully minimalist arboreal structure, stripped down to the few branches that convey the most appropriate messages in the most efficient way.

Of course, it is teenagers who have to live through this pruning process. We know this can be a difficult experience, so why does our brain develop this way? As it turns out, 'overgrowth followed by pruning' is a very common way to grow brains, and it occurs in other parts of the human brain, and in other vertebrates' brains too. It may seem wasteful to grow all those synaptic connections only to remove most of them again, but this method is powerful because it gives the brain immense flexibility. During the first phase, synapses develop in an almost uncontrolled way, but in the second, pruning, phase, the architecture of the brain can be sculpted to reflect the demands being put on the teenager. Thus, for a few years, teenagers have plastic brains which can wire themselves up not according to a preordained genetic blueprint, but in the light of experience. Teenagers can learn how to behave, communicate and succeed, and then preserve the connections that support those processes – as we will see in Part Four of this book, we learn many of our adult patterns of behaviour while we are teenagers, and adolescent pruning may be the reason why. The teenage brain is a 'behaviour establishing machine', leaving adulthood as nothing more than a slow decline into mental and emotional inflexibility.

The regions of cortex which undergo the most pruning during adolescence are the ones we most associate with teenage behaviour. The parietal cortex is savagely pruned in the second decade, a time when we start to ascribe extremely subtle and complex interpretations to our perceptions of the world around us – this is why a ten-year-old could not write a sonnet. The prefrontal cortex is subject to even greater attrition, and it has been suggested that this leads to increased analytical abilities, as well as the more disruptive aspects of the teenage mind – lack of foresight, emotional volatility, impulsiveness and lack of thought for others. The concordance of grey-matter reconfiguration and teenage psychological change seems too striking to be a coincidence.

There is yet more change underway in the teenage brain. So far we have considered only the changes in the grey matter. Also delayed into the second decade of life is the maturation of the white-matter fibres beneath, which can carry information over great cerebral distances. White-matter fibres are white because they are coated in a fatty substance called myelin which electrically insulates them. There is more to myelin than insulation, however: it alters the way nerve fibres carry impulses so that signals 'leapfrog' along nerves up to a hundred times more quickly. Myelination is the neuronal equivalent of replacing the pony express with a fibre-optic cable, and this upgrade is being installed throughout the developing adolescent brain. We used to think that myelination was nearly finished by adolescence, but MRI has now shown that this was wrong.

So, just as the grey matter is thinning out, the white matter beneath is fattening up, literally, with lardy myelin. In fact, we think that the thinning of the grey matter is caused not only by synaptic pruning, but also by compression by the white matter growing underneath it. Indeed, MRI measurements show that many areas of grey that appear to be thinning are simultaneously being pushed outwards from the centre of the brain by white matter expansion – paradoxically, grey often thins in brain regions that are growing. However, white matter myelination follows a different pattern from grey matter pruning – not so focused on the prefrontal and parietal regions, and with different relative timings in different regions. In general, the back of the brain myelinates earlier and the front later, with a 'wave' of maturation surging from back to front over the course of the second (and third) decade of life. This trend neatly follows the evolutionary tendency of humans to 'frontalize' – to progressively concentrate more and more novel functions in the frontal lobes over millions of years.

In the human brain, particular pathways seem to receive special attention – being preferentially myelinated, perhaps because of their importance for the human way of life. During adolescence there is very marked myelination of the pathways between Wernicke's and Broca's language areas, for example. Also a major site of change are large bundles of nerve fibres called the 'corticospinal tracts', which in humans carry most movement instructions to the muscles of the body, allowing coordinated locomotion and fine manipulation. And links between memory and emotion areas are also speeded up, perhaps to allow emotional responses to be tempered by the light of experience. Finally, a major step is taken towards adulthood with the myelination of the huge bundle of white matter connecting the high-level interpretation regions of the parietal cortex with the concentrating-and-planning regions of the frontal cortex – the original information superhighway.

There is obviously an enormous amount of neuronal rearrangement taking place in the adolescent cortex – this is certainly not a quiet hiatus between childhood proliferation and adult stability. Rather it looks like the most crucial phase of perfecting that all-important human brain. Whether it is pruning an overabundance of grey-matter synapses, or accelerating the sluggish fibres of the immature white matter, major brain reconfiguration is a central feature of being a teenager.

However, before I hastily leap to state that such-and-such change in the adolescent brain is responsible for so-and-so antisocial teenage behaviour, I must sound a note of caution. There is a large gap in our understanding of the teenage brain. We now know a great deal about how its structure changes over the teenage years. We also all know how teenagers behave. However, I must emphasize that we have almost no hard evidence linking structural change to actual behaviour. Yes, it is tempting to link maturation of the Wernicke's–Broca's pathway with the newfound articulacy of late adolescence. Yes, it is tempting to ascribe the unpredictable emotional and social reactions of adolescents to the frantic pruning of the prefrontal cortex. Yet the fact remains that we have not yet demonstrated any of these links. The links may indeed be there, and the circumstantial evidence is compelling, but we simply cannot carry out the necessary experiments to confirm them. We cannot inject human adolescent brains with chemicals which suppress or promote pruning or myelination in particular regions, so we must settle for cautious interpretation of correlation and anecdote.

Another caveat is that although human teenagers are powerhouses of nervous development, they are not unique. As I have already said, synaptic overgrowth followed by pruning occurs not only in humans, but is a popular system of brain development in many species. The same is true of delayed white-matter myelination. However, the extreme delay in pruning and myelination is an unusually human characteristic, and the way these processes occur in different cortical regions at different times may be a defining human characteristic, too. In addition, I must emphasize that the process of change kick-started in adolescence continues into adulthood, albeit in decelerated form – some regions of grey matter shrink continuously into the seventh decade of life.

Finally, it is important to realize that we do not yet know what drives the different phases of teenage cerebral maturation. It has been proposed that adrenarche, the onset of sex steroid hormone secretion by the adrenal glands in late childhood, drives the formation of all those synapses. And it has also been suggested that the steroids produced by the ovaries or testicles at puberty drive the pruning process. The evidence put forward to support these hypotheses is indirect, however – it is based on the effects of sex steroids on mood and memory in the adult brain. Also, failed adrenarche and failed puberty do not cause a collapse of adolescent brain development. And finally, common sense suggests that adrenarche and puberty would be very erratic phenomena by which to time the complex chronology of brain development – after all, some normal teenagers undergo puberty eight years later than others.

Despite these reservations, it is clear that something very big is going on in the teenage brain. And it is hugely tempting to link that change to the unpredictable, distinctive and anti-social things that teenagers do. You may like to consider this link the next time there is some adult–teenager conflict in your household. Could the slamming of the door and the shouting be just as much a result of the 'inflexible staidness' of the adult as the 'exuberant flexibility' of the teenager?

This view of adolescence as the meticulous organizing of an overgrown brain gives us new perspectives on the role of teenagers in the evolution of the human life-plan. Maybe the two-orange *Homo erectus* brain had stumbled along for two million years at the very limits of how big a run-of-the-mill primate brain could be. For the brain to become bigger and brighter still, perhaps we had to evolve teenagers. They were a wonderful new innovation which gave us an extra decade of paced cerebral reorganization which allowed the *sapiens* brain to attain its unprecedented size without going off the rails. Maybe this is why teenagers appeared just before the modern brain did – without them we would all be huge-brained, incoherent dullards.

Why all the sleep, risk and anger?

It all seems so reasonable at the time. Rolling out of bed on Saturday afternoon, shouting at your parents, and then going straight out to meet up once more with the 'wrong sort of people'. All these things make perfect sense when you are a teenager, yet all would evoke at least a pang of guilt in an adult. Such apparently unreasonable behaviour has done more than anything else to give teenagers a bad name. Spots, hair and smelliness are simply unfortunate – it is behaviour which brings teenagers into conflict with everyone else.

We have just seen that the adolescent brain is a 'work in progress', pruning its grey matter and myelinating its white matter. Yet teenage behaviour does not seem much like a halfway house between childish and adult behaviour patterns, nor does it look like a vague 'general underdevelopment' of an adult brain. Adolescents exhibit some very distinctive behaviours, which are so consistent between individuals that parents can joke about their lazy, grumpy, irresponsible teenagers knowing that other parents will know exactly what they mean. This stereotyped nature of teenage behaviour suggests that there are certain ordered, consistent changes that take place in all teenage brains. It also hints that some of this behaviour may, heaven forbid, actually take place for a reason.

So let us work our way through the Saturday afternoon terrible triad of laziness, risk-taking and anger.

Laziness

As well as a constant source of parental humour and frustration, teenage sleep patterns are also a striking exception to the rule. In general, we sleep less as we get older. Human fetuses sleep almost all day with a few short breaks for some wiggling about. We all know that newborn babies sleep most of the time, and that infants and children need less sleep as they get older. Adults need a few hours less sleep than children, and as they age a further couple of hours are chipped off their daily sleep requirements. Yet teenagers stand in apparent contrast to this trend – first they turn all lazy and find it difficult to get up in the morning, but towards the end of adolescence they seem to need less sleep than anyone else; or at least they appear to cope better with sleep deprivation.

The teenage inability to get out of bed is more important than just the parental frustration it causes. It has been shown that teenagers who find it harder to get up in the morning feel more sleep-deprived than their peers, fall asleep more during the day, are more likely to miss school and perform less well academically. Also, they feel unhappy more often, are more drawn to risky activities and suffer more accidents and injuries. It is important to be clear about cause and effect here – the research shows that these symptoms are not caused by actually getting up late; instead they are commoner in teenagers who report that they have difficulty getting up at the same time as everyone else. This distinction, along with

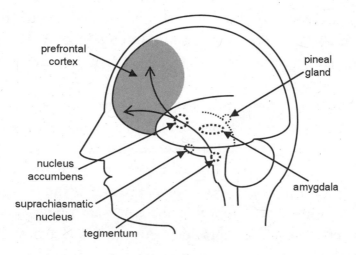

prefrontal
cortex

pineal
gland

nucleus
accumbens

amygdala

suprachiasmatic
nucleus

tegmentum

the wide variety of symptoms, suggests that these teenagers are not simply lazy. We now think that teenagers' sleep needs are different, and that they vary between individual teenagers.

Of all the mental processes investigated by the formidable tools of modern neuroscience, sleep has proved to be one of the least willing to give up its secrets. We are still not sure why we sleep, nor exactly what is going on inside the sleeping brain. However, we have had some success studying teenage sleep patterns because we know which two parts of the brain impose our twenty-four-hour day–night 'circadian' cycle. The first of these is the 'suprachiasmatic nucleus' in the ancient hypothalamus, which contains a tiny circuit of cells working as a twenty-four-hour clock inside your head. If you went to live in an underground cave, your internal clock would make you wake at approximately twenty-four hour intervals, and you would still subjectively feel that there was a cycle of 'day' and 'night'. And, once you re-emerged from your troglodytic vacation, your inner clock would be reset by the ambient circadian cycle of light and dark, should it have erred from an exactly twenty-four-hour rhythm. When I did my PhD at the London Institute of Zoology, there was a room next door to my lab where hamsters were housed in constant darkness (which hamsters seem to enjoy). Computers hooked up to the running wheels showed that the normal hamsters woke up and went for a run every twenty-four hours. However, there were also hamsters with damage to a single gene used in the suprachiasmatic nucleus, and they went for a spin every twenty-two hours. And hamsters with two damaged copies of the gene went running every twenty hours. The suprachiasmatic nucleus is almost certainly the central clock controlling the brain, but it is an inaccessible thing, and impossible to study in human teenagers.

Instead we study the suprachiasmatic nucleus by proxy. By a circuitous route, daylight entering the eye controls the activity of a second region, perched on top of the brain stem: the pineal gland. The pineal exerts its effects by secreting an unusual hormone called 'melatonin' during the night, and this is why the pineal is easier to study – we can measure melatonin in teenagers' blood and saliva. Thus the activity of the pineal is more measurable, famous (people take melatonin tablets to alleviate jet lag) and tangible – for example, seasonal animals like sheep and deer use the increasing amounts of melatonin secreted during the lengthening autumn nights to tell them to breed. However, we must bear in mind that, of the two, the secretive suprachiasmatic is probably more important than the probeable pineal in teenagers.

So what happens to the circadian clock in adolescence? We already had a hint in Part One that something strange is going on when we saw that pituitary reproductive hormone secretion follows a unusually circadian pattern in teenagers. Also, the pineal gland shrinks noticeably during adolescence. Most remarkably of all, when melatonin secretion was measured in teenagers, it was discovered that the night-time peaks and daytime troughs of melatonin occur approximately two hours later than they do in adults. Obviously this teen-lag could explain a certain unwillingness to get up in the morning – maybe 8 a.m. feels like 6 a.m. to a teenager – but the evidence is not as clear-cut as some press articles and books might suggest. Melatonin is only a very indirect indicator of the activity of the all-important suprachiasmatic nucleus, and these results could just as well indicate a disconnection between the suprachiasmatic nucleus and the pineal during adolescence. We are not allowed to stick electrodes in teenagers' hypothalami to find out more, but I must admit it would be interesting to put some teenagers in a cave to see if they think days are twenty-six hours long.

There are other possible explanations which could turn out to be just as important. For example, sleep is not entirely controlled by the inner clock. We do not slavishly go to sleep at the same time every day – instead, we sleep when we want to or when we think we should. Everyone knows that they get tired faster when they are busier, and also that they recuperate better when they sleep soundly. One can almost imagine a repeating 'sawtooth' pattern of fatigue accumulating during the day and then being expunged as we sleep, only to build up again the next day. This sawtooth model of sleep is now thought to act alongside the internal circadian clock to drive sleepiness, and it may be just as important in explaining adolescent morning sleepiness. For example, sleep could be less restorative in teenagers than adults, making them need more of it. Alternatively, teenagers may somehow accumulate tiredness during the day 'without realizing it', and thus go to bed with more sleep requirement than they expected. This could also explain why they like staying up late as well. However, this wish to stay awake in the evening could also be explained by another factor – the sheer excitement of the teenage world. Teenagers may stay up late simply because they feel they have so much to do, including the thrill of interacting with other teenagers. In short, when you are a teenager, the night is exciting and the morning is boring. Finally, another factor gradually starts to disturb sleep patterns in teenage girls – quality of sleep varies throughout the menstrual cycle and will continue to do so until the menopause.

So there are many possible explanations for teenage morning sleepiness, although as yet only some have firm evidence in their favour. Whichever of them is the culprit, it is clear that the phenomenon does not reflect simple adolescent laziness as is often assumed. Next time the parents among you are angrily wrenching off the duvet, do bear in mind that the poor dears probably cannot help it.

Risk-taking

One of the great triumphs of neuroscience has been the mapping of particular functions of the brain to specific pathways within it. Over the last few decades, scientists have established what is effectively a roadmap of almost all our mental functions. While it remains tentative in places – we still do not know what traffic travels along some of the roads – this map gives us a striking sense that the brain is potentially comprehensible.

Some of the most important routes on this map are the bundles of nerve fibres which achieve their effects by releasing the chemical dopamine. There are four such bundles in the brain and they perform a wide variety of functions, from controlling movement to controlling lactation – doctors prescribe dopamine-affecting drugs to treat conditions as diverse as Parkinson's disease and excessive milk production. Other dopamine systems will appear repeatedly in this book, because they control the way our brains deal with incentive, motivation, risk, reward-seeking, enjoyment and mood. In fact, it is astounding just how many of our everyday mental processes are controlled by dopamine, especially in teenagers.

Incentive, motivation, risk, reward-seeking, enjoyment and mood are interlinked phenomena. Indeed, we can start to see why this is so if we view dopamine pathways being there to make us seek out things we have previously enjoyed. Enjoyment is an important process, because it makes us happy and drives us to seek out the same enjoyable things in the future. If you consider that those enjoyable things could be food, or sex, or social interaction, then you can see why these dopamine pathways have been essential for human survival through the ages. Although we might like to think of ourselves as complex beings, much of our time is spent just looking for things we like, albeit in sometimes convoluted ways. And as we grow up, risk-taking becomes an important part of mature reward-seeking. As we enter adolescence, the things we want are no longer simply lying around us, or in the gift of our parents – we must risk failure, injury, embarrassment or even death to fulfil our desires. Risk-taking is when an animal gambles with loss in the hope of making a greater gain, and adolescence is when humans start to learn the skill of exploiting risk.

The dopamine-secreting brain pathways involved in reward-seeking course between three regions: an area in the brain stem called the 'tegmentum', clusters of nerve cells higher up called the 'accumbens' nuclei, and the huge, seething adolescent prefrontal cortex. We assume that the tegmentum–accumbens pathway is of an older evolution, perhaps derived from an ancient food-seeking system, whereas the tegmentum–accumbens–cortex pathway may be newer, allowing us to bring our intellect to bear on the challenge of finding desirable things. But these dopamine pathways are not themselves directly involved in acquiring things from a teenager's environment; instead they are more like a control knob, increasing or decreasing such behaviour.

Great change is afoot in the dopamine pathways during adolescence. Some of the evidence for this comes from studies in lab animals, but what information we do have from human teenagers tells the same story. The data is fiendishly complex, but can be summarized by saying that the activity of the old tegmentum–accumbens dopamine pathway decreases in the early teenage years, while the newer tegmentum–accumbens–cortex system becomes more active. The effects of dopamine are complicated, but this shift from the old to the new is dramatic, and we believe that it is the cause of much of the mental change that occurs between childhood, adolescence and adulthood. For children and adults, these changes make perfect sense – a shift from visceral, gut-reaction desire fulfilment to a more intellectual, considered, planned approach. However, teenagers have to cope with the transition in between.

In young rats – inquisitive, intelligent, sociable creatures rather like human teenagers – the dopamine shift occurs just as it does in humans. And the shift causes many familiar-sounding effects – an interest in ingesting mind-altering substances, a greater willingness to encounter the unknown, a desire to meet new and interesting rats. Human teenagers are probably experiencing similar changes. One way that the dopamine shift could cause human adolescent behaviours is that it may suppress the old accumbens system before the newer cortex system is fully functioning, leaving teenagers without any way to control their behaviour. Combine this with a large, unrefined mass of prefrontal cortex, and teenagers start to look like a dangerous combination of inquisitiveness and carelessness. Alternatively, another possibility is that the dopamine shift renders teenagers relatively unable to experience pleasure, so they seek more and more risk and stimulation in an attempt to overcome their adolescent emptiness and grumpiness. No surprise, perhaps, that sad teenagers often lock themselves in their rooms and listen to loud music – a stimulus known to activate the tegmentum–accumbens–cortex dopamine system.

However, suggesting that teenage risk-taking is an unfortunate side-effect of brain maturation is to ignore the fact that taking risks is an essential part of life – and a skill that human teenagers must master. Much more likely is the possibility that a period of risk-taking is deliberately built into human adolescence – to allow us to develop these skills at a time when the likelihood of actual permanent damage is relatively low. Supporting this idea that 'risk is good' are studies which show that teenagers who undertake risky behaviours tend to have higher self-esteem and social competence. Also, a desire for risk is obviously built deep into the human mind. Many people enjoy dangerous sports throughout their lives, often saying that it gives them something absent from the rest of their lives. Others enjoy gambling, even though they know that bookmakers and casinos make huge profits from their customers. Of course, everyone is different and some individuals can take things too far. For example, under experimental conditions, teenagers who have shown anti-social behaviours in the past are more likely to take unreasonable risks for the tiny chance of a large gain. (So are lotteries simply an institutionalized way of exploiting the antisocial?)

But if risk is inherently good, why are so many teenagers killed, injured or permanently thrown into lifelong cycles of damaging behaviour? How can risk-taking be a normal part of teenage life when it causes so much damage? I think there are two answers to this question. The first is that, as with everything in evolution, the advantages of risk-taking must outweigh the disadvantages. A risk-taking teenager may learn so much more about exploiting their environment and inter-acting with others, that the risks are simply worth taking. Secondly, humans no longer inhabit the world in which they evolved their teenage risk-taking behaviour. In the hunter-gatherer world of a million years ago, teenagers probably encountered risks that were easier to assess – being caught by a lion, falling from a tree, being rejected by a hoped-for sexual partner. Today, our Stone Age *sapiens* brain must deal with risks that it did not evolve to assess – injecting heroin, unprotected sex, driving on wet roads.

So teenage risk-taking is an unavoidable part of life, and presumably a desirable one too. However, it is an example of the *Homo sapiens* brain not coping with the modern world it has created – modern humans are notoriously poor at assess-ing modern risks. As we will see in the rest of this book, some much-feared teenage activities are rather harmless, whereas some apparently innocuous ones can cause long-term damage. Yet no matter how unpleasant it may feel, we must accept that teenagers take risks, and all we can do is try to reduce the potential consequences. This acceptance may seem bleak, but it springs from all the scientific evidence showing that teenagers should be expected to do things that adults find unreasonable. Some have even suggested that this acceptance should be incorporated in the legal system – that teenagers should be considered 'biologically' less culpable for their crimes.

The dopamine controversy is only just beginning.

Anger

Third on our Saturday-afternoon teenage list, anger is a complicated thing. Teenagers get angry or aggressive for several different reasons, and we must differentiate between these causes to understand adolescent behaviour. At the outset, I must emphasize that aggression confers very clear evolutionary advantages – it protects us from potential predators, it goads us into catching our prey, and it allows us to assert ourselves and react against social unfairness. And as a sign of its importance, the hypothalamus contains several regions for aggression, anger, hunger and sexual behaviour, all in close proximity.

A major cause of aggression is fear – in most animals the last defence against being eaten is to attack. Fear is so important that it has its very own part of the brain, two blobs of grey matter of the size and shape of almonds, called the 'amygdalae'. The amygdalae have complex internal structures and play diverse roles, but fear is at the centre of their existence – they become active when animals experience direct physical threats; destruction of the amygdalae renders wild animals tame; MRI studies show that they become active when we are shown frightening images. The amygdalae even have a 'social' aspect to them too – they respond to fearful expressions on other people's faces. Because of their role in perceiving threat, the amygdalae are important in social interaction and attributing emotional weight to people or events. In humans they do not do this job on their own, because the prefrontal cortex takes over some of their long-held functions, but the amygdalae are important all the same.

Early in human development, differences appear between the sexes. The amygdalae bear receptor molecules for androgens and as a result they grow faster in boys. Some other regions involved in behaviour have oestrogen receptors and grow more quickly in girls. Do teenage girls and boys respond to perceived threats from authority in different ways because of these differences? Of course there may be good reasons why boys need larger amygdalae to make them more sensitive to threat – in hunter-gatherer societies men spend more of their time dealing with dangerous animals, or jostling for position in the male hierarchy.

Recent MRI studies have looked at the development of the adolescent amygdala. It seems to have distinctive characteristics, but the results are more complicated than is often claimed. When shown images of fearful expressions, children and adults show similar levels of activation in their right and left amygdalae, whereas adolescents show preferential activation of the right amygdala. The nearby regions of prefrontal cortex show similar trends in boys, but the two sides of the prefrontal cortex respond equally at all ages in girls. These right–left asymmetries are difficult to explain, although as we will see, the right side of the cortex is usually the inarticulate side. These intriguing results are a long way from demonstrating a specific neurological reason why teenagers are quick to anger, but they do show that the anatomy of adolescent fear is different from that of children and adults. It is tempting to suggest that a shift is occurring, from the 'gut reaction' amygdala to the more circumspect cortex – like what we saw happening to risk-taking during adolescence – but the evidence is not yet clear. One likely reason for this uncertainty is that the amygdalae are not homogeneous blobs, but complex aggregates of many dissimilar parts, each with different roles in assessing threat and attaching emotional weight. Our imaging techniques are simply not precise enough to dissect changes in all the different subsections of the living human amygdalae.

Another cause of teenage aggression is jealousy, and here there is a clear difference between the amygdala of girls and boys. In some ways, humans are easy to study because they understand stories. We can show people filmed narratives, expect them to empathize with the protagonists, and study how their brains react to the artificially constructed situations. When people are shown stories about sexual infidelity, certain parts of the brain light up. The male brain shows greatest activation in the amygdala (fear) and hypothalamus (aggression, among other things), whereas the female brain is activated in the temporal cortex. Thus men may have a more direct link from sexual jealousy to fear and aggression. Could this explain why men are more likely to attack sexual partners, become pathologically jealous, or engage in stalking?

Regardless of what induces anger, I think many of us subjectively think there is some sort of threshold which must be reached before we become angry – a level of summated fear/frustration/jealousy at which we are pushed over the edge. It also seems as if this threshold changes over time, and that it varies between people – we are touchier when we are tired, and some people snap more easily than others. Also, individuals differ in how they express their anger – a teenage girl may become verbally aggressive; a teenage boy may resort to violence. However, the biological basis of anger is only slowly being elucidated, and here at last we have clearer evidence of a hormonal effect on teenage behaviour.

Some of this evidence linking hormones to anger comes from studies in teenagers with under-active gonads, who thus have inherently low concentrations of sex steroids. These teenagers report that they become more physically (but not verbally) aggressive when they are treated with androgens or oestrogens. Also, girls exposed to high levels of androgens (made by overactive adrenal glands) before they are born are more competitive and aggressive. Together, these results suggest that hormones act both directly on teenage behaviour, and also indirectly by hard-wiring the brain very early in life. Also, these studies tie in with data gathered from athletes. Not only do circulating androgen levels show a link with competitiveness, but losing at a sport causes androgen levels to fall. And conversely, winning causes androgen levels to increase, especially when winning is accompanied by an especially euphoric mood.

The links between androgens and competitiveness have led to some worrying suggestions. If androgens cause competitiveness and success causes androgens to increase further, then perhaps the same could be true of another risky, demanding, committing behaviour: crime. Could a single successful crime lead to a vicious circle of increased criminal motivation and yet more crime, with androgen stimulation fuelling the loop? We have already seen that teenagers are often authority-ignoring risk-takers, and now we have a possible mechanism by which that incaution and resentment could spiral into crime. Worse still, some controversial studies show that violent criminals tend to have an underactive prefrontal cortex, as well as unusual amounts of various brain chemicals. Of course all this is rather speculative, but the fact remains that most crime, and most violent crime, has its origins in adolescent boys.

Teenage boys have yet more problems, of course – they are more sexually frustrated, they are frustrated by their own slow development, they tend to overestimate their own abilities and they have an inbuilt drive to show off those abilities to others. Because of this, it has been suggested that the link between hormones and the brain is not in fact directly related to anger, aggression or violence, but to dominance. We humans all like to establish our place in the social hierarchy, and many of us are able to do it by intelligence, humour, appeasement or ingratiation – for most of us anger is an admission of social failure. But some teenagers find that they are simply not very good at intelligence, humour, appeasement or ingratiation, and maybe that is why they opt for a more aggressive route.

The hormonal and anatomical causes of teenage behaviour are gradually becoming clear, and many scientists now believe it is also possible to explain this behaviour in terms of evolution and reproduction. After all, the sexual roles of boys and girls are fundamentally different, and this difference may explain why teenage boys find life so difficult. According to most theories of human reproductive ecology, boys are competitive with each other, they initiate courtship and sex, but they are vulnerable to rejection by girls. Also, males invest less in reproduction than females, and this makes them potentially more promiscuous, yet at the same time they are more sexually protective of their partners – an unattractive inconsistency which teenage girls often resent. This general lack of male sexual discrimination may explain why men are more likely to derive pleasure from pornography, to use prostitutes, and to want to investigate unusual sexual practices. On a lighter note, it may also make boys less modest about their bodies than girls – after all, teenage boys jumping naked into a lake is funnier and carries a less sexual overtone than teenage girls doing the same thing.

So there are many factors that, in concert, may make teenagers angry or aggressive: unusual ways of processing fear, a tendency for jealousy, the possible effects of sex hormones. Combine these effects with impetuousness, partially developed mechanisms for controlling emotions, and even, as we will see later, the onset of many mental illnesses, and adolescence becomes a dangerous time. We always hear when an armed teenager runs amok in an American school, and we often hear about teenage fights, crime and suicide. And the parents among us sometimes have to deal with apparently random outbursts of ire. Yet adolescent mood can seem unpredictable and inexplicable for one good reason: the human species is mentally complex, and teenagers are simply trying their best to grow up into adult humans.

We started with adolescent anger and we ended up taking a journey through aggression, competitiveness, violence, dominance and sex. In the complex human brain all these things are tangled together whether we like it or not, and adolescence is usually our first encounter with this worrying tangle. In a later chapter we will see how one of the greatest challenges faced by teenagers is to accept that they have this unspeakable conflict within them, yet still construct a self-image they can live with.

Why do teenagers start to think in new ways?

If there is one thing society expects teenagers to do, it is to develop their mental skills. We humans cherish our advanced thought processes for good reason: we have created a world in which our success is often determined not by crude physical effort, but by our ability to solve intellectual, practical and social problems. Centuries ago we invented educational systems to encourage cognitive development in children and teenagers, and ever since we have been searching for the best way to make schooling work.

Yet surprisingly little of what is done in school is based on scientific evidence. Most has its roots in anecdote and experiences of teaching in the past. A large part of the contemporary educational system dates back to the eighteenth and nineteenth centuries – long before we had any idea what biological attributes actually constitute 'intelligence'. In fact, we still have only a patchy, disputed understanding of cognition and intelligence. Considering how much importance we attach to higher mental functions in teenagers, it is amazing how little we have studied the biological basis of those functions. What work has been done has often focused on obvious abnormalities of learning, rather than studying the mainstream mêlée of adolescent academic success and failure. Add to these problems two worrying facts – that we have no clear idea why teenagers think differently from children; and the suspicion that for the first time in history, teenagers' bodies are maturing faster than their brains – and you can see why our need to study teenage cognition is so urgent.

Defining intelligence is almost impossible. For many children passing through the modern educational mill, intelligence may seem to be defined as academic achievement. Of course, academic ability is a useful skill in modern life (and is conveniently easy to measure), but equating intelligence with academia seems a narrow thing to do. The world is full of people previously written off as academic underachievers, but who have established successful businesses or thrived in unexpected careers. Many people's intelligence lies in their ability to analyse themselves, capitalize on their strengths, remedy their weaknesses and interact with others. This has led to more general theories of intelligence, emphasizing things such as the ability to succeed in one's social context or in one's own opinion. And for us too, it might be best to take a very flexible approach to intelligence in teenagers. Perhaps for the sake of argument we should think of intelligence as the end-product of cognition – our mental ability to approach and solve problems.

Just by observing young people, educational psychologists have developed many theories of how teenagers learn and think, and in the rest of this book we will see that some of the simplest ideas have proved to be the most powerful. For example, it has long been proposed that young animals are 'hard-wired' to copy adult behaviours – a suggestion so simple that it is easy to underestimate how important this process can be in humans. Similarly, crude forms of learning based on reward and punishment are just as effective in people as they are in puppies. Another form of learning that always strikes us a ludicrously simplistic is Pavlovian conditioning, in which an animal's responses (drooling) to a stimulus (food) may be transferred to another, irrelevant stimulus (a bell ringing). All in all, we may think we are very complex creatures, but our obsession with role models, our compulsion to seek reward, and the prevalence of self-defeating 'Pavlovian' abnormal human behaviours, all show what very simple roots underlie the ways we behave.

Yet however crude the drives behind adolescent learning, the mental skills we develop in the second decade of life can be spectacular. For decades, educational psychologists have argued that human cognitive development progresses in a series of neat stages, and the stage in which teenagers are supposed to find themselves is called the 'formal operations stage' (although some suggest that many people never reach this stage). Giving the stage a name makes it seem more discrete and less complex than it really is, but teenagers do start to tackle many mental tasks that children simply cannot attempt. They can create and manipulate abstract concepts, cope with shades of grey in arguments, generate novel arguments based on initial assumptions, approach tasks methodically and set themselves distant goals. They can also perform the powerful feat of analysing their own thought processes – generating their own ideals, criticising and improving their own thinking and analysing their own worth. And to top it all, they develop a strong social dimension to their thinking: they can analyse relationships, verbally articulate all their new thoughts to others, and 'mentalize' – create mental models of how other people think.

Children may be charming little people who can talk and think a little, but we do not become fully mentally human until we are teenagers. Because powers of self-analysis and mentalization develop during adolescence, it is tempting to suggest that they are characteristics which humans could evolve only once we had evolved teenagers, several hundred thousand years ago. This is why I think teenagers have been the secret of our success as a species. However, as we will see in Part Four of this book, there is a downside to these skills – self-analysis and mentalization can come to obsess teenagers to a point at which they can no longer function in society.

So if adolescence is the launch pad for adult thought, where and why does all this new mental agility take place? Although some features of teenage intellect may seem subtle or intangible, psychologists have been very successful at developing methods to test them under laboratory conditions. We can now objectively measure how these skills change after human brains are injured, or which tasks light up which parts of the brain in an MRI scanner. Surprisingly, we can even assess many of these abilities in monkeys and rats too. And the results of all these studies can be distilled down to one statement: teenagers develop many of their cognitive abilities because the prefrontal cortex is activated by dopamine pathways ascending from lower parts of the brain. There may be other processes involved as well, but once again the primacy of the prefrontal cortex and dopamine is clear. For example, in some cognitive tests teenagers use their prefrontal cortex more than either children or adults.

Teenagers do not develop all these skills in a neat synchronized ascent towards maturity. Instead, different cognitive abilities develop at different rates. The ability to ignore irrelevant information and process salient data reaches adult-like levels early in the teenage years; but not until nineteen or so do we fully develop our ability to hold many competing, interacting concepts in our mind at once. Also, the speed with which we can interpret the emotions expressed in the human face is actually lower in the early teens than in either children or adults – perhaps because of the messy over-exuberance of brain synapses at that time. And of particular interest to me in my role in selecting students for university is the claim that teenagers become fluent in the 'formal operations' of physical entities before they can do the same for analysing social relationships, raising the fascinating possibility that scientists may become intellectually mature before artists do.

So why are dopamine's effects on the prefrontal cortex so important? Maybe picking apart all the separate strands of teenage cognition will help us find out.

First of all, if a teenager is to undertake an act of cognitive brilliance, he or she must pay attention and concentrate. This may seem obvious, but getting a brain to ignore the enormous mass of irrelevant incoming information and focus on the job at hand is actually a miraculous feat of computation. The brain must decide what is salient, and then blank out everything else – consider how easily a child gets distracted from their work. Imaging studies and experiments with drugs which block the action of dopamine suggest that the prefrontal cortex is a major site of 'attention', and that dopamine is its main controller. Blocking dopamine reduces our ability to focus. The results are not quite that simple, however, and the borderlands of the parietal and temporal lobes may be involved too – hardly surprising, as this is where most of the irrelevant sensory information and memories are distractingly buzzing about.

Establishing goals, and the satisfaction of achieving them, are also hugely important in human cognition. Humans have risen above the simple short-term seeking out of food, shelter and sex seen in other animals – and we often maintain goals in our heads for long periods of time while we formulate elaborate intellectual, technological and social plans to achieve them. As a result, the old tegmentum–accumbens system for reward-seeking has been supplanted by a newer tegmentum–accumbens–prefrontal system to allow us to carry out our uniquely convoluted forms of desire-fulfil-ment. Indeed, recordings of the activity of individual nerve cells in the primate prefrontal cortex suggest that there are specific neural circuits that generate goals and respond to their attainment – once again, we suspect, switched on by dopamine during adolescence. And just as important as the identification of goals is the ability to change tack: once a goal is set, we retain the ability to set it aside temporarily and work towards other goals if necessary. For example, injury of the prefrontal cortex can lead to a tendency to persevere exces-sively with tasks, when the 'sensible' thing to do is to disengage and concentrate on something else for a while. And tellingly, drugs which alter the dopamine system can be used to cure this futile doggedness.

Another part of the cognitive process that seems to be required for many different tasks is 'working memory' – not the long-term storage of memories, but the collecting together in a temporary conscious 'workspace' of any con-cepts, memories and perceptions we wish to think about. Only when these elements have been assembled in 'the front of our mind' can we start to compare, contrast, link and rearrange them. This ability to toy with several different ideas increases dramatically during adolescence and is probably what allows us to discover underlying themes, develop conceptual frameworks, and think laterally. It may even be what allows us to be creative, by combining and juxtaposing dissimilar concepts. Indeed, it seems that teenagers' minds are often more creatively free than adults', and this may explain their creative leaps in fields as diverse as mathematics and popular music. In fact, I have always suspected that most people's lives follow paths dictated by moments of adolescent insight and creativity.

The teenage years are a time of wonderful mental experiment, when many of us decide who we are and where we are going. And working memory, which allows teenagers to achieve this, seems to be another prefrontal cortex/dopamine phenomenon. During adolescence, the regions of the brain active during working memory change dramatically from a childlike distribution in the deep nuclei of the brain and a region of infolded cortex called the 'insula', to a more mature localization in the prefrontal cortex. This region remains predominant in adults, although working memory becomes more tied to specific little areas – a trend which it is tempting to blame for the loss of the untrammelled mental processes of adolescence. And the role of dopamine in stimulating all this working memory is now known in some detail – neuroscientists are now elucidating how different dopamine-binding molecules in the prefrontal cortex control the development of working memory. Indeed, depletion of those binding molecules reduces working memory as severely as surgically slicing off the frontal lobes.

Again and again we have found aspects of teenage and

adult cognition that are carried out in the prefrontal cortex –
tasks which light up MRI scans; tasks which are hampered by
prefrontal injury; tasks which are altered by drugs which
change the activity of dopamine in the prefrontal cortex.
Decision-making seems to be located here. Thinking about
one's own thought processes is here. 'Mentalization', the
ability to ascribe mental thought processes to others and then
to predict those processes, is here. There even seem to be prefrontal areas that are the seat of processes as specific as
arithmetic – tangible cerebral locations for our sense of
number. So much of the mental machinery we need to
succeed is packed into the prefrontal cortex, fired up during
adolescence by the dopamine sprinkled upwards from the
brain regions beneath. Yet while the role of dopamine is not a
simple one – it may have different effects in different contexts, and it can sometimes give us a tangle of contradictory
experimental results – its importance is certain.

One aspect of human mental activity which separates us
from the beasts is language – the ability to articulate all those
clever thoughts we have. You may remember that language
was an important item on our list of what is unusual about
humans in Part One. There is no good evidence that any
other animal species has what we would define as language (a
flexible way of articulating almost any thought using a small
array of simple sounds), yet language is universal in *our*
species. There is no known human society which does not
have language, and this is probably because humans are loath
to discard the enormous advantages that language confers.

In many animal species, information is only passed from
one individual to another by genetic inheritance – offspring
inheriting behaviours and skills in the genes they inherit

from their parents. Many mammals improve on this by learning from each other by observation and play. Yet language allows humans to go one step further – to warn, advise, charm, threaten and inform each other in a powerful new way. We do not just inherit genes from our parents, nor simply copy behaviours from our peers. Most of what we get from others comes in the form of language. Humans are different because they have a non-genetic, non-behavioural means of conveying information.

Humans' strikingly unique acquisition of language mostly occurs during childhood. It is not a phenomenon of adolescence. Many of our linguistic skills are established by the age of ten – much of our vocabulary, most of our grammar, almost all our pronunciation, and some of our ability to create and interpret meanings. And there is a large inbuilt mass of cerebral machinery which allows children to acquire these basic language skills. The language centres of the human brain simply do not exist in other species: specialized regions for interpreting and generating speech, staked out on our cortex. These regions usually predominate on the left cerebral hemisphere, especially in right-handed people, and cause the most dramatic left–right asymmetries in the human brain. Very noticeably, however, the regions of the brain directly involved in speaking and listening are not part of the prefrontal cortex. Childhood language acquisition, therefore, is fundamentally different to adolescent cognitive development.

So where does this leave teenage language? Even though ten-year-old children can speak perfectly well, they do not communicate like eighteen year-olds. Clearly there is *something* happening to language skills in teenagers. Rather than altering the basic processes of speech generation and comprehension, teenagers are instead connecting their language systems to the formidable cognitive armoury developing in their frontal lobes. In other words, they are not so much learning to 'speak better' as having more complex thoughts to articulate. Gradually they start to adapt the skills they acquired as a child to their new mind and their new world. For example, they start to discover the subtleties of nuance, sarcasm, irony and satire.

An important feature of teenage language is the ability to linguistically manipulate other people, and the newfound ability to mentalize means that this manipulation is often mutual and consensual. Teenagers start to gossip and tease, and they soon learn the difference between doing these things with affection and with malice. Humour and manipulation become teenagers' favourite way of getting inside other people's heads – testing the boundaries of what others will and will not accept. And of course flirting is the most delightfully elaborate form of teenage communication, one in which all the post-childhood skills are brought to bear – humour, teasing, tone, style and astounding feats of circumlocution.

Another striking adolescent linguistic change relates to the way that teenagers start to communicate less with their families and more with their peers. Although they retain the ability to communicate in a readily comprehensible way, they also develop novel forms of communication for different social situations. The most important of these is the language they use in social groups with other teenagers – usually based on slang, idioms, in-jokes and codes. This new, idiosyncratic communication emphasizes the integrity and importance of teenage social groups, affirms individuals' presence within those groups and also excludes undesirables (including adults and children!). We all know that teenagers often speak to each other in a language almost incomprehensible to anyone else, but they can usually revert to more orthodox communication when they want to. The most elaborate expression of this excluding teenage language is pop music, and successive generations have had the great pop music of their youth – the music which 'spoke to them in a language they could understand' – etched into their memory.

In the last decade, human teenagers have had yet another chance to demonstrate their immense linguistic adaptability. The ease with which they have seamlessly incorporated new technologies into their communication can be startling to adults. Of course, adults can control a computer mouse and send text messages, but the speed with which teenagers use simple trial-and-error to learn electronic communication is astounding. They are quickly able to juggle the conflicting demands of being intelligible to their friends, being incomprehensible to their parents and asserting an electronic linguistic individuality, all with a subtlety that adults just cannot match. New forms of communication simply blend into their way of dealing with the world, with no clear demarcation between talking, texting, phoning and e-mail – for example, most adults would never carry on simultaneous conversations with one friend on the phone and another standing in front of them. And the idea that a presence on sites such as Facebook, MySpace or Bebo (some of which will presumably seem hilariously antiquated after the few short months between this book leaving my computer and landing on the shelves) could be anything other than an extension of the self is entirely alien to the teenage mind. There is even evidence that key-tapping adolescent thumbs have become more dextrous and muscled in the last decade – a physical mutation that has allowed a whole new age of teenage expression.

So teenagers are not learning language, but they are learning how to use it. The appearance of teenagers in the human life-plan allowed us to evolve the full expressibility of language which defines our species. Human language is complex – as complex as the human brain can comprehend – and adolescence is where that complexity starts. One effect of this is that abnormalities of language such as dyslexia start to become more apparent in teenagers, even if they were 'hidden' during childhood. Another striking change is that teenagers start to use linguistic skills to think in other ways – creating verbal arguments about abstract concepts, for example. The intertwining of language and thought that takes root in teenagers is so intimate that some have suggested that human consciousness may actually be defined in terms of an internal verbal conversation taking place inside our head.

Despite all the linguistic changes going on in teenagers, there is not much evidence of structural change in the brain to explain them. Perhaps this is because teenage language development is caused by reorganization and switching-on of the prefrontal cortex, rather than a complete rebuilding of the language centres further back. But one exception to this is the linguistic difference between girls and boys. There are very clear differences between the sexes in the thickness of grey matter in some cortical regions associated with language – differences so dramatic that a brain may be reliably 'sexed' on the basis of its cortical anatomy. These sex differences are intriguing because they may explain differences in verbal skills between the sexes. For many years we have known that, on average, girls perform better in verbal tasks, whereas boys perform better in visual and spatial tasks. Also, I wonder if recent changes in education have led to a 'feminization' of teaching, in which female-preferred ways of working (organized progress and continuous assessment) have become more valued than male-preferred approaches (risk-taking and terminal exams). Evolutionary biologists have suggested that cognitive and linguistic differences between the sexes exist for a good reason, equipping them for their roles in hunter-gatherer societies – with women interacting and raising children in large social groups and men needing to communicate only to hunt. Some radical theories even suggest that human language evolved as a way for women to communicate with each other, and that boys only learn to speak as an unexpected side-effect of listening to the women who rear them.

Whatever the evolutionary reasons, it often seems as if adolescent girls and boys communicate in different ways. Girls often talk to each other in a more intimate fashion: their way of 'getting into each other's heads' is to share their feelings and experiences directly. Teenage boys tend to study their peers more indirectly, by discussing opinions of more abstract phenomena, like sport or music. It is also tempting to speculate that linguistic differences also affect how teenagers interact with their parents. My teenage experience was that when parents impose some heinous new restriction on their teenage offspring's liberty, girls react with long articulate arguments challenging the perceived injustice, whereas boys express their rebellion by simply defying the new restriction and then mutely accepting any resulting parental retribution. Maybe the screams and sulks of adolescence should be seen as fossil evidence of our species' quest for superiority.

We now have a better understanding of what adolescence is. Not only is it an elaborate and protracted set of bodily changes, but even more importantly it is the most crucial phase in the ponderous and demanding development of the huge human brain. Compared to other animals, and contrary to popular opinion, young humans have evolved to be remarkably free of the control of hormones. Instead, the adolescent brain is special because it is a site of a spectacular restructuring. Dopamine drives new ways of thinking, living and taking risks, and the pinnacle of its effects is the maturation of the prefrontal cortex, where humans hatch complex plans to achieve what we want and avoid what we do not.

The emotional, cognitive and linguistic changes of adolescence make it the central part of the human life-plan – this is the cerebral crossroads at which all the aspects of our mental life meet. However, in the rest of this book we will see that many teenage problems result from this convergence. Teenagers change so fast that their life can become a precarious balancing act – and we will see that this makes them intrinsically unstable when confronted with drugs, relationships and sex. Many of the things teenagers do are just harmless investigation of the world around them, but others can have repercussions that will live with them for the rest of their lives. In many developed countries the most common causes of teenage death are accidents, homicide and suicide. Clearly things can go very wrong. Teenagers can pay an enormous price for being the pinnacle of human evolution.

3 Out of the Ordinary

The truth about alcohol, nicotine and other diversions

You know, my friends, with what a brave carouse,
I made a second marriage in my house;
Divorced old barren reason from my bed
And took the daughter of the vine to spouse.
The Rubaiyat of Omar Khayyam

Drug addiction is an inherently teenage thing.

Over the last few decades many people have tried to dissuade
the public, and young people in particular, from taking
drugs. Yet among these earnest advisers of youth, I think one
stands head and shoulders above the rest in the sheer strange-
ness of her role as narcotic doomsayer: Nancy Reagan.
Teenagers probably start to experiment with drugs either
because they want to fit in with their peers, or because they
are exercising their teenage urge for experimentation.
Presumably, if they are to be dissuaded from taking drugs,
they need to hear it from people with whom they feel some
affinity. And in the eighties, when I was a teenager, what we
had was the shiny, grinning yet strangely skeletal face of the
first lady. Somehow her 'Just Say No' campaign made the idea
of speedballing more, rather than less, appealing.

Nevertheless, the focus on adolescence makes sense
because, as it happens, this is the most important time in our

lives as far as drugs are concerned. It is thought that more than three-quarters of drug, tobacco and alcohol addicts (I will count all of these as 'drugs' from now on) first experience their chosen substance in their teenage years. We can probably all think of reasons why people try drugs when they are teenagers, but as we will see, teenagers are probably also especially vulnerable to many of their effects – presumably because of the changes to body and brain we discussed in the first two chapters. Maybe drugs really do hook us when we are least able to resist them. And although, as a laissez-faire, non-proscriptive type of person, it pains me to say it, scientific discoveries within the last five years have made us think that we really should be very cautious about teenagers and drugs.

Few things scare people as much as a loved one becoming an addict. Addiction seems to take people away from us – they lose their inner control and drive, and in the process somehow lose themselves. They move out of the world in which the rest of us live, and there seems little we can do about it. To the rest of us, addiction is outside the ordinary experience of everyday life. But how did modern human society get to this strange, uncontrollable state? Where did all the drugs come from? Why, at this stage in our species' history, do so many young people become addicts? Why do drugs wrench people away from their normal lives, and why are the young so susceptible? These are the questions I will tackle in this part of the book.

From the seventies to the present day, while fashions for individual drugs have come and gone, total drug use in adolescents has been running at a fairly constant level. However, while the numbers are not increasing, many clinicians are worried that the teenagers now entering treatment are more severely affected than in the past. There is a subjective sense that things are getting worse. Also, many of us worry that our inability to cope with the increasing availability and potency of drugs is a sign of some deep human failing. Can the evolutionary heritage that has served us well in so many other ways, not help us deal with drugs?

In fact, I believe that an evolutionary approach will turn out to be our saviour, because it will explain why humans interact with drugs in the way they do. And humans are good at taking action once they understand things. Certainly explaining risks to teenagers is more likely to be successful than just telling them blankly that drugs are 'bad'. 'Just Say No' has proved to be a singularly unsuccessful approach, and many of the child actors recruited to its bright and breezy campaign later fell into their own cycles of drug abuse and rehabilitation. Maybe 'Just Say Why Not' would have been more effective. Thanks a bunch, Nancy.

Where did all the drugs come from?

Modern humans have an astounding variety of psychoactive drugs at their disposal. Chemists have attempted to classify them into neat chemical families and pharmacologists have grouped them according to their effects on the body, but the plethora of substances often spills out of the columns of the classifiers' tables. There are some drugs which fit the ordered scheme, but there are others that fall between groups, and a few more which defy any attempts to fit them in at all. The quotation at the start of this third part of the book is but a hint of the chemical variety out there – there seems to be a drug for every occasion, every nuance of the psychedelic's quest. When one drug drops out of fashion, there is always another to take its place.

In this part of the book I will use alcohol, tobacco, cannabis, cocaine, amphetamines and opioids as my examples. This is mainly because they have predominated throughout the historical vagaries of drug fashion, and are also the most studied. However, it is important to remember that they are but a small part of a veritable cornucopia of mind-altering substances. The array of drugs available to teenagers is startling, but my aim in this chapter is to draw out the features that link them all. If we focus on three self-evident aspects that are common to all these chemicals – that they are available; that they affect the brain; that they can cause addiction – then we can pick out themes which will explain the teenage drug phenomenon.

The first issue is, of course, the very existence of all these substances. It has often struck me as strange that the world about us just happens to contain a variety of chemicals apparently perfected to interact with human brains. Indeed, this natural abundance of drugs goes against the Copernican and Darwinian view underlying modern science: that human beings are *not* at the centre of existence. If the universe was not designed to suit humans, then why do all these naturally occurring substances seem like they are designed expressly for us? Worse than that, addictive drugs are not just occasional freaks of nature – they are abundant; they are everywhere.

There is a simple reason for the existence of most drugs, and that is plants. Plants have been around a lot longer than humans, and they have been evolving all that time. Plants are the basis of almost all the biological systems on earth, but they have had a hard time of it. They may have the unique ability to build themselves out of sunlight, but they have paid a considerable price. Immobile, energy-rich plants look like a free lunch to animals, so to a plant it must seem as if everyone out there is trying to eat it. To counter this continual attack, plants make special chemicals. As well as containing all the biochemical machinery needed to run the primary planty functions of using sunlight, growing and producing offspring, plants also contain an enormous array of 'secondary compounds' which protect them. These secondary compounds may be waste products that have simply been allowed to accumulate in the plant's cells, or they can be complex molecules especially constructed by the plant, at great cost in resources and energy.

Many of these chemicals are poisons, often concentrated at high levels in the parts of the plant most exposed to attack by animal herbivores. Nicotine, for example, is a potent nerve toxin to herbivorous insects, made in the roots of tobacco plants but stockpiled in the bug-exposed leaves. Nicotine may constitute 0.5 per cent of the weight of a tobacco plant, so it is a foolish insect that nibbles on it. We also believe that cannabis, cocaine and opioids evolved as toxins to deter herbivores from eating hemp, coca and poppies, respectively (cannabis may also act as a sunscreen for hemp leaves – it absorbs ultraviolet light). Indeed, most addictive drugs come either directly or indirectly from plants – even MDMA, or 'ecstasy', a derivative of amphetamines, is artificially synthesized from sassafras plants.

In most ecosystems, insects present far more of a herbivorous threat to plants than bigger animals do – there are simply so many insects around. Because of this we believe there is a continual evolutionary arms race between plants and insects, with plants putting valuable resources into deterring insects and insects developing new ways to resist plants' deterrent chemicals. So we mammals have been parachuted into a chemical battlefield where insects and plants are slugging it out for survival, and we must try and survive in this ravaged place. Some of the insect poisons are poisonous for us as well, and plants also make some toxins specifically directed at us: this is why yew and rhododendron kill browsing mammals. However, mammals are just as good as insects at cheating the defences – for example, rabbits make an enzyme that destroys the poison in deadly nightshade.

Among all these insect poisons, there are some which are only partially effective against mammals. Instead of killing mammals stone dead, they cause less dramatic effects. They bind to molecules in the mammalian nervous system just as they would in an insect, but instead of completely destroying it they cause less dramatic and more complex alterations to its function. Thus many mind-altering drugs are in fact plant-derived insect poisons which retain only partial potency in humans. They evolved as lethal weapons in the plant–insect war zone and humans are just collateral damage. This idea of drugs as 'accidents of war' also says a great deal about our similarities to insects – drugs affect our brains because we share many of our molecular brain processes with insects. This means that psychoactive drugs act on extremely ancient mechanisms in the human brain – mechanisms we inherited from the common ancestor of humans and caterpillars, a creature which wriggled about many hundreds of millions of years ago. And these mechanisms have survived in both insects and us because they do something extremely important. Addictive drugs do not target random lumps of the human brain; as we will see, they act on the very processes which drove our evolutionary success.

The evolution of drugs has not been entirely a story of conflict, however. There are some examples where plants have produced chemicals to attract animals. Plants are rather inconsistent in their approach to predation, and they often produce structures specifically to be eaten: fruit. Fruit are parts of a plant which invite consumption so that animals will disperse the seeds they contain. Because of this, fruit are attractive to animals – they look, feel, smell and taste good.

In particular, animals like them because they are full of energy-giving sugars, and the riper the fruit the more sugar it contains. Over-ripe fruit are the sweetest of all and they often burst open enticingly. Once open, they accumulate yeasts which ferment the sugars into our most prevalent psychoactive drug: alcohol. Yeasts do this for their own good, but the smelly alcohol acts as an indication to hungry animals that the fruit is packed full of sugar. Also, animals can extract almost as much energy from the alcohol as they can from the sugar, so they eat that too. Just think of wasps in an autumn orchard.

An extreme form of this mutual cooperation between plant and herbivore has developed within the past few thousand years of human evolution. Humans have started deliberately to cultivate plants which make psychoactive chemicals, and as a result these plants have been more successful than ever before. There are far more opium poppies and hemp plants in the world now than twenty thousand years ago. Agriculture has meant that the gentle co-evolution of humans and the plants we love has slipped into a higher gear. And the price these plants have paid for their propagation by humans is that we have changed them. We have bred our 'drug crops' to contain ever higher amounts of the secondary poisons we crave – completely the opposite of what we have done with the poisons in our 'food crops'.

So who first started taking drugs? The fossil history of drug abuse is admittedly rather thin – there are no fossil teenage hominid skeletons guiltily gripping a joint between their teeth – but we know enough to place human drug use in context. For one thing, humans are certainly not the only animals to use psychoactive drugs – among mammals, we know that wild sheep lick narcotic lichen, water buffalo graze on opium poppies and elephants eat, even argue over, certain fermenting fruit. The drive to ingest chemicals for their psychoactive properties rather than their nutritional content seems to be a general one. In humans we have evidence of charred remains of drug plants such as cannabis in New Stone Age settlements – this is as close as we get to the guilty fossil teenager. Of course, drug use may have been going on for some considerable time before then, and it may be only one aspect of our species' ongoing use of plant secondary toxins. We inquisitive, experimenting great apes are prone to this activity – gorillas are known to swallow unchewed leaves for medicinal reasons, for example. Indeed, we may have learned what plants to try by observing the drug habits of other animals.

A major shift in human drug use came when our ancestors started actively to cultivate drug-yielding plant species. In this context it is worth mentioning that although most historical accounts of agriculture focus on food plants, some anthropologists have suggested that 'drug plants' may have been the subjects of our first attempts at cultivation. Cannabis is a popular, if controversial, candidate for precipitating the dawn of agriculture. It is, after all, very easy to grow in hot countries, and it has been claimed that it was used to counter the extreme boredom of some elements of the hunter-gatherer lifestyle such as ambush hunting and spear fishing. Even if human agriculture did not have its origins in such risqué crops, the agricultural revolution certainly allowed great advances in human alcohol consumption. Some of the earliest cultivated food crops were the wild grasses that gave rise to modern cereals, and it did not take long for humans to discover that cereal grains can be split open and fermented just as easily as fruits. We have written and archaeological evidence that alcohol has been our constant solace for perhaps ten thousand years.

Over much of this time, drugs have been a largely positive influence. As well as their boredom-relieving effects, drugs have a long and documented history in the development of religions throughout the world – their effects resembling the expected experience of religious transcendence. Many artists today still claim that drugs are a crucial part of their creative process. Drugs were often used for their positive mental effects – cocaine as a stimulant, alcohol encouraging social facilitation, nicotine inducing a sense of mental clarity (I once worked with someone who only smoked when he was writing research grant applications). Possibly the greatest contribution of drugs to human life has been the disinfectant effect of alcohol. The word 'civilization' means 'living in cities', and the last ten thousand years has seen a process of ever-increasing human urbanization. However important for our advancement, gathering large numbers of people in one place carries great health risks. Worst of these is that people start to defecate in each other's water supply, a process which still causes millions of fatal infections around the world. For people living in pre-sanitation cities, water was simply not safe to drink. On the other hand, fermented beverages were far safer partly because they contained alcohol, which kills microbes (including the yeasts which make it). For thousands of years booze was the best way for city-dwellers to avoid illness.

But if humans started to use drugs because of their pleasant and undoubtedly beneficial effects, why have drugs now become a scourge of modern society? In the rest of Part Three, when I describe how drugs affect teenagers, it is worth remembering that large-scale addiction of the human population is a relatively new phenomenon. People have taken drugs since at least the start of the agricultural revolution, yet only in recent decades (or centuries, in the case of alcohol) has addiction of large numbers of people become a social problem. What, in short, has changed?

I think there are two reasons for the upsurge in addiction. The first is that, as we will see, drugs addict us by latching on to an extremely important system in our brain – a system so crucial to our survival that there has been absolutely no question of us losing it within the evolutionary 'blink of an eye' of the last ten thousand years. The second reason is that drugs are now more accessible, affordable and potent than ever before. Instead of laboriously acquired hemp, cider and coca leaves from distant lands, we now have local providers of cheap skunk, vodka and crack. In other words, modern drugs cheat the system – they work outside the ordinary rules of gain and loss, cost and benefit. For the first time in the history of our species, we all have easy access to chemicals so powerful that they can permanently distort the way our brains work.

Why do drugs affect teenagers differently?

People usually start taking drugs during adolescence, but the effects of psychoactive drugs on teenagers are in some ways complex, and in some ways simple.

Drugs are complex because they can act on many different parts of the teenage body and brain to produce their desired effects. (We will, as people usually do, worry about the undesired effects later.) For the most part, drugs act on receptors in the brain – large molecules on the surface of nerve cells which evolved to bind small neurotransmitter molecules. Neurotransmitters and receptors are how information gets from one brain cell to another – one nerve cell secretes a neurotransmitter into the tiny space or 'synapse' between it and a second nerve cell; that neurotransmitter then binds to the receptor molecules on the second cell; this binding may either increase or decrease the activity of the second nerve cell, and thus its tendency to secrete its own neurotransmitters on yet more nerve cells. As it happens, most nerve cells in the brain receive neurotransmitters from many nerve cells, and themselves secrete neurotransmitters which bind to the receptor molecules of many other nerve cells. Although I have simplified the story somewhat, this is the cellular and molecular basis of how the brain works: an interlinking mesh of billions of discrete nerve cells, each taking the information given to them in the form of neurotransmitter molecules, and producing an output signal in the form of other neurotransmitters.

Because receptors are spread throughout the normal brain, drugs can exert their varied effects all over the place. Amphetamines and ecstasy, for example, cause a widespread secretion of the neurotransmitters noradrenaline, dopamine, serotonin and oxytocin to generate a subjective feeling of stimulation, euphoria and even affection – rather like a state of optimistic excitement. Cocaine promotes dopamine release in a variety of areas, including those involved in movement and higher mental processes. Nicotine mimics the natural neurotransmitter acetyl choline and binds to receptors in many different parts of the brain and body to exert its diverse stimulatory effects. Alcohol has, if anything, even broader effects, binding to receptors for glutamine and GABA (remember them?) as well as suppressing brain metabolism and secretion of stress hormones. Its net effect is to suppress brain activity, but at low doses its main action is to suppress our social and sexual inhibitions.

Cannabis and opioids have proved to be among the most interesting of 'recreational drugs' because of the discovery that they mimic neurotransmitters that are natural versions of cannabis and opioids produced in the drug-free brain. For example, cannabis slots into the CB1 and CB2 receptors which usually bind to a complex system of 'endocannabinoids' to control many processes in the brain and immune system. This explains how a single drug can induce relaxation, pain relief, increased appetite (the 'munchies') and also reduce the inflammation of multiple sclerosis. The brain's own opioid system is, if anything, even more complicated, with a wide range of natural opioids binding to several different types of opioid receptor molecule. Natural opioids control the transmission of pain signals in the brain, and doctors administer opioids to reduce pain; there are opioid receptors in the intestines, and morphine relieves the symptoms of diarrhoea; natural opioids are involved in mood, and people take opioids because they like the euphoric feeling they induce.

So drugs are complex because they cause their effects by binding to a varied assortment of receptor molecules throughout the brain. The pattern of binding is different for different drugs and it may even be different for different people too. In contrast, there is one way in which drugs are simple. When we think of the adverse effects of drugs, one effect in particular springs to mind because we think of it as common to all of them: addiction. Addiction is a theme which runs throughout our dealings with drugs. Almost all 'drugs of abuse' can be obviously addictive, and even in less clear-cut cases we still do not know exactly what makes people repeatedly use drugs such as cannabis. While drugs can cause any of a wide array of mental and physical effects, addiction is the phenomenon that links them all together. And it is what frightens us most about teenage drug use.

So what is 'addiction'? It is a word we use all the time and it has strong connotations, but nailing down a definition has been difficult. Over the years the scientific definition of addiction has evolved to a point where many experts would rather avoid the word altogether. Some opt instead for a more colloquial definition of addiction as the compulsive use of psychoactive drugs in a way that interferes with normal life. This is what I will mean by 'addiction' in this book.

Addiction is often misunderstood because there are some related concepts that can easily get tangled up with it. The first of these is drug 'dependence', which means that stopping taking a drug leads to unpleasant physical or psychological withdrawal symptoms. But dependence is itself a complex thing. Drugs do not have to be psychoactive to cause dependency – one can become dependent on laxatives, for example. Also, withdrawal symptoms can be terribly unpleasant without actually presenting any risk of death or injury – such as those of opioid withdrawal. So dependency is obvious strongly tied to addiction, but it is not the same thing.

Another idea related to addiction is 'tolerance'. Tolerance describes the phenomenon whereby drug users must take more and more of a certain drug to experience the desired effects – because their body slowly starts to 'tolerate' and ignore the drug. Although addiction often runs alongside tolerance, once again the two are not the same. One can develop tolerance to many medicinal drugs that are not psychoactive: and some psychoactive drugs do not induce tolerance. Indeed, users of nicotine and cocaine may become more, not less, sensitive to their effects with repeated use.

A third aspect of drugs that is difficult to tease apart from addiction is drug 'craving'. Drug craving is often the main sign of drug addiction in teenagers – when the need to take more of the drug becomes a compulsion that overwhelms concern for everything else: money, success, loved ones, even survival. Drug craving can seem like an almost automated overriding response, and as we will see, it does reflect a rewiring of the brain systems involved in seeking rewards. However, drug users also crave their drug for other reasons. Some of these reasons are, to be honest, entirely sensible. First of all, teenagers may seek out a drug because they like its effects – they simply want to experience the kick, the euphoria, the relaxation, the hallucinations, the numbing, or the way it makes them feel about themselves. This is the feeling I have when I want a beer – I just want the pleasant experience induced by fermented cereal. Secondly, and again entirely reasonably, people crave drugs because they want to avoid withdrawal symptoms. Withdrawal symptoms are unpleasant, so it is eminently sensible to want to avoid them. This is a reasoned craving, and it works in the short term or long term: heroin addicts shy away from the sheer immediate nastiness of going cold turkey, and female teenage nicotine users know that quitting will make it harder to stay skinny. One of the most insidious parts of this wish to avoid withdrawal symptoms is that drug users know that the very best cure for them is to take more drugs.

An especially alarming feature of craving is that drug-taking behaviour shows a striking propensity to be 'learned'. In Part Two of this book, you may remember that I mentioned that animals often learn by surprisingly simple mechanisms. They can be rapidly trained to do things by a rigid system of reward or punishment, and they can also be trained to carry out a behaviour (drooling) in response to any given stimulus (bell) if that stimulus is initially closely followed by a more natural stimulus (food). This apparently simplistic view of learning has few basic rules – as long as the stimuli, behaviour, rewards and punishments occur in the right order, and over a short period of time, animals can be taught to do just about anything. Surprisingly, and perhaps disquietingly, we now believe that these simple rules apply to people just as much as they do to other animals. One example of this is that drug users can come to associate the paraphernalia of drug administration, or the location of previous drug taking, with the pleasure of the drug itself. They have trained themselves to link objects or places to the urge for drugs. And this training can persist for years, hidden deep in our memory bank of learned behaviours. Years after quitting a drug and overcoming the withdrawal symptoms, just seeing a syringe or standing in an old haunt can trap ex-users into a new cycle of drug use.

So addiction is not the same as dependence, tolerance or even craving. It is linked to all of them, but it is worse. I do not wish to sound smug, but I think that if most heroin addicts knew they could save their own lives by suffering a few days of extreme discomfort, consciously resist the lure of the drug's pleasant effects, and avoid syringes and drug dens for the rest of their lives, then giving up heroin would be considerably easier than it actually is. There is something about addiction that takes it far beyond the level of making a simple conscious commitment to give up an unpleasant habit.

The reason why drugs are so terribly addictive is that they act directly on the parts of our brain which control our behaviour. You may remember from Part Two that there is a bundle of nerve connections deep in the brain that drives us to seek out what we have previously enjoyed. These nerve fibres run from the 'tegmentum' in the brain stem to the 'accumbens nuclei' at the core of the cerebral hemispheres, where they secrete dopamine. Probably evolved from an ancient system that trained our fishy ancestors to seek out the food they had previously enjoyed, this tegmentum–accumbens pathway now fires off whenever we encounter something we like – such as food, drink, sex, shelter, or even video games.

Despite its humble origins, the tegmentum–accumbens

remains as important for us as it was for our ancestors. When you think about it, a great deal of life revolves around seeking out what we want, even though the things humans want and our ways of getting them are often abstract and complex. We cope with this abstraction and complexity by linking up the old tegmentum–accumbens system to the cerebral cortex, and we like to think that the resulting tegmentum–accumbens–cortex system gives us some conscious control over our desires. As we saw earlier, these newer connections explain why tinkering with dopamine levels in the brain affects our conscious cognition. Yet however clever we are, the old tegmentum–accumbens pathway still lies beneath, subconsciously driving us to satisfy our urges. Our conscious mind is no more than a veneer of respectability covering our ancient selfish lusts.

So dopamine is the key to seeking out the things we like. It is worth mentioning at this point that, paradoxically, dopamine may not be very important in actually liking things. This may seem strange, but it reflects a very real difference. When you first eat chocolate, it gives you great enjoyment. You are then driven to seek it out again. The 'enjoying' and the 'seeking of more enjoyment' occur at different places in the brain, and involve different neurotransmitters – seeking enjoyment is a dopamine phenomenon, whereas enjoyment itself is caused by other things, maybe endocannabinoids and natural brain opioids. Of course, initial enjoyment is important because the first few times teenagers take drugs they are not addicted – they are simply enjoying them. The data is less clear-cut in humans than it is in lab rats, but this distinction between liking and wanting may explain why many pleasurable experiences are not addictive.

Several decades of drug research have led to one startlingly unifying conclusion: all recreational drugs increase the amount of dopamine in the nucleus accumbens. Whatever else they do, fermented fruit, coca leaves, hemp, poppies and tobacco all act here. Suddenly the accumbens re-enters the limelight, this time as the common focus for all drugs – the place they all act. This is a chilling discovery, because the accumbens controls the way we seek out the things we want. This is why drugs change who we are – they subvert our natural system of wanting and striving, and redirect it towards finding more of the drug, always more drug, with everything else pushed to the bottom of our list of priorities. They strike directly at this deep, ancient place which drives the behaviours which define so much of our individuality. It is hard to over-emphasize the power that accumbens dopamine wields over us, but one experiment is very telling: rats wired up so they can administer electrical jolts to their own tegmentum–accumbens will do so repeatedly, neglecting every other desire until they die of starvation or thirst.

The drugs teenagers use all increase levels of dopamine, but they do it in fiendishly different ways. Cocaine acts in perhaps the simplest way. Once dopamine is squirted out of nerve cells, any that does not bind to a receptor is quickly sucked back into cells, thus cutting short its effects. Cocaine blocks that sucking-back process, so excess dopamine is left sloshing about outside the cells, binding to receptors and over-activating the dopamine-sensitive nerve cells. Amphetamines probably do the same thing, but they also make more dopamine squirt out in the first place. Nicotine acts by over-stimulating receptors normally present on the dopamine neurons. Alcohol alters the way natural neurotransmitters bind to their receptors on the dopamine neurons. And cannabis and opioids pretend to be endocannabinoids and natural brain opioids and influence the dopamine neurons indirectly – unsurprisingly, the brain systems for 'liking' are connected to the systems for 'wanting'. Whatever devious route they take, all these drugs are driving up dopamine in the accumbens.

But a simple rise in dopamine does not seem much on its own – perhaps no more than a little mental note to try the drug again some time. A newfound liking for Turkish delight would be expected to have that sort of effect. The reason why drugs can 'hook' us is that dopamine can have permanent effects on the cells on which it acts. Huge drug-induced surges of dopamine hitting cells in the accumbens cause a long-term reduction in the number of dopamine receptors on those cells. At first this may seem sensible, as it makes the accumbens less sensitive to another dose of the drug. However, this insensitivity to dopamine has some unfortunate effects. First of all, it means that the drug-taker needs to take more drug to achieve the same effect – leading to a need for ever-increasing doses of it. Secondly, it makes the accumbens less able to respond to the enticing effects of sensible things like food, sex and achievement – making them seem less desirable than the drug upon which the brain is slowly becoming fixated. The ups and downs of dopamine and dopamine receptors are probably more complicated than this, but we believe that some sort of unbalancing of the dopamine system explains the sheer tenacity of addiction.

So drugs cheat us because they act directly on our 'wanting' pathways. They overpower them and leave damage that lasts long beyond the initial hit – we think that the long-term imbalance in the dopamine system caused by drugs is the reason why they skew our 'wanting'. Our 'wanting' pathways evolved for a very specific reason, to make us seek food, drink, sex and all things nice – but we rarely get addicted to those things. There is a characteristic inflexibility to the craving for addictive drugs that makes them fundamentally different from our more everyday, natural desires. Admittedly your desire for water may be pretty inflexible after five days in a desert, but in general our non-drug urges are more sensible and appropriate. We compulsively want food, drink, sex and shelter, but they do not continually try and edge each other out of our affections. Of course, the fact that some people do indeed get addicted to food or sex or various behaviours suggests that the dividing line between drugs and healthy things is rather more blurry than we might like, but the fact remains that heroin is more addictive than bread.

We now have a clear model of addiction, a theory of how all those weird botanic insect toxins hijack our brains. This now puts us in a good position to study teenage drug abuse. Although we may argue about why teenagers try drugs for the first time, we can discount claims that addiction is an indication of an individual's inner weakness of character. Instead we can see addiction for what it is – an inner human imperfection, exposed only now our global technological economy has made drugs so potent, available and cheap. Addictive drugs act on the goal-seeking systems in the brain that helped us survive and succeed for millions of years, so from the evolutionary point of view, it is not the teenage brain that is the problem. The fault lies with the drugs which deceive it.

At the start of Part Three I claimed that drug addiction is a teenage phenomenon. You were probably not surprised to hear that most people first try drugs when they are teenagers, nor that addicts usually encounter their own chosen drug during those years. After all, if young children are prevented from encountering drugs by their protected place in the family, then adolescence is simply the first time that most people *can* try drugs. And most people seem to try them pretty quickly. However, we often worry that teenagers are especially vulnerable because drugs attract them more and affect them more than adults. So is this true?

Earlier we saw that risk-taking is a healthy, and indeed essential part of teenage life, but it is often claimed to explain why teenagers start to take drugs. After all, the first time a teenager uses a drug is completely different from all the subsequent times: they have no idea what the positive or negative effects will be, and their accumbens dopamine system is entirely pristine. This first time is as close as they ever get to an unclouded decision to take the drug, and we assume that it has nothing to do with the addiction mechanisms that kick in with repeated use. We know that teenagers like to take risks, but the problem with taking a drug for the first time is that the risks are entirely unknown: some will never take the drug again; some will take it repeatedly, enjoy it and suffer few adverse effects; some will become addicted; some will suffer severe effects or die of an overdose. I am sure that many teenagers think hard before making this leap into the dark. Because of this, although it seems obvious to suggest that teenage risk-taking is an important factor in the first episode of drug use, I am not convinced. For example, we have seen that 'risk-taking' teenagers often feel more socially confident and stable, whereas drug use is more likely to be a problem in teenagers who feel insecure.

Despite my scepticism, there is evidence suggesting that some teenagers are just too inclined to try new things. Maybe they retain a playfulness and inquisitiveness from childhood that is dangerous when confronted with drugs – and a quest for novelty is not the same thing as a wish to take risks. In this context, it is interesting that children who exhibit 'pica', or eating non-food items, are more likely to grow up to be addicts. Also, studies in rats have shown how risk and novelty might be handled differently by different individuals. When lab rats are offered cocaine or amphetamines on demand, the individual rats differ markedly in their tendency to take them. The rats who use the most drugs also tend to 'gamble' when playing games which involve winning or losing rewards. Crucially, these impulsive rats have lower levels of dopamine receptors in their accumbens before ever taking a drug, not unlike a human who has already undergone several drug-induced dopamine surges. Is the same true of human teenagers? Are some born less able to be stimulated by pleasurable experiences, more susceptible to the quick dopamine hit of drugs?

There are differences between teenage and adult addicts that make me even more suspicious of the idea that adolescents take drugs because they are risk-takers. Teenagers who seek treatment for drug problems are more likely to have had various other problems in their life *before* they ever took drugs. Teenage drug users more often have family problems, mental illness and psychological abnormalities than adult drug users, and they more often use multiple addictive substances. Also, they are far more likely to have attempted suicide. Whereas adults usually enter treatment programmes voluntarily, often after a drug-induced crisis such as a divorce or losing their job or house, teenagers are usually unwilling participants and their 'final straws' are often more subtle – perhaps underperformance at school or being caught stealing. To me the patterns in teenagers and adults look so different that they suggest that the very causes and mechanisms of drug use in teenagers may be different too. Teenagers rarely seem to get drug problems 'pure and simple' – they are often tangled up with social, emotional, health and psychological problems instead.

Social stress and poor self-esteem are other factors which have been claimed to be important, and perhaps crucial, in teenage drug-taking. Many teenagers say that they first took drugs to fit in with what their peers were doing, or what was expected of them. And of course the ability to stand up for yourself and say no is dependent on self-esteem. It takes a lot of guts to be seen to ignore the cool kids and listen to Nancy Reagan. Some animal studies back up this idea – subordinate monkeys are more likely to self-administer drugs than dominant ones. Also, the area of the brain that mediates social stress (the hypothalamus) and the area that underlies addiction (the accumbens) have many connections running between them – and indeed, social stress is known to be a potent cause of relapse in teenagers who have quit drugs in the past.

These newer 'self-esteem theories' are gaining support, to the point where some are suggesting that teaching teenagers how to withstand peer pressure may be the best way to reduce drug use. The big problem with this approach is that it sounds too wishy-washy for politicians to put much money into it, but then again, the expensive, macho 'war on drugs' approach has hardly been a success.

(On a lighter note, one phenomenon of adolescence which prefigures substance craving is the menstrual cycle. Although it has proved surprisingly difficult to demonstrate in scientific studies, everyone knows that women crave chocolate during the premenstrual phase. Chocolate is a delightful mix of all sorts of things that humans like – fat, sugar, a little caffeine, the stimulant theobromine, something just like an endocannabinoid, and several chemicals claimed to be raw materials for making neurotransmitters. Add to this the fact that chocolate feels, tastes and smells better than just about everything else, and you can see why so many people crave it. However, there have been no clearly defined cases of chocolate addiction. The premenstrual craving for chocolate is hard to explain, especially as the xanthines in chocolate may worsen the symptoms of premenstrual syndrome, yet I am told that the craving is quite specific for chocolate. Despite this, careful scientific study has shown no more than a general tendency to prefer high calorie foods at that part of the cycle. Also, attempts to fend off chocolate cravings by administering progesterone to counter its premenstrual decline have proved ineffective, and perhaps rather excessive. One of the most important questions of womanhood remains unanswered.)

So, to summarize, there are several possible triggers to teenage drug-taking – risk-taking, social and mental stress, low self-esteem and even the menstrual cycle – but *starting* taking drugs is only half the story. Recent studies have told us that teenagers react differently to drugs than adults, and much of the research has been done on alcohol. In the trusty lab rat, patterns of alcohol intake are very different between young and adult rats. For example, young rats consume more alcohol than adults under a variety of conditions. Also, putting adult rats in solitary confinement reduces their alcohol intake, but this reduction does not occur in juveniles – maybe grown-up rats are social drinkers. Importantly, alcohol causes less sedation and uncoordination in young rats than adults, and similar claims have been made for teenage humans. If teenagers are less sleepy and wobbly after drinking, then they are more able to carry on drinking. Also, teenagers who drink seem to experience more social 'loosening' than adults, and their memory is more affected too. These two findings mean that drunk teenagers are more likely to do things they do not really want to, and not remember it afterwards – and we know that teenage girls are more likely to experience non-consensual sex if they drink.

There are similar differences between teenagers and adults in the effects of other drugs. One of the most striking is ketamine, a strange hallucinogenic, pain-killing sedative (which I use to anaesthetize cats and horses). Teenagers are extremely susceptible to its effects, but children do not experience its hallucinogenic effects at all. Also, although it is difficult to measure these things, amphetamines and opioids may induce less 'buzz' or euphoria in teenagers. Many report that the drugs just make them 'feel different'. Unfortunately, the relative insensitivity of teenagers to drugs' effects is not a good thing, as it makes them more likely to take high doses in their search for psychedelic fulfilment.

Teenagers may be even more susceptible when it comes to the long term effects of drugs. We saw in Part Two that teenage sadness has been ascribed to low sensitivity of the tegmentum–accumbens pathway to dopamine. We can now see how this could also make teenagers more prone to becoming addicted once they start using drugs. Such general statements about dopamine are probably great oversimplifications, but the fact remains that the dopamine system, and also several other systems involved in wanting and liking drugs, are in a state of flux in teenagers. Their checks and balances are differently set to those of adults, so it should not surprise us that teenagers respond differently to drugs.

Indeed, some scientists now view adolescence as a particular window of vulnerability to addiction, when the teenage brain is more likely not only to try, but also to be subverted by drugs.

Again, much of the evidence comes from studies on alcohol. Although I hate to admit it, popular opinion is correct, and teenagers are more likely to binge drink than adults. And we now think that it is the repeated after-effects of heavy drinking that cause much of the brain degeneration associated with alcohol use. Also, some parts of the teenage brain, including regions involved in memory, are far more susceptible to the toxic effects of alcohol than in adults. To make matters worse, while adult alcohol users gradually develop a partial tolerance to many of the short-term effects of alcohol, teenagers do not seem to do this.

Tobacco likewise seems to get a hold of teenagers much more easily than adults. Studies in mice show greater changes in neurotransmitter systems when nicotine is administered to young animals than to adults, and teenage smokers tell a similar story. Intermittent low-level nicotine use can induce significant craving within a few weeks in teenagers; and perhaps only 3 per cent of adolescent nicotine addicts are able to quit within two years. These figures are much worse than those for adults. Equally worrying is the fact that we know almost nothing about the differences between adults and teenagers in the effectiveness of drug treatment methods.

The fact is that teenagers are simply less able to resist drugs. Their brains are still developing, so they respond differently. Also, many teenagers want to escape social, mental and physical turmoil, and drugs can seem like a way out. Maybe they simply do not want to resist.

So is teenage drug use really a bad thing?

Adults worry a great deal about teenagers harming themselves. On the morning I wrote this, the British Prime Minister was pronouncing in a live radio interview about the ills of teenage binge drinking. However, the media are so bad at explaining risk that it is unlikely that most teenagers are well informed about the implications of what they do to themselves. In this book, I want to be realistic about the risks of teenagers' various activities – some are relatively harmless, others have long-term severe consequences, and many are somewhere in between.

Also, it is pointless to claim that drugs have entirely unpleasant consequences: if that were so, teenagers simply would not use them. Teenagers use drugs for simple reasons – to make them feel good, to act as 'social lubricants', to link them to a particular social group – and the pleasure they derive from them should not be underestimated. Of course that pleasure is immediate and dramatic, whereas the adverse effects of drugs are delayed and unpredictable. And when we animals are trying to learn the consequences of our actions, immediate and dramatic beats delayed and unpredictable every time.

Over the past few decades we have collected many statistics about drug use, although most are not derived exclusively from teenagers. First of all, we can arrange the major drug groups according to frequency with which they are used by the population of the Western world, from most common to least common:

alcohol tobacco cannabis cocaine amphetamines opioids

It is possible that cocaine and amphetamines should be the other way round, but apart from that the list is probably as one would expect. We can also arrange the drugs in order of how likely one is to become addicted to them, with the most addictive at the start of the list and the least addictive at the end:

tobacco opioids cocaine alcohol amphetamines ?cannabis

With its ready availability and remarkable addictive proper-ties, tobacco is starting to look worrying, and this is confirmed by the next list. This is the estimated numbers of deaths caused by the various drugs (in order of decreasing number of total deaths in the population).

tobacco alcohol opioids cocaine amphetamines ?cannabis

This last list is of course dependent on many things – how many people use the drug, how often and in what doses it is used, and its toxic effects. Some drugs, such as alcohol and tobacco, kill mainly by their long-term effects, whereas others kill by sudden toxicity.

So drugs can be viewed in different ways. There is no doubt that drugs have adverse effects, but just grouping all the drugs and all the effects together and saying they are uniform is a ridiculous oversimplification which teenagers simply will not believe. So, for the rest of Part Three, I will pick apart the different ways in which drugs can affect teenagers, starting off with the obvious way: how drugs can kill them.

The simplest way that a drug can kill is by short-term or 'acute' toxicity, and there are striking variations between different drugs in this respect. The big killer, tobacco, is extremely 'safe' as far as acute toxicity is concerned: it is very unlikely that anyone would suddenly kill themselves with the nicotine doses available from cigarettes. Alcohol is slightly less clear-cut because it is possible, but uncommon, to kill yourself with excess alcohol. The amount of alcohol required to poison a human is not beyond the realms of possibility, but the sedative effects of alcohol mean that it is difficult to keep drinking long enough to ingest a fatal dose. As we have seen, however, teenagers may be more vulnerable because they are less susceptible to that sedation – less protected by inebriation. Cannabis is an unusual case, because it may actually be impossible to overdose: there are very few cannabinoid receptors in the parts of the brain which control vital functions such as breathing.

Acute toxicity is more important for the other drugs on our list, mainly because there *are* receptors for them in the 'vital functions' parts of our brain. For example, opioids suppress breathing, probably by making the brain insensitive to the carbon dioxide we accumulate when we hold our breath. Many opioid users die because they simply stop breathing. Acute cocaine toxicity is less common but it usually centres on the cardiovascular system, causing heart rhythm irregularities, heart attacks and strokes. People often argue about the acute toxic effects of ecstasy, and this is probably because they are strange, unpredictable and rare, but nonetheless real.

The drug kills by dangerously raising the core body temperature, although the number of deaths is small compared to other drugs.

By sheer force of numbers, long-term or 'chronic' toxicity is far more important, because this is how the most commonly used drugs kill. Although lung cancer is the best known chronic toxic effect of tobacco, other effects are, if anything, more worrying. Tobacco-induced heart disease can seem a less clear-cut effect because many other things cause heart disease, but the effects of nicotine on the heart and circulatory system are horrifyingly common and severe: chemicals in tobacco cause arteries to block, disrupt blood chemistry and damage lungs. We all know that chronic alcohol use has serious consequences too, usually targeted on the sensitive brain or the diligent liver, the organ entrusted with the job of disposing of it. Alcohol is also calorific and is a common cause of obesity. The problem with deciding how much alcohol a teenager should drink is that its chronic effects are unpredictable. Obviously the more you drink, the more likely you are to lose your memory and die of cirrhosis, but some people suffer these effects at lower doses than others. Also, there is no 'threshold' level below which toxicity cannot occur, so government guidelines are no more than estimates, pitched pragmatically on a sliding scale of toxic (and pleasant) effects – after all, complete abstinence from alcohol is safest, but teenagers are unlikely to heed such ascetic advice.

The long-term effects of many other drugs are less well understood, partly because they may overlap with those of tobacco and alcohol. A good example of this is cannabis, whose chronic toxic effects may blur into those of tobacco, with which it is often smoked. Despite this overlap, it now seems likely that cannabis may cause long-term impairment of cognition, affecting a wide variety of skills and decision making processes.

Drugs can have chronic adverse effects other than simple toxicity, and in teenagers the most important of these is self-neglect – which teenagers are often pretty good at anyway. Of course, self-neglect occurs as part of addiction, but some drugs encourage self-neglect regardless of whether the user is addicted or not. Drinking alcohol provides so many calories that drinkers can, strangely, become obese and malnourished at the same time. The main drive to human appetite is a desire for energy and alcohol provides that in abundance, but without other constituents of a balanced diet. Many drugs cause weight loss and malnutrition because they suppress appetite – nicotine, cocaine and amphetamines, for example – and sadly this is often one reason why teenagers like to use them. In addition, all drugs can cause more general forms of self-neglect, such as diversion of funds from food, hygiene and clothing into buying drugs. Adolescent drug users may miss out on the key time in their lives when they are meant to learn to look after themselves. General lack of care, along with cognitive impairment, is also the cause of a further effect of drugs, and perhaps the most important of all: adolescents who drink or take drugs are far more likely to be injured in accidents and fights.

The self-neglect caused by drugs can spread even wider to cause many forms of social failure. Drug use, whether addictive or not, has been linked to educational failure, impulsive violence, eating disorders and self-harm. Perhaps 70 per cent of teenage suicides have drugs as an underlying cause. Even if drugs do not directly cause these signs of teenagers' failure to cope, it is likely that they exacerbate them. In particular, drug use has been claimed to set up stress/drug cycles in which teenagers habitually turn to new drugs to cope with stress, which may itself be caused by giving up other drugs. And periods of social failure are especially damaging for teenagers because this is the time when they are supposed to acquire the social and emotional skills that will support them for the rest of their lives. If they lose enough of their adolescence to drugs, they may never get that learning opportunity again. Another ramification of drug use is that teenagers may turn to crime, a move often precipitated by the need to fund further drug use. And in areas where drug distribution has become gang-dominated, teenagers are seen as useful gang members because they are difficult for the authorities to control and prosecute.

Sexual self-neglect is an especially disturbing part of the drug-induced inability to cope. Many studies have linked alcohol intake to number of sexual partners, or frequency of sexual intercourse. Of course this does not prove that alcohol causes promiscuity, but alcohol is known to suppress inhibitions, and as we will see in Part Five the context of early sexual encounters in incredibly important. Yet teenagers will always want to have sex whatever they are told, so rather than banning adolescent sex perhaps we should be encouraging sober, thoughtful sex instead. Also worrying are the links between alcohol and 'high-risk' sexual behaviours – unprotected sex, infidelity to partners, excessive sexual experimentation and trading sex for money. More specifically, stimulant drugs can also induce increased sexual cravings, to the point that excessive masturbation can lead to genital injury.

Mental illness is perhaps the most extreme manifestation of adolescent failure to cope, and this is an area where our views have changed recently. When I was a teenager I was entirely unaware of any link between drugs and mental illness. In weighing up the attractions and risks of drugs, it simply did not feature. Yes, many told stories of friends who had used drugs as part of their slump into mental illness, but no one claimed that drugs *caused* that slump. The causal link is still not definite, but recently more and more evidence has accumulated linking drug use to mental illness. Perhaps surprisingly, many of the data relate to the drug my generation thought was safe: cannabis. There are now well-established statistical links between cannabis use and cognitive impairment, depression, reporting of psychotic symptoms, and subsequent diagnosis of schizophrenia. Cannabis has also been implicated in a more specific 'amotivational syndrome', a psychological definition of what many of us might picture as a 'lazy stoner'. Cannabis is not the only drug under suspicion however, and amphetamines, alcohol and cocaine have also been linked to psychosis. In addition, nicotine is known to have a complex involvement with depression and anxiety. Many teenagers use it to 'self-medicate' depression and anxiety yet its own withdrawal symptoms include both those effects, so it is proving very difficult to discover whether its long-term use actually makes these problems worse.

Despite all these links, there is complete disagreement within the scientific community as to whether drugs actually cause mental illness. They may do so, but mental illness could just as plausibly drive teenagers to use drugs. A third possibility is that some teenagers have a shared predisposition for both drug use and mental illness. The controversy stems from the fact that we simply cannot perform drug experiments on human teenagers – so all we have are statistical surveys. However, we do have some circumstantial evidence that the endocannabinoid system is important in the healthy development of brain systems which function abnormally in mental illness, and this is where the scientists take sides. Some say this means cannabis impairs brain development and thus causes mental illness, while others say that the causal link is not at all clear. This debate is important because it informs our attitudes to teenage drug use: for an individual teenager it makes the stark difference whether or not drugs will increase their chances of suffering mental illness. Parents might prefer to play safe and discourage drug use, but as yet they cannot say, hand on heart, that drugs cause mental illness.

One of the most important skills that teenagers acquire is scepticism, and many are suspicious of the things adults say. One claim that rarely rings true with teenagers is that using drugs will inevitably lead them to take new and nastier drugs, leading into a downward spiral of addiction and collapse. They look around them and see many drug users experiencing few ill effects, and they also see many of their peers using alcohol and nicotine without apparently being sucked uncontrollably into the world of 'hard drugs'. Many teenagers also realize the hypocrisy of an adult world in which legal 'soft' drugs kill far more people than illegal 'hard' drugs. So, at a time in their lives when they are hard-wired to stop believing everyone else and start believing in themselves, perhaps it is no surprise that many teenagers confidently expect that they will not be 'the one' who becomes the drug casualty. Addiction and the progress to 'harder' drugs is for weaker souls than them, surely? And of course, although we do not like to admit it, many of them are proved right in this assumption. But is this just luck – or is it true that some teenagers are more likely to become ensnared by a series of ever more potent drugs?

Campaigns to reduce teenage drug use have often made great play of the 'gateway drug' concept. This is the idea that 'soft' drugs like alcohol and tobacco encourage teenagers into an escalating sequence of newer and 'harder' drugs, passing through cannabis and stimulants to cocaine and opioids. The gateway drug idea implies either that drugs invariably induce further mischievous narcotic experimentation, or that some drugs actually render the brain more 'addictable' by others. Yet here also, this popular idea has many critics who think that no causal link has been demonstrated. Using alcohol may indeed encourage heroin use, but conversely teenagers could instead have common biological or socio-economic predispositions to both alcohol and heroin. We are back to the problem of not being able to carry out experiments on people, and resorting to circumstantial evidence. The statistical links are clear but the reasons are not.

There are clear links between early drug use and use of the *same* drug later in life. For example, cocaine administration in young rats increases the rate at which rats self-administer cocaine in later life. Similarly, in humans there is a strikingly clear link between the age at which teenagers first drink alcohol and their later chances of becoming alcoholics: starting to drink at fourteen corresponds to a fourfold increase in the chance of addiction than drinking at twenty. However, showing gateway links between *different* drugs has been more difficult. Nicotine use in young rats has been shown to increase alcohol use in adulthood, but this is not a 'soft'-to-'hard' transition. Also, in humans, teenage nicotine use shows strong links with subsequent cocaine use, but as usual this could be explained by certain teenagers having a general tendency to try any drug available. Anecdotally, we know that two different drugs can become intertwined in users' minds, such as when an ex-nicotine addict craves a cigarette whenever they drink alcohol in a hazy bar, but this is not the same as a teenager 'progressing' to use nicotine for the first time. From a more mechanistic point of view, early cannabis use has been shown to induce a degree of tolerance (insensitivity) to opioids, cocaine and amphetamines – but as we have seen, tolerance is not the same thing as addiction. Indeed such cross-drug tolerance is almost to be expected if all these drugs are indeed acting on the same reward-seeking tegmentum–accumbens pathway. Perhaps this is the best evidence we have for the gateway theory of drug progression.

The second half of adults' threat of the 'inevitable downwards spiral' is the bit that teenagers are least likely to believe. Many know from experience of the world around them that drug addiction is not an inevitable consequence of taking drugs. This clear inconsistency between adult threats and adolescent experience is one of the greatest causes of friction between teenagers and the rest of society. It seems that some people are inherently more likely to get addicted, and every teenager likes to think they are not one of those people. With their strangely mixed feelings of weakness and invincibility, they prefer to think that they are one of the many who can cope – those who can 'deal with it'.

There are certainly variations between people's responses to drugs. These often result from basic biological differences between individuals, either in the brain systems which respond to drugs, or in the mechanisms the body uses to destroy and discard them. For example, there are well-characterized variations in the genes which make enzymes to destroy alcohol, and this means that some people can tolerate alcohol better than others. Also, because the alcohol destruction pathway entails a sequence of biochemical steps, in some people that pathway can 'back up' and make them temporarily accumulate toxic breakdown products of alcohol. These variations between individuals are also mirrored in differences in alcohol sensitivity between subgroups of the human population. This is why I was considered a hard-drinking man in Japan, but rather a lightweight in Britain.

In fact, there are so many differences in individual susceptibility to drugs that we now wonder if variability has been built into human biochemistry because it is in itself advantageous. People need biochemical resistance to the mind-altering plants growing in their local environment; however, they do not need resistance to plants they are never likely to meet, and in fact it would be a waste of resources to have such resistance. So modern variations in drug susceptibility may reflect adaptations of our ancestors to their planty, druggy milieux. In this context it is tempting to suggest that Europeans metabolize alcohol well because of two thousand filthy years of city living when the only safe sources of water were wine and beer. After all, natural selection must work well when teetotalism is commonly fatal. So perhaps the human variability in drug susceptibility (about which teenagers love to remind us) is the natural consequence of our species having evolved in a wide variety of environments.

With recent advances in molecular biology, we can now see the geographical and botanical diversity of human history etched into our genes. Many gene variations have recently been linked to susceptibility to the effects of alcohol, nicotine, cocaine, amphetamines, opioids and cannabis. And there are signs of further discoveries to come: one study in rats showed links between amphetamine sensitivity and forty-three genes – that number is 0.2 per cent of all the genes present in a human. Many of the genes implicated in drug susceptibility are involved in making receptor molecules in the brain, and as we have seen these are exactly the molecules on which drugs act. Furthermore, if we all have inbuilt genetic susceptibilities to individual drugs, then can we not also vary in our general propensity for addiction? If all drugs addict us by the same dopamine-secreting tegmentum–accumbens pathway, then it is reasonable to suspect that the molecular details of this addiction machinery may also vary between individuals. Indeed, psychological and genetic studies both suggest a strong genetic basis for addiction, so perhaps we should think of 'addictive genes' as well as 'addictive personalities'.

But I still think we have tended to underestimate the social aspects of drugs in all our agonizing about them. We are, after all, an essentially social species – one in which individuals only function in relation to others. And when we are teenagers, socialization is more novel, immediate and formative than at any other time in our lives. Because of this, I think we should worry more about the roles of self-esteem, peer pressure and social inadequacy in teenagers' decisions to take drugs. Of course, adolescent self-esteem, peer pressure and social inadequacy may have strong underlying genetic influences – a teenager's personality may certainly be decided in part by their genes, and by how their parents' genes affected their upbringing – but in an individual, everyday teenager, it is the personality we see rather than the genes. Also, if a teenager's life is taken over by drugs, it is their social development that will suffer, or fail completely. Blaming their genes will not help them. If we are to help an individual teenager, it is the personality, not the gene, we must address and encourage to defend itself, believe in itself and not yield.

Adolescence evolved as a wonderful novelty of human evolution, a stage in the life-plan to acquire new physical, mental and, as we will see in Part Four, social skills. However, the adventurousness, social rebellion and sheer cerebral flux that define teenagers have accidentally rendered them vulnerable to the cheap, potent drugs that have appeared in the past few decades. Drugs give them undoubted pleasure and bolster their inclusion into social groups, and this is why they try them. But recent research shows that drugs subvert the teenage brain in an exceptionally aggressive and unrelenting way. The evidence is so concerning that, although this has come as an unexpected epiphany to me as I wrote this book, perhaps the old advice that taking drugs 'is best left until college' might turn out to be correct.

The attack on ancient teen brains by modern teen drugs has exacerbated the conflicts between teenagers and the rest of society. Parents are always driven to protect teenagers, but those teenagers often see drugs as an exciting and enjoyable way to declare their independence and enter the social world in their own sweet way. Still, for many teenagers the story of drugs does not have a tragic ending. Our huge prefrontal cortex often summons up enough control to overcome the ancient reward-seeking pathways deep beneath, and many people *do* quit or control drugs successfully. The prefrontal cortex often 'knows what is right', but it seems that a certain level of confidence, strength and support is needed for it to win through. In Part Four we will look at the things that give teenagers this confidence, strength and support – the relationships that flutter between themselves, the world around them, and other people.

4. Love and Loss

Why teenage relationships can be the best and worst things in the world

But I like very few people. And even fewer of your age and sex. Liking other people is an illusion we have to cherish in ourselves if we are to live in society. It is one I have long since banished from my life here. You wish to be liked. I wish simply to be.

John Fowles, *The Magus*

Being a teenager is a confusing experience.
The whole world opens out with new vistas of social and intellectual opportunity, yet at the same time it closes in on us. Many of us start to see ourselves as individuals at this time – a mind imprisoned within its own body, always reaching out to others, yet forever isolated from them. There is a sudden realization that we must make do with the mind that nature has given us, and a suspicion that if things go wrong, we are on our own. This is also the time when the human penchant for self-analysis really kicks in; always in the mind of the teenager there is the occasional thought, the frequent worry or the constant panic that they are 'not good enough'.

Teenagers often seem as if they are off in a little world of their own, and perhaps they are – busily making sense of other people, the world and their own concerns. Wondering if they are normal. Most adults have strong memories of the way they felt during adolescence, and I am no exception. The last thing I want to do is fill this book with the reminiscences of a thirty-something white Caucasian male, but those are the only memories I have. As a teenager I remember having three or four good friends, but sometimes wondering if I was supposed to have more, or whether we were meant to support each other in a more overtly emotional way. Romantic life seemed encouraging, although I did wonder if I was destined for a life of indefinite serial monogamy – which in hindsight strikes me as a rather charming fear for a sixteen-year-old. School and work seemed okay, but I always wondered how unexpectedly 'burn-out' could strike. And although I was generally very relaxed, I got this weird panic attack thing whenever I ate in public – a problem from which I could benefit now that middle-age lardiness has set in.

There you have it – the ruminations of a teenager not so far from where I am sitting. Looking back, the main impression I get now is that I was keen to analyse everything and accept nothing. Any facet of my life that was on an even keel was mentally checked for falsity, instability or abnormality, while anything overtly worrying was met by vague helpless bemusement. But one strong feeling filled my teenage years – a sense of uncertainty about myself. Newly aware of how trapped I was inside my own head, how could I ever know if my experiences of adolescence were normal?

Of course no one can ever know for sure how others feel, but that does not make teenage uncertainty any easier to bear. When we are teenagers we feel uncertainty especially keenly, and it is compounded by the embarrassment of having our stumbling physical and mental development on continual display to the watching world. Considering this, it is little wonder that adolescence is often viewed as a time of turmoil and negativity – although I believe turmoil can be a positive force too. In addition, the new feelings and self-awareness that come with adolescence may explain why things can go very wrong indeed – mental illness shows a vicious predilection for the teenage years, and can cast a shadow over a whole lifetime.

But if we are to understand the task faced by the teenage mind – that summit of human achievement – we will have to think hard about what it must do, what can go wrong and how we should study it. As teenagers, we all have to develop the ability to deal with all three of a triad of phenomena: our selves, our world and other people. All three are difficult to deal with, and all three are interlinked. Also, corresponding to those three phenomena are the three major mental illnesses that may result when we fail to deal with them – depression, schizophrenia and anxiety – and we must also find out what they can tell us about the more widespread teenage failings of sadness, confusion and worry.

Most importantly of all, we must work out the best way to view teenagers and their minds. Should we study them as individual patients fretting on the psychotherapist's couch? Or as electrical-chemical vessels of cerebral mechanics fizzing in the physiologist's lab? Or are they, as evolutionary biologists would have it, simply immature nude apes disoriented because they came into the world expecting to spend their lives scampering about on the ancient plains of Africa? In this section we will work through these possibilities one at a time, and we will see that teenagers manage to be all three things at once.

Why do teenagers get so sad?

Teenagers used to be overlooked by psychotherapists. Freud and the early psychoanalysts focused on childhood as the fount of later behaviours, attitudes and problems, whereas adolescence was seen as an uninteresting transition into adulthood. Childhood was targeted as the time when our relationships were somehow internalized into our way of dealing with the world – becoming part of the fabric of our personality. We still believe that personalities are partially constructed in this way, but the result of decades of study of child development is that we now have a simpler approach to the whole process. The building of the self is not as hidden and mysterious as we once thought. Also, we have realized how important adolescence is for learning the behaviours that will last the rest of our lives. Really, it is hardly surprising that the crucial time for learning how to deal with ourselves and our peers also happens to be the time when we are becoming increasingly self-aware and interacting more with people our own age.

Psychotherapy has an unusual status in modern science. It may seem obvious to say so, but it is rooted in the practical, everyday process of treating mental illness. Because of this, it is based on anecdote and trial and error. Psychotherapists develop models of how the mind works, which they test by using them to treat people with psychological problems. However, they simply cannot perform 'proper' experiments to test the validity of their theories in a cohort of people all in the same mental state – after all, no two human minds are alike. Also, they cannot carry out 'controlled blind experiments' in which patients do not know what treatment they are receiving, or if they are receiving any treatment at all – the whole point of psychotherapy is that the patient is aware of what is going on.

Another problem with using psychotherapy to tell us how the teenage mind works is that, for obvious reasons, therapists concentrate on people who are 'unwell', rather than the majority of the population who are 'well'. And we simply do not know whether the unwell minority can be used as a model of how everyone else's minds function. Indeed, that criticism could be levelled at this very chapter, part of which will focus on the dramatic increase in mental illness that occurs in teenagers. However, I will try to balance this by constantly harking back to how things change in teenagers who are not mentally ill.

Still, during adolescence the link between illness and normal mental processes is especially close. Because of this, many teenagers suffer symptoms that would be considered pathological in adults – prolonged unhappiness, compulsive self-criticism, disordered thought processes, undirected anxiety – that the boundaries between normal and abnormal are especially fuzzy. Also, mental illness so often starts during adolescence that it can appear frighteningly like a regular part of growing up. Even with mentally 'well' teenagers, adults can find it difficult to explain the illogic of adolescent experience and behaviour. This might explain why there is still no consensus about whether the old cliché of adolescence – that it is an inherently and unavoidably painful experience – really is true. Some studies claim that it is every bit as stressful as is often claimed, while others think that the chaos and pain of adolescence are hugely overstated.

Despite all this anecdotal, disease-obsessed vagueness, there are two very good reasons why we should value the therapist's view. The first of these is that the teenage mind is unarguably complex, and we simply do not possess any neuroscientific tools that can fully interpret that complexity. Instead, we try to understand it in a detailed, subtle way, using a detailed, subtle but unscientific tool called a therapist. Therapists may oversimplify, generalize and leap to conclusions, but they are the closest thing we have to a mind-measuring machine. And this leads us on to the second reason to value psychotherapy, which is that it often works. In recent decades, neuroscientists have identified many anatomical, genetic and chemical processes that underlie the mental illnesses that afflict teenagers. Sometimes these discoveries have even led to effective treatments for these diseases. However, as we will see, the success of these treatments can give us a misleadingly simple view of those diseases. And the best evidence that psychotherapy is a valid approach to the teenage mind is that despite the abundance of other treatments available for mental illness, psychotherapy – just talking to someone – remains one of the most effective.

So how do teenagers learn to deal with themselves? I am not sure if you can really have a 'relationship' with yourself, but common experience tells us that teenagers have to develop ways to understand, evaluate and accept themselves. This sense of self is hugely important – essential, in fact, for every other part of our mental well-being. Without it we would be rootless automatons, blindly reacting to the world around us without any reference to who we are. There are two elements of this sense of self which are especially important to teenagers: self-analysis and autonomy.

Children are self-analytical from time to time. They learn the difference between what is going on in the world and what is going on in their head – although the child who covers his own eyes so he cannot be found is a striking example of how long this realization can take. As the first ten years of life elapse, children occasionally refer to how they see themselves and how they think others see them, but these flickerings of self-analysis are interspersed with long periods of endearing ignorance of the self.

All this changes at the start of adolescence. Not only do teenagers spend more time looking inwards, but it starts to become something of an obsession. Early-teens may sit for long periods mulling over their own hopes, fears, abilities and defects. This newfound self-obsession is, of course, entirely normal. Indeed, far from being the irritating narcissism it is often claimed to be, it is a sign that teenagers are doing what they evolved to do. One of the keys to human success is that we are able to analyse ourselves – both as individuals and as an entire species we self-criticize, solve problems and adapt ourselves until we can achieve what we want. While children are rather poor at self-analysis, preferring instead for an adult to show them the correct way to do things, adolescents are the complete opposite. This explains why they sometimes aggressively reject outside advice – so they can learn how to modify their own thought processes.

How frustrating must it be to have to learn, from scratch, how to do that?

In Part Two we saw that a dramatic reconfiguration of the brain is taking place at exactly the time when teenagers are becoming self-analytical. It is tempting to think back 250,000 years to the time when the appearance of teenagers first allowed the evolution and configuration of the huge *Homo sapiens* brain, and to speculate that this was the first time that such self-analysis had ever existed on earth. Self-analysis gives humans immense mental flexibility, and it is teenagers who first see the advantages of that flexibility. If they cannot do something, then they can strip apart and reassemble their own mental processes until they find a way to succeed. They learn the power of being able to solve their own problems – to develop their own code of beliefs, to learn how to cope with adversity, to calm themselves, and to *enjoy* self-reliance. Self-awareness opens up a whole new world of mental possibilities – and a new mature, teenage, personality.

But self-analysis brings its own problems. With it comes the opportunity for excessive, damaging self-criticism. Teenagers are more prone to self-criticism than adults, perhaps because they are still cognitively immature, socially inexperienced and often belittled by the adults around them. Many therapists worry that psychiatric disorders often stem from a failure to construct a viable, coherent sense of self in the teenage years. The requirement for teenagers to set their own mental agenda means that, inevitably, some of them get it wrong. And as a result they can spend the rest of their lives locked in futile, obsessive attempts at trying to come to terms with themselves.

From personal experience, I believe that most psychological problems do indeed stem from a mis-setting of these internal self-analysis mechanisms during adolescence. So many of the troubled teenagers I see are, quite simply, criticizing themselves to pieces. They are bright, charming, attractive people who seem to have no way to view themselves in a positive light. They have a self-image they find it painful to live with, but cannot seem to change. I worry that if they do not seek help (and they may not, as that would add to their sense of worthlessness), then they will go through life chronically unhappy. They may never show symptoms severe enough to be diagnosed as mentally ill, but the flawed relationship they formed with themselves could stay with them for ever.

The other half of the yin and yang of emerging teenage self, complementary to self-analysis, is autonomy. Autonomy cannot develop without self-analysis, and the converse is probably also true. During early adolescence, teenagers withdraw from their parents both mentally and emotionally. Although they still need them for occasional material and emotional support, they start to actively exclude their parents from their lives – a process which may be painful for all involved, but is nonetheless entirely normal.

Later on I will refer to this parental rejection as part of the changing teenage social world, but I mention it here because the shift is more than just a simple change in social preference. Many have gone as far as to claim that it is a complete internal restructuring of the mind's view of itself. If a teenager is ever to be able to function as a normal adult, it is thought that they must pass through this stage of self-determination to a state where they can stand alone as an emotionally autonomous being. This voluntary act of dislocation from parents is itself empowering, and by leaving teenagers precariously isolated, it forces a radical review of their self-image. Maybe this is why parental support is so valuable for teenagers – it gives them something they can feel they are throwing back in their parents' faces.

The rewards of a teenager's proclamation of autonomy are enormous: a new, more profound state of consciousness that was never available to them as a child. They can now glide from childish self-interest, through a teenager's desire for social approval to an adult sense of altruism and self-sacrifice, accumulating the beliefs and behaviours that will define them as individuals. Along the way, they start to develop the confidence to maintain their inner emotional stability without demanding support from others. They will then be free to experiment with emotional independence and dependence, and to control how much they let others into their lives. This may all sound rather esoteric, but it is crucial: some therapists believe that a great deal of later emotional turmoil results from people striking the wrong balance between emotional attachment and detachment during adolescence. Many people react to relationship problems by trying harder and harder to fight their way into others' affections, when the best thing may actually be to stand back and be the old independent person that others once found so attractive.

So autonomy is a good example of how conflict and upheaval are a healthy part of teenage life. Active rejection of parents opens up adult choices about independence and emotional relationships; indeed, some biologists have claimed this reveals a central emotional dichotomy built deep into the human brain. It has been suggested that as primates evolved, they allocated the functions of independence and attachment to different halves of the brain. According to this theory, the right side of the brain accumulated the machinery of emotion, positivity and attachment, whereas the left side acquired analysis, negativity and autonomy. As a result, the right side is prone to social obsession and anxiety, while the left is withdrawn and antisocial. And this tension between the two sides is claimed to have reached its pinnacle in humans – the master manipulators of social context, inquisitiveness and communication. So the social life of humans, the most social monkeys of all, can be seen as a left–right tension between emotional dependence and autonomy. Unfortunately, modern neuroscience has suggested that this idea of a strict right–left split is an oversimplification, perhaps resulting from technical limitations in early experiments on the living human brain. Yet it is still possible that opposing regions tangled up in *both* sides of the brain are continually slugging it out to decide how to interact with the outside world: spiky, independent Lennons and naïve, charming McCartneys of the mind producing an eloquent output neither could create alone.

So I suggest that self-analysis and autonomy are the two tools teenagers must develop to create a sense of self that will support them for the rest of their lives. Admittedly, people can change the way they see themselves later in life, but it can be incredibly difficult to repair the failing sense of self so often formed in adolescence. Surely this is all the more reason to help teenagers form a self with which they can be comfortable.

Although self-analysis and autonomy are the cornerstones of teenage development, they can also cause one of the major psychological problems of adolescence: depression. Depression is sometimes claimed to be the most burdensome illness in the world, and this is almost certainly the case in the developed world where it affects perhaps a fifth of the population. And intriguingly, this scourge of the *Homo sapiens* brain often starts in the teenage years – and thereby hangs a tale.

'Depression' is a complicated concept, and this is especially true in teenagers. First of all, it is entirely reasonable for people to react to bad things happening in their lives by becoming sad, and of course this sadness can be profound. In this case, grief, loss or failure trigger a process sometimes called 'reactive depression'. In contrast, the term 'clinical depression' has been used to describe a condition in which people feel extremely depressed, but with no obvious external cause. Classically, clinical depression was thought to start without provocation, and to cause characteristic symptoms involving the whole body: fatigue, headaches, loss of sex drive, appetite changes, and waking early in the morning but not being able to get back to sleep. However, many now believe that the distinction between reactive and clinical depression is not as clear as once thought – reactive depression can lead to clinical depression, and the symptoms of the two can overlap. Yet many patients still seem to be in a 'clinical' category in which their deep black sadness appears completely out of proportion to the adverse things that happen to them. They become locked into a distinctively vicious cycle of negative thinking and hopelessness, especially about themselves. Conversely, although many people feel reactively depressed at some point in their life when something goes wrong, they are still able to articulate exactly why they are sad, they can often 'count their blessings' and they may even 'see the light at the end of the tunnel'.

Adding to this debate about clinical and reactive depression is a third phenomenon, which I will call 'teenage sadness'.

Mood is a fundamentally different thing in teenagers, and I think it warrants a new category. Many psychologists have reported the replacement of the essentially optimistic bias of children by a more negative teenage outlook – almost an adolescent 'fall from grace'. Between a third and a half of all US teenagers report being 'sad' or 'in turmoil' at any one time – a staggeringly high figure which indicates that something changes dramatically in the second decade of life. I cannot believe that the outside world becomes much more horrible during adolescence, so it is unlikely that external factors can explain these dramatic changes in mood. Also, bodily changes at puberty can be worrying, but even these seem insufficient to explain these dramatic alterations in mood. 'Teenage sadness' is such a distinctive and profound thing that it must result from changes taking place within the brain itself. Whether it can be blamed on the extensive anatomical restructuring of the teenage brain, or more 'psychiatric' concepts such as the development of self-analysis and the quest for autonomy, it seems clear that teenage mood alters because the teenage brain alters. And if the teenage brain is *supposed* to change, should we not expect teenage sadness to occur?

If we think of teenage sadness as an unavoidable side-effect of the maturation of the huge *sapiens* brain, then that brain starts to look like a terrible evolutionary gamble. Humans have been successful because of our brains, but are we, and teenagers especially, now paying the price of that success? Teenagers are walking a psychological tightrope – their sadness blurring frighteningly into clinical depression. Many 'normal' teenagers exhibit symptoms that would be considered evidence of mental illness in adults. Indeed, teenagers are good ammunition for those who claim that no one can ever be psychologically 'normal'.

Yet teenage sadness is also different. For example, depressed teenagers are often irritable, whereas depressed adults are usually more melancholy. Also, adolescence is a time of characteristically dramatic mood swings, for reasons which may relate to the anatomical reorganization of the brain circuits controlling emotion. And because of this, teenage sadness is often expressed loudly for the world to hear.

Adolescence is a cruel time for depression to strike because this is a time when there is so much to do and try, and no time to be lost. Teenage depression shows strong statistical links to anxiety, suicide, drug use, eating disorders, promiscuity, teenage pregnancy and failure at school. In fact, more than half of depressed teenagers also show signs of anxiety disorders, and this implies that, rather than being a clearly defined condition, adolescent depression is just one large knot in the awful tangle in which many teenagers find themselves. Depressed teenagers miss out on so many things that they have to do, and their depression very often continues long into adulthood – as with so many aspects of adolescence, setting the tone for an entire life. And sadly, other teenagers can be so wrapped up in their own quest for happiness and success that they are often not much help. An unfortunate social consequence of teenage depression is that sufferers can appear to become inward-looking to the point of selfishness, and other teenagers can find it hard to sympathize with them.

Psychotherapists have given us great insight into the thought processes that characterize 'clinical' depression, and there seem to be certain 'thinking abnormalities' which crop up again and again. Contemporary diagnosis of depression may be based too much on the 'tick box' approach of determining how many of the 'required' symptoms people show, but there certainly are features that crop up again and again in clinical depression. None of these symptoms on their own defines clinical depression, and we all show some of them at some time in our lives, but in combination they add up to a pattern of thinking that is distressing, self-defeating and difficult to escape.

Negativity is a thread which runs through depression. We must all learn to deal with bad things happening to us, often by putting them in perspective so we can remedy or bypass them in some way. Yet people with depression often focus exclusively on adverse events, and indeed there is good evidence that their memory for positive events is measurably impaired. They also tend to react to adverse events with predictably negative emotions. This in itself would not be too bad – after all, we all feel down sometimes – but teenagers with depression often draw unreasonably negative inferences about events. They feel that they are evidence of the general hopelessness of life, and this can freeze them into a state of passive inertia which they find difficult to escape. Worst of all is the way that they often interpret adverse events as a sign of their own inadequacy and weakness. If you believe that everything bad happens because you are incurably worthless, then it is hard to see a way out.

Clinical depression's ocean of negativity has many currents. Depressed people often think in an all-or-nothing way, in which phenomena are either 'good' or 'bad', which reinforces a sense of hopelessness when so many things fall into the 'bad' category. Similarly, depression also commonly involves tendencies to jump to conclusions and over-generalize. It can also be linked to changes in values and goals – for example, depressed teenagers are more likely to think that happiness comes from material possessions and social acceptance, whereas other teenagers are more likely to value their own attitudes and goals.

The role of negativity in teenage depression has even led some psychologists to suggest that the disease is, at its heart, an addiction to negativity. Early exposure to failure and negativity in others has been claimed to lead to a teenage inability to appreciate pleasure and a stifling fear of failure. This may lead to misdirected attempts to 'defend' themselves from pleasurable things and challenges, and even derive perverse reassurance from inflicting pain and deprivation on themselves. It may be difficult to understand why people behave like this, because it does not seem to make sense. But we have already seen that the ways people learn behaviours can be frighteningly simple and inexorable. Besides, entering a self-defeating cycle of negativity is, by its very nature, unlikely to 'make sense'.

If we are to stop teenagers entering a lifelong struggle with depression, we must first work out why depression so often starts at this particular phase of the human life-plan. One explanation often suggested is that the teenage body undergoes many unnerving and distressing changes during puberty, and it is these which trigger teenage depression. The body is unstoppably and very publicly becoming sexualized in ways that can be embarrassing, and occasionally disfiguring. Acne, for example, is strongly associated with depression and even suicide. Other 'biological' reasons for depression have also been suggested – adolescence is a time when glandular fever and post-viral fatigue syndromes often take hold. These conditions may either cause depression directly, or they may cause it indirectly by depriving teenagers of contact with their developing social world. Yet all these physical causes of depression, while important for the people who suffer from them, seem too crude to be the root cause of widespread teenage sadness and the adolescent dawn of clinical depression.

Much more convincing is the link between depression and self-esteem. As part of the teenage development of self-analysis, we all acquire a sense of self-esteem, and it is clear that this process can go badly wrong. So many attractive, intelligent, charming teenagers have a self-image that appears, to any independent observer, to be ridiculously low. Self-esteem is an excellent candidate for the cause of teenage depression for good reasons: like depression it comes to the fore in adolescence; it is low in some teenagers for no good reason; it is easy to see how it might cause negativity to be ascribed to one's own worthlessness; and studies show that depressed teenagers often have low self-esteem (although it is not clear what is cause and what is effect). Of course, because we are an inherently social species, teenage self-esteem is not just an inward-looking phenomenon, but also has a strong social dimension. Because teenagers worry so much about how others see them, it is easy to understand why early symptoms of depression can weaken their confidence so much that their self-esteem falls even more. Social failure reduces self-esteem which breeds yet more social failure and the cycle is complete.

There is one striking feature of teenage depression which adds support to the idea that depression is built into the fabric of growing up. During childhood, depression is rare and is, if anything, slightly commoner in boys. But by thirteen years of age there is a remarkable skewing of depression towards girls, so that they are twice as likely as boys to suffer it. This sets the trend for adult life, as the discrepancy persists until middle age. Although psychologists are not sure why girls are more prone to depression than boys, this sex difference does imply that there is something about depression that is 'inbuilt'. By the age of thirteen, most teenagers are only just starting out on the process of learning socio-sexual interactions, and the fact that the sex discrepancy in depression is already established by then suggests that depression is caused by changes going on inside the brain rather than any external influences. As the female brain develops, it acquires behavioural traits demonstrably different from its slower-developing male equivalent. Teenage girls react more to negative events than boys, and they are more likely to explain them in terms of their own failings, especially their physical unattractiveness. They are also less likely to ignore stressful events than boys. They dwell on their own weaknesses more than boys, both alone and in social groups – which may be why girls worry more about their friendships (more on this later). And intriguingly, depressed teenage girls tend to have more sexual partners than other girls, whereas depressed boys tend to have fewer.

So the evidence is mounting that there is a grumbling weakness in the proud human brain as it edges into its second decade. The flexible, self-constructing human self of the teenage years must develop its self-esteem and learn to articulate its emotions and cope with adversity, all at a time when the very fabric of the brain is being rebuilt. This complex process of psychological development is essential to becoming fully human, but it exposes the brain's own failings. A major reason why depression often starts during adolescence is that this is the first time when the brain has sufficient cognitive abilities to be able to suffer it. You cannot use your own worthlessness to explain adverse events until you can analyse yourself; you cannot have a sense of hope-lessness until you have a sense of your own personal future; you cannot shy away from intimidating tasks until you understand what striving for a goal actually means.

Depression, like most mental illnesses, is an abnormal functioning of the mental abilities that define us as human. This is why humans are the only animals to get clinical depression and teenage sadness. Also, because we acquire most of those human abilities during adolescence, depression cannot start in earnest until we are teenagers – before then we simply do not have enough brainpower. Thus the things that have made humans so successful are also what make teenagers' lives a misery. Teenage depression exposes a fright-ening instability in the huge human mind: we have evolved our brains to the very limits.

In our quick look at teenage depression, we have tried to look through the eyes of a therapist. However, it is worth men-tioning that there are other ways of viewing depression, and these do not always lead to the same conclusions.

First of all, evolutionary biologists have tried to develop a theory of why depression has evolved. Rather than seeing it as an unfortunate by-product of the exuberant enlargement of the human brain, they have tried to identify a useful role for depression in human life. Much of this quest has been based around the idea that displays of sadness carry important social messages to others. According to these ideas, we exhibit sadness to elicit a response from others – and indeed most of us respond to a sad person with help and sympathy. However, although we may explain the evolution of *reactive* depression as a way to encourage social support in difficult times, it is harder to explain why *clinical* depression should be advantageous. For one thing, it is just so debilitating – it is difficult to imagine a human surviving the condition in the cut and thrust of the ancient African plains. Moreover, when people discover that another's sadness has no tangible cause, I think their instinctive reaction is not sympathy, but confusion. People do not immediately know how to help someone with clinical depression, so I doubt that it performs a useful social function. One morbid theory even suggests that it exists to encourage suicide, because an individual's suicide has been argued to be evolutionarily desirable if it frees resources for their surviving kin.

A second theory of depression is far more mechanistic, and it springs from the finding that clinical depression is often effectively treated by drugs called 'selective serotonin reuptake inhibitors'. These drugs increase the amounts of the neurotransmitter serotonin available in the brain, and their effectiveness has been claimed, quite reasonably, to suggest that something is wrong with the brain's serotonin system during depression. However, this argument has been extended, often by people who feel very strongly about it, as evidence that abnormal serotonin levels are the actual cause of depression. This is an enticing theory because it establishes a specific physical abnormality at the core of depression – far easier to comprehend than vague speculations about self-esteem or negativity. It can also be used to remove much of the stigma of depression, by implying that having 'broken serotonin' should be no more embarrassing than having a broken leg. However, just because the theory is attractive does not mean it is correct. There are some simple, technical problems with the serotonin theory of depression – selective serotonin reuptake inhibitors act on potent neurotransmitters other than serotonin, for example. Also, the brain reacts

to these drugs with a complex rebalancing of its neurotransmitter systems, and maybe it is this rebalancing which 'cures'
depression. Indeed, there are genuine fears that the serotonin
theory is simply too much of an oversimplification – just
because a drug appears to work does not mean that it strikes
at the very root of a disease.

Why do teenagers get so confused?

It is not just our relationship with ourselves that changes during adolescence: we also develop a new relationship with the outside world.

We saw in Part Two that a profound restructuring of the brain is taking place during the second decade of life, and that this fundamentally changes the way we interact with our surroundings. Part of this change is due to a recasting of the tegmentum–accumbens–cortex pathway. This array of dopamine-releasing nerves ascends from the depths of the brain to temper and guide the activity of the huge *sapiens* cerebral cortex. The cortex is a fizzing electrochemical sea of enormous computational potential, but it must be carefully controlled if it is to learn to analyse, abstract and describe the world outside. When teenagers learn to do these things successfully, a whole new realm of consciousness becomes available to them for the first time. However, so profound are the mental changes required to reach that realm, that teenagers may experience years of disordered and disturbing thoughts during the transition. And some never reach their destination, but are left stranded along the way: schizophrenia usually starts during adolescence. Teenagers have a tough time because it is they who are responsible for wiring up our species' huge brain, and because of this, teenage confusion can come in many forms. Perhaps we should try to break this confusion down into a few different types. First of all, we all have an idea in our head of how the world works, and it confuses us when that idea is challenged. Anyone can become confused when something does not make sense. Secondly, many of us, and especially teenagers, go through phases when our life does not seem to make sense – when we feel that we are missing something, or that there must be some secret to which we are not privy. Maybe we all feel like that, but do not like to admit it. Things can get worse, however, and when our model of the world and how we interact with it becomes disordered and unpredictable, we use the term 'schizophrenia'. Finally, when a mind entirely loses touch with reality, we call it 'psychosis'. It may or may not be correct to think of these four phenomena – transient confusion, 'life' confusion, schizophrenia and psychosis – as points on a continuous spectrum of confusion, but certainly they all start in earnest when we are teenagers. And to teenagers, whose brains are very much a work in progress, it can be worryingly difficult to work out which type of confusion is which.

So what causes the fizzing electrochemical sea of the cortex to fail to establish normal relations with the outside world? Already we have seen that depression may be a sign that the human brain is now overstretched, and schizophrenia may be an even better example of this. Typically starting between the ages of thirteen and eighteen, schizophrenia is a distinctive set of psychological abnormalities. Unlike depression, in which many symptoms can look like extreme versions of the mental processes we all undergo, the disordered cognitive processes of schizophrenia appear obviously 'strange'. Also, schizophrenia seems to be built into the human condition: animals do not get it, but the condition crops up with remarkable consistency throughout recorded human history, and in all cultures around the world. Schizophrenia is our best evidence that the human brain has got too complex for its own good, and that it is teenagers who bear the brunt.

Something obviously goes wrong in schizophrenia, and as a result schizophrenia is the mental illness most often viewed in physical terms. Viewing the schizophrenic brain as a diseased organ – a measurably dysfunctional form of the normal human brain – has allowed us to make great progress in understanding the mind. Indeed, to me some of the strange features of schizophrenia look as if they are trying to tell us something about how the teenage mind works. After all, schizophrenia is quite common – 0.5 per cent of the population is a lot of people in total – common enough to suggest that it is a sign of an inherent weakness of the developing human brain. Also, as we will see, there is considerable evidence that overt schizophrenic symptoms are preceded by years of more subtle abnormality – you can 'see the disease coming', as it were. Most intriguingly of all, not only does the condition usually start during adolescence, but it even *looks* like failed development of the mental processes we are all supposed to acquire as teenagers. People suffering from schizophrenia do not understand where their own chaotic thought processes come from; they lose their ability to enjoy things; their conversation becomes limited; they become socially withdrawn, emotionally unresponsive and unmotivated; they lose the ability to plan. They become incomprehensible to people around them. I am certainly not suggesting that all teenagers are schizophrenic, but there are some obvious common features between schizophrenia and those difficult years when the teenage cortex is desperately trying to develop its new consciousness.

So what causes schizophrenia, and what does it tell us about the lesser forms of confusion that afflict all teenagers? It is worth saying at the outset that there have been more causes proposed for schizophrenia than for any other disease. The scientific literature on the condition is enormous, and there sometimes seem to be as many theories as there are researchers working in the field (one scientific paper even claims that schizophrenia has cursed the human population ever since we started to wear shoes with elevated heels). The huge number of schizophrenia theories suggests that the condition is complex – certainly too complex for us to have a simple, single understanding of it. Maybe schizophrenia is actually many different diseases that just happen to look the same. Or, perhaps schizophrenia reflects a single weak link in the evolution of the human brain, which can be stretched to breaking point by a wide range of other problems. Whatever the truth, as you read through our theories about schizophrenia (and I have ten of them here!) you might like to consider what they tell us about the more general question of why so much mental anguish starts during adolescence.

Ten theories about schizophrenia

1. The first theory suggests that the brain cannot undergo much mental illness or confusion until the cognitive changes of the teenage years have taken place. As we saw in Part Two, as we pass from childhood to adolescence the brain starts to develop in a strikingly new way. The brain stops growing and starts to prune away the exuberant childhood thicket of nerve branches; starts to coat previously unused pathways with fatty myelin insulation; activates its dopamine control systems. As a result, the teenage mind acquires new forms of thought, self-awareness, emotion and socialization that were not possible in the child. According to this first theory, the major mental illnesses of mankind are failures of the mental abilities we develop in our teenage years – the very abilities which make us human. For example, depression may be a failure of our self-awareness circuits, and perhaps schizophrenia is a failure of teenage thought systems. Whatever the details, this theory suggests that mental illnesses cannot really start until adolescence because before that time we simply do not possess the mental machinery which can fail. Thus children are largely protected from our species' scourge of mental illness, as well as teenagers' feelings of sadness and confusion, because they are not yet fully mentally human.

2. The second explanation of why schizophrenia, and mental illness in general, often strikes in adolescence is subtly different from the first. According to this theory, mental illnesses are built into the developing brain from a very early age, in the form of malformed circuits which lie dormant until the brain first tries to use them during adolescence. Thus mental illness does not develop anew during the teenage years – rather, it is there from the start, hidden by the immaturity of the childhood brain. Good evidence for this dormant phase of mental illness is the 'prodrome' (or premonition) of schizophrenia – months or years of subtle psychological abnormality which precede the full-blown illness, but which include social withdrawal, anxiety, depression, poor concentration, irritability and unhappiness. Although these symptoms may seem vague, the prodrome of schizophrenia is the best understood of any mental illness.

And it gives us a big clue to the nature of the disease: schizophrenia is lying latent within children's brains, often evident from an early age as minor psychological problems, but waiting for adolescence to reveal its full ferocity.

3. The third theory of teenage confusion and mental illness centres around the idea that teenagers are meant to develop in different ways at different times. In Parts One and Two we considered the idea that different aspects of teenage physical and cerebral development might be deliberately staggered, so that they occur in sensible, helpful stages, and even that teenage boys and girls are meant to develop out of synchrony with each other. These ideas may be extended to mental development, to imply that we have evolved a system of social skill acquisition that is also carefully arranged into a neat sequence. And scattered around the brain are 'social circuits' which fall into three main groups, each of which matures at different times – those which perceive the teenager's social world develop first, those which allow emotional reactions to that world mature next and those which allow more considered, thoughtful responses to the social environment develop last. For example, such a sequence of events could explain why mid-teenagers can be so unabashedly sensitive and emotional, yet unable to analyse their social situation. But as well as explaining this 'normal' teenage confusion, the staggered development of these processes could also explain the adolescent onset of mental illness. Indeed, brain scanning techniques have shown that several of the areas involved in social perception, emotion and analysis have an abnormal structure in teenagers with mental illness. However, we should be cautious about this evidence, as it may not be as strong as it first seems. As we will see, so many brain structures appear altered in schizophrenia

that it would be surprising if some of the 'social regions' were *not* abnormal.

4. The fourth theory is also about the timing of teenage development, but it suggests that the chronology of modern adolescent life has become fundamentally unnatural and harmful. Throughout this book I have argued that the teenager is a uniquely human phenomenon, undergoing a sequence of physical and mental changes, carefully orchestrated to occur in a defined order over a prolonged period. So if timing is so important in teenage development, what happens if modern life disturbs that timing? Probably the most clear-cut example is that humans are better nourished than at any time in their history, and this has hastened some aspects of adolescent development but not others. Best documented is ever-earlier puberty, which means that teenagers now become sexually mature when they are relatively mentally immature. I will discuss this issue again in more detail in Part Five, but it serves to show how modern teenagers are developing at 'unnatural times' and in an 'unnatural order'. What if a premature surge of sex hormones renders the brain susceptible to schizophrenia? What if a physically developed body precedes its inhabitant's ability to accept a sexual body image? What if good nutrition hastens development of emotional but not analytical brain regions? The human brain is already unwieldy and unstable, so subtle mistimings could be enough to tip it over the edge into mental illness. You only need to visit a zoo to see what good nutrition and unnatural surroundings can do to once-wild animals.

5. The fifth theory, like the fourth, focuses on a deep failing of modern life, but in this case that failing is social and cultural, not biological. The concern is that modern teenagers are thrust into social environments and cultural systems that are so unlike those in which they evolved, that many of them simply cannot cope. They try to make their way in the world, adapting to the modern system as best they can, but eventually the strain becomes so great that they fail mentally. This theory is appealing but it is difficult to test, mainly because we do not know what humans' 'natural social and cultural system' was. We often think of pre-agricultural humans living in scattered, multi-extended-family communities, partly because this is what modern hunter-gatherers do, but we can never be sure. Does a teenager need just one parent, or a nuclear family, or an extended family, or a more dispersed 'commune' system to be mentally stable? Do parents impose more or fewer constraints on their children's self-expression, privacy and sexuality than they did fifty thousand years ago? We simply do not know. It is easy to idealize the old hunter-gatherer life, but there is some evidence to support the idea that its loss is indeed partly responsible for mental illness. For example, schizophrenia is commoner in urban environments, and especially so in socially disordered urban communities. Were the old ways, whatever they were, the best?

6. The sixth explanation is strangely positive: it suggests that we have schizophrenia for very good reasons. Creativity is central to human life. Without it, we could never have achieved so much. Also life would be, well, extremely boring. But creativity is an unusual mental process. It involves breaking free from run-of-the-mill ideas and making strange intellectual connections. Finding new solutions to practical problems and developing new forms of artistic expression require the mind to think in an essentially confusing, nonsensical way. To make new mental links, the mind must be free to toy with apparently unrelated concepts. It must run wild in an unfocused, disordered hope that it might stumble on some wonderful new truth. Evolutionary biologists have suggested that because creativity is so important, disordered and nonsensical thinking is an essential element of the human mind. Some of us do it less (the reliable plodders) and some do it more (the unpredictable visionaries), but human society works best when we have both types of person. This has led to the suggestion that schizophrenia is just one extreme of the range of human creativity – people who are so disordered and nonsensical that they can no longer function. Yet the genes they carry are maintained in the population because they create the occasional genius. Some have even extended this idea to claim that religious revelation is a product of human evolution – after all, people who hear divine voices in their head may be considered to be either God's chosen one, or psychotic.

7. Now we are moving into some of the more mechanistic ideas about teenage schizophrenia. For some time it has been suggested that schizophrenia is a genetic disorder, something written into the molecular script of individual sufferers. Some of the best evidence for this theory is that schizophrenia seems to develop over time, perhaps even from before birth. I have already mentioned that it may be preceded by a long 'prodromal' phase, but the disorder can have even earlier roots than that. For example, there is a link between schizophrenia and problems with the birth process. Intriguingly, it is the job of the baby's brain to ensure that it is positioned correctly for birth, so could a difficult birth be a first sign of brain abnormality? Also, there have been suggestions that children who develop schizophrenia in later life are more likely to experience prenatal infections, or have minor physical abnormalities than other children. Yet proving a genetic

cause has been difficult, partly because the disease could just as well be triggered by any aspect of a child's upbringing – and that upbringing is usually carried out by the same parents who bequeathed their genes to the child. However, a consensus is slowly developing that there is indeed an important genetic component to schizophrenia.

8. One of the problems with schizophrenia is that, although linked to genes, it cannot reliably be predicted by them. This unpredictability strongly suggests that while children may be born with an increased susceptibility to the disease, they only develop it as teenagers in response to another trigger – the so-called 'second hit' hypothesis. And many scientists now believe that this second hit might be a stressful adolescent event. Teenagers split stress into two components: they 'experience' stress with their amygdalae (almond-shaped blobs deep in the brain) and 'deal with it' using their prefrontal cortex (the corrugated sheet on the front of the brain). It is important that the amygdalae respond to worrying things, but it is also important for the prefrontal cortex to control that reaction – it is good to worry, but not too much. And there is good evidence that the prefrontal cortex is less active in schizophrenia, probably because there is not enough dopamine stimulating it from beneath. So according to this theory, some teenagers are inherently less able to cope with stressful situations because of a dopamine 'deficiency'. Because of this, instead of shrugging off adversity like most other teenagers, they get their second hit: the trigger that drives them into schizophrenia.

9. The ninth theory is that the cause of schizophrenia is far more complex than this dopamine theory would suggest, but that it may still be caused by a tangible, physical abnormality of the brain. Yet the problem with studying the brain during schizophrenia is that just about anything that can go wrong does go wrong. There is no single change in the brain that is of itself a sure sign of schizophrenia. Instead, schizophrenia may involve shrinking hippocampi, under-stimulated prefrontal cortex, poorly developed cerebral cortical cell layers, poor communication between regions of the temporal lobe, receding grey matter and enlarged fluid-filled spaces at the core of the brain. And studying brain chemistry is no less confusing – dopamine levels are indeed abnormal, but drugs which affect serotonin also help to treat the disease, and recently attention has turned to glutamate as a culprit as well. The schizophrenic brain is, to be honest, an anatomical and chemical mess. This is not to say that detailed picking apart of the working teenage brain will never tell us the cause of the disease, but at present it is hard to tell what is cause, what is effect, and what is the brain's desperate attempts to compensate for its failings.

However you look at it, the odds are stacked against the teenage brain. Adolescence is a time of new vulnerability; adolescence is a time when hidden defects emerge; adolescence is vulnerable to mistiming of biological changes; adolescence is the victim of the unnaturalness of modern life; adolescence is a time of failure to cope with stress; adolescence can be a time when a deep-seated chemical failing of an anatomically flawed brain occurs. All in all, it is little wonder that teenagers get confused sometimes. Rather, it is a testament to their resilience that they can carry out any rational thought at all. Which brings me finally to the tenth theory, and this is the one that links schizophrenia and adolescence more intimately than any other.

10. According to this theory, schizophrenia is an extended, exaggerated adolescence. We have already seen that there is

overlap between adolescent and schizophrenic behaviour, but I stopped short of equating the two. Well, some psychologists are not so cautious. They point out that a large number of teenagers find this period in their lives distressing, and even more are emotionally confused. Many cannot tell the difference between striving for autonomy and delusional behaviour. Others show a degree of egocentrism that would be considered abnormal at any other age, and some justify this behaviour with disordered, fantastic trains of thought.

But is schizophrenia really an abnormal extension of adolescence, or are the similarities merely coincidental? Just because schizophrenia is a failure of the thought processes we happen to acquire as teenagers, this does not mean that adolescence is some sort of 'phase of normal psychosis'. Teenage confusion may share some features with schizophrenia, but the two are not the same. Instead, the reason why adolescence lies at the heart of this illness is that this is the time when we build most of our uniquely human abilities. And schizophrenia is what happens when that unstable human cerebral edifice comes crashing down.

Why do teenagers get so worried?

All teenagers worry, and the thing that worries them most is their relationship with other people. Their newly elevated level of consciousness and social self-awareness means that there are more potential mistakes to worry about making. Of course anxiety is useful because it protects us from doing silly things – it has saved us from predators and accidents for millions of years. Yet predators and accidents are relatively simple things. The most complex and unpredictable phenomena in our environment are other people, and worrying about other people is a tangled, fraught, exhausting affair, especially for teenagers. So once teenagers have established a coherent relationship with themselves and the world around them, they face the greatest challenge of all – to develop relationships with other people.

A great deal of medical evidence supports the popularly held idea that adolescence is stressful, at least for some. In a repeat of what we have seen with other psychological disorders, anxiety-related psychological problems usually start during the teenage years. As many as one-fifth of teenagers may show signs of extreme anxiety – phobias of social situations, agoraphobia, panic attacks, fear of situations that involve scrutiny by others. As a result, many exhibit anxiety-reducing behaviours which either perpetuate their problems, or stymie their mental and social development – perhaps by avoiding contact with other teenagers. Social worries usually also feed into a diminishing sense of self-esteem. Some teenagers, especially girls, resort to self-harm – cutting, poisoning – to help them gain some sort of control over their emotions, and perhaps one in twenty of these will attempt suicide. There are also clear links between anxiety and other mental illnesses, including depression and schizophrenia.

Evidently, adolescent worrying can become horribly exaggerated, but why? Also, why does this happen to some teenagers but not others? In moving on to consider how teenagers develop relationships with other people and why it makes them anxious, we should take an evolutionary point of view. We need to think like evolutionary biologists, to view teenagers as young primates who, until relatively few generations ago, were expected to scratch a living on some ancient savannah. And unlike depression and schizophrenia, which also usually start during the teenage years, anxiety can be *helpful*: it undoubtedly helped us survive on that savannah. From the social point of view, being anxious about other people is eminently sensible – we all have to consider how others see us, and also bear in mind that some people may be out to get the better of us. Anxiety can obviously be useful, but why does it sometimes get out of hand in teenagers?

We know a great deal about the biology of stress and anxiety because although stress in teenagers is often due to their social relationships, stress can also be caused by non-social cues. That type of stress is much easier to study experimentally because it is simpler to simulate the risk of bodily harm, pain, or the presence of a predator, than it is to simulate a socially embarrassing situation. Because anxiety is such an important protective mechanism, it should come as no surprise that stress research has shown that there are several parts of the brain involved in it. Previously we have mentioned the amygdalae, which perceive and remember fear. Also, further down in the brain is a structure called the nucleus coeruleus (the 'sky blue place') which plays a role in vigilance and reacting to fear. The amygdalae and the coeruleus may exist in a constant state of disquiet, mutually stimulating each other with the neurotransmitters noradrenaline and corticotropin-releasing factor. They also connect to the cerebral cortex to allow conscious perception of, and emotional reactions to, fear. However they also drive a multitude of changes in the bodies of stressed animals and teenagers.

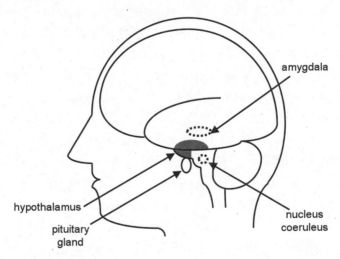

These bodily effects of stress can be the most inexplicable, uncontrollable and frightening reactions to cope with. Stress and anxiety cause the release of noradrenaline and adrenaline throughout the body, either from nerve endings or the adrenal glands (two small ovoid organs next to the kidneys).

These hormones cause the pupils to dilate, the heart to pump harder and faster, saliva secretion to stop and blood to drain from the skin and genitals. In other words, they cause the symptoms of panic, which may become so severe that people worry that they are having a heart attack. Anxiety also activates the hypothalamus – the master controller of the body's hormones on the underside of the brain – to secrete corticotropin-releasing factor. This percolates through to the pituitary gland to induce secretion of another hormone which eventually reaches the adrenal glands where it, in turn, causes secretion of the hormone cortisol. And cortisol exerts powerful and complex effects on almost every part of the body – redirecting its metabolism, the immune system, and the growth of skin and hair, for example. Because of this, cortisol may be responsible for many of the adverse effects of long-term anxiety.

All this may seem very unpleasant, but anxiety and stress affect the teenage brain and body for very good reasons. In our hunter-gatherer days, it was very important for some worrying things to be able to grab our attention and demand a solution – be it escape, avoidance of danger, or diffusing a socially difficult situation. Some things really can be a matter of life and death, so it makes sense that anxiety can be all-consuming. The bodily effects of stress also make sense – there is no point in salivating, digesting or being sexually aroused when the best thing is to be vigilant, flee or fight. So, all things considered, it is not teenage anxiety that is abnormal: it is its extent, or the things which trigger it.

Because anxiety is such a crucial protective response, teenagers' brains are wired up to learn to respond to new, worrying situations. This high state of alertness to possible threats probably explains why they can accidentally 'learn' to show anxiety in response to irrational things. As we have seen, like Pavlov's dogs, humans can easily be conditioned to become anxious in response to apparently innocuous cues. All that is needed is for those cues to coincide with a different, truly worrying cue. The simplest example of this is phobias, in which children start to associate extreme fear with something like spiders or enclosed spaces. Later on, just the suggestion of an arachnid or a small room can trigger the full dry-mouth, pounding-heart stress experience. And because of this, phobias can usually be cured by training people to link the cue with something more pleasant. Panic attacks are an especially dramatic example of learned stress responses – I remember feeling the early signs of an attack triggering an uncontrollable wave of anxiety flooding over me, building and feeding off itself so that all I could do was wait helplessly for the storm of tension to subside. Anxiety can make you a spectator in your own body.

Teenagers are always learning responses to things in the outside world, and I think this drive to learn comes to dominate their psychology. Adolescence can be a time when teenagers use simple Pavlov-like mechanisms to learn behaviours that may later seem complex and inexplicable. This is not just about phobias and panic attacks, but the basis of almost all our adult behaviours. The process starts very early, and there is good evidence that young animals learn many of their initial stress responses by imitating their parents. Also, a stressful early life has been shown to be linked to increased anxiety responses in later life – it is as if we assume that the rest of our life will be about as stressful as our childhood. We then start to learn stress responses to all sorts of things during our adolescent years, sometimes becoming increasingly anxious when we meet someone of the opposite sex, or when we fall behind in our work, or when we sense social embarrassment. Conversely, people can develop 'learned helplessness' in response to bad things happening. If a neglected dog is left shivering out in the rain for long enough, it will eventually learn that it cannot avoid its fate and later on, when offered the chance to walk under shelter to warm up, it will not take that opportunity. I suspect that these alarmingly crude forms of learning explain the weird behaviours that some teenagers acquire and then exhibit throughout their lives – why they avoid intimacy; why they seek out people who have misled them in the past; why they tolerate and even draw comfort from abusive relationships.

But what is it about teenage social life that causes so much worry in so many people? The first great teenage social upheaval is that their relationship with their parents changes. As we have already seen, during the early teenage years parents change from being the central force in our lives to being far more peripheral. The most basic, genetic explanation for this – that separation from parents prevents incest when offspring reach puberty – may be true for many other animals, but it seems too simple for humans. Instead, teenagers do not just 'drift away', but undergo an active process of rejection of their parents which is probably essential for their development as individuals. They become naturally defensive, aggressive and often downright unpleasant in their dealings with their parents – as do many other juvenile primates.

Girls and boys may differ in the way they reject their parents. We have already seen that boys develop slowly, and because of this they must wait longer to challenge their father in social dominance – a delay they may find irritating but which prevents conflict within the family. However, studies suggest that teenage boys' opinions start to take precedence in the family setting over those of their mothers long before girls' opinions do. Girls, who develop their mental abilities more quickly, may therefore find their aspirations frustrated throughout their adolescent years. Maybe this explains why teenage girls often emotionally distance themselves from their parents more actively than boys do.

Also, the rift between teenagers and parents may be made more stressful by certain aspects of modern life. It is clear that teenagers are becoming sexually, and possibly mentally, mature at an earlier age than at any other time in our species' history. This may mean that they now reject their parents at a younger age – a shift that parents find painful, and that teenagers find hard to cope with. At the same time, the structure of many modern societies means that teenagers are financially dependent on their parents for longer than ever. The joint effect of earlier puberty and delayed financial independence is that the potential period of teenage–adult conflict has now been extended at both ends. Add to these problems the suggestions that modern teenagers get less chance to contribute to society, and get to communicate with adults less than at any time in the past, and you can see why teenage anxiety might be on the increase.

At the same time that teenagers are rejecting their parents, they are also undergoing a second profound social upheaval: they are becoming more attached to their friends. Teenagers have been estimated to talk to their friends for four times as long each day as to adults. There is no reason to think this drive to commune with adolescent peers is a strange effect of modern life, and I suspect our hunter-gatherer teenage ancestors did exactly the same thing.

However, it is worth mentioning that friendship is an extremely rare phenomenon in the animal kingdom. Individuals of other species usually associate with others because they are parents, offspring, mates, or because they derive safety in numbers. The human habit of seeking out others of a similar age (and usually sex) for protracted discussion and rumination is unique. Indeed, many teenagers report that they are happiest when chatting to their friends. Also, many of the misdemeanours perpetrated by teenagers are explained (often truthfully) as the result of peer pressure. So what is it that drives humans to start forming these special, intense, yet not obviously productive relationships in their teenage years?

The first theory of why teenagers make friends is that they derive some gain from the arrangement. This idea comes from the observation that most non-family alliances in other species involve cooperation in acquiring food, or some other resource. Although this makes sense, it is hard to see what immediate material gain teenagers derive from having friends. Yes, friends do occasionally help each other out, but this occurs surprisingly infrequently. In fact, individuals who court friendship by offering immediate material gain such as gifts are often greeted with suspicion – if they are accepted into teenage social groups at all, they are usually only tolerated as long as the material gains continue, after which they are unceremoniously dumped. However, the idea that friends are there to help you out is still a good one, even if humans often hide this scheming reciprocity behind the nobler façade of altruism. Indeed, many teenagers say that a friend is someone who will support them in times of need. And intriguingly, some psychologists have claimed that modern teenagers feel socially unstable because their life is 'too easy' –

danger rarely threatens, so their friends never get the chance to show their support.

A second possible reason for teenage friendships is that they are a learning experience. Humans are an extremely social species, and to a great extent our individual success depends on our ability to function well in society. Thus adolescent friendships could be viewed as a way to practise social skills in a relatively risk-free environment. Teenage friendships are so important in allowing us to slide seamlessly into the world of adult social interactions that I suspect we often take them for granted. In fact, the best evidence of this is the one social interaction for which platonic friendships do *not* prepare us: just think of the frisson of inexperience and vulnerability we all experience when we first start romantic and sexual relationships. And teenage friendship gives us much more than practice at socializing. It means we do not have to build our little internal model of the world alone. We can share our experiences and ideas about families, friends, activities, life and death with others of a similar age to see if they agree or disagree. Groups of teenage friends are co-constructing a view of the world which will last them throughout their life.

A final theory of teenage friendship is that it supports our sense of self. By engaging with other teenagers, we learn that society accepts us, even validates us, and that as a result we have some social value. Previously we saw how self-esteem is enormously important to normal psychological development, and that having a place in a group of friends – a sense that one is, to some extent, irreplaceable – is crucial in developing self-esteem. Not surprisingly, having a nucleus of good friends has been strongly linked to happiness, and some psychologists have even suggested that there is an optimum number of friends for teenage mental health.

So now we can see why friendship is so important to teenagers. Friendship is central to teenage development, and the urge to avoid loneliness is incredibly strong. Teenagers value the triad of reciprocity, social learning and self-esteem so much that studies show that they instinctively evaluate other teenagers for the three corresponding outward signs of common interests, mutual understanding and positive communication.

Teenagers' unremittingly strong urge for friendship also explains many of the weird things they do. Most teenagers seek out a recognized place in a social group of their peers, and will go to great efforts to secure one. Appearance is important to them, and one way they register their social position is by fashion. Obviously teenagers select their clothing and accessories to make themselves look attractive to competitors and suitors, but there is much more to it than that. After all, teenage girls do not all wear 'cute' clothes and teenage boys do not all wear 'macho' ones. Instead, they choose clothes they think say something about themselves, be it their membership of a social group, their ability to keep up with the times, or some selected aspect of their individuality. One example of this is piercings, a form of self-mutilation presumably intended to convey a certain social spikiness, as well as a refusal to conform. Another is the enduring appeal of the Goth, a fashion for dark clothes, pale skin and striking makeup that has lasted, with a few changes in terminology, for a quarter of a century – a veritable eternity in the world of teenage fashion. I suspect that being a Goth is appealing to teenagers because not only does it allow them to disparage much of society in a clearly advertised way, but it also allows them a relatively harmless communal forum in which to experiment with, and maybe even revel in, teenage negativity. And I should know – I married one.

The formation of gangs is often viewed as a more alarming aspect of the adolescent drive for inclusion in peer groups. Yet aggregating into exclusive social groups is an almost unavoidable part of growing up. As an adult it is easy to ignore the fact that for much of the time, there simply is not very much for teenagers to do with their leisure time. Groups of teenagers *have* to hang around on street corners and in parks: they are drawn to be with their friends, they are barred from places where alcohol is served, and the last place they want to be is in the parental home. After all, that would be too much like children going round to each other's houses 'to play'. A similar trend can be seen in the fragmented and slightly marginal groups of juveniles who mope around the periphery of many primate communities. In humans, most 'gangs' are entirely harmless, and present teenagers with a perfectly viable way to develop socially. Of course, humans in isolated groups can occasionally spur each other on to behaviour they would never countenance individually – but we cannot change the simple facts that humans operate in social groups, and sometimes they do the wrong thing. And unfortunately, when the world outside becomes a dangerous place, we often react by becoming ever more dependent on our social group for protection – in the process becoming more susceptible to being part of the mob.

Despite the central importance of teenage friendship, it can be a very different phenomenon in girls and boys. My own anecdotal experiences of friendship seem to agree with the published studies. On average, girls are much more open with their friends, and share more intimate details of their own emotions and biology than boys. Because their friends know so many of their embarrassing secrets, trust often becomes extremely important in female teenage friendships. Loss of a friend can be a stressful and frightening experience for a girl, and is often even viewed as a betrayal. Conversely, boys seem less obviously open and emotional with their friends, and their conversations often focus on shared interests, such as sport, music, or the more superficial aspects of female attractiveness. It is tempting to suggest that male friendships are somehow shallower than female friendships, but I am not sure that is the case. After all, friendship is all about getting inside other people's heads and letting them inside yours, and just because boys do this more obliquely than girls does not mean that their feelings are any less strong or warm (although of course we would never admit it).

This girl–boy difference always seemed obvious to me – I even remember selectively seeking out my female friends when I wanted to discuss emotional matters. Because of this, I now wonder why girl–boy teenage friendships are so neglected by psychologists – they are, after all, an interesting counterpoint to same-sex friendships. Of course, they carry the exciting risk of sliding into a romantic or sexual consummation, but they are also less likely to suffer some of the problems associated with same-sex friendships. Without the insecurity that can sour girl–girl friendships and the crippling indirectness of some boy–boy friendships, teenage inter-sex friendships can be refreshingly simple and open, as well as offering an invaluable insight into 'how the other half thinks'.

Of course, the downside of the importance of developing relationships with peers is that problems with friends can be the major cause of anxiety for teenagers. Lack of friends can be devastating, leading to anxiety, low self-esteem and depression. Also, as I have already mentioned, breaking up with friends can be a bitter blow, and especially worrying for girls. The phenomena of loss and loneliness affect teenagers so badly because they often see them as reflections upon themselves – implying that they cannot acquire or retain friends because there is something wrong with them. Adults who have more of a 'track record' of good friends in the past, can view upheavals in their friendships with a more relaxed attitude.

As well as rejecting their parents and acquiring friends, there is a third great social upheaval with which teenagers must deal, and that is competitiveness. Like many animal species, human societies spontaneously organize themselves into dominance hierarchies, with socially dominant individuals and socially submissive ones. And just like other social animals, modern humans retain our evolutionary heritage of enjoying being high in the pecking order and putting effort into getting to the top. Anyone who observes teenage interactions cannot fail to see hierarchies being formed and maintained – it really is like watching a pack of monkeys. Human teenage hierarchies are fluid, with individuals clambering their way up and slipping down, and they are also divisive, because teenagers compete with friend and non-friend alike. Friends can tacitly 'negotiate' some sort of rapprochement whereby they stop competing directly, but even this may be illusory, as two friends usually still have to stake their claims to places in the same hierarchy. Of course, adults have dominance hierarchies too, but because they are more long-standing, and the individuals in them are undergoing less physical, mental and social flux, they tend to be more stable – less clambering and slipping means less anxiety.

Interestingly, mixed groups of teenagers seem to partition themselves into separate male and female dominance hierarchies, and the criteria for achieving high status differ in the two sexes. Boys become more overtly competitive in their early teenage years, and initially their status depends on physical strength and skills, and to some extent their social skills and looks. Moving up and down the hierarchy depends on clear-cut episodes of success or failure in various physical activities, including the occasional fight. It is noticeable that high status does not necessarily require leadership abilities, and often it is boys slightly lower down the pecking order who take the initiative. Intriguingly, boys' intelligence appears to have little effect on their position in the hierarchy, which is hard to explain from the evolutionary point of view, as it should be of crucial importance in a species whose intellectual abilities have been the key to its success.

In comparison, girls' hierarchies are complex, implicit and even more stressful. Perhaps because overtly dominant behaviour is unattractive to boys, it is uncommon in girls and is usually reserved for phases of painful social change. Instead, girls have been reported to assert their status by criticism and ridicule (often in the form of imitation) and shunning targeted individuals. Another surprisingly frequent method of self-betterment is allegations of promiscuity against other girls – something that would presumably not have the required effect in boys. All in all, teenage girls' hierarchies can be a difficult zone to inhabit.

Studies suggest that the criteria that determine status are different for girls, with physical attractiveness outweighing physical, intellectual and even social prowess. The importance of physical attractiveness to girls can be a cruel feature of adolescence. While the physical changes of puberty gradually (if belatedly) draw boys towards our societal ideals of what a man should look like, they often drag girls away from any resemblance to the images of skinny, slim hipped models that infest the media. In Part Five we will think further about what girls and boys consider attractive in the female form, but it is clear that many teenage girls worry too much about losing weight (in contrast, as many teenage boys want to gain weight as lose it). This inherent tendency to worry about becoming overweight probably contributes to the remarkably high incidence of eating disorders in teenage girls, although how much of a contribution it makes is controversial. Eating disorders – anorexia, bulimia and other combinations of self-starving, binging and purging – are difficult to explain in terms of evolution. Some have suggested that anorexia represents a disordered form of a natural behaviour which made our ancestors desist from food gathering to spend time courting and mating. Conversely, excessive exercise, which often accompanies female teenage anorexia, has been claimed to reflect an abnormal form of increased wandering in search of food in response to famine. However, these 'reasons' for eating disorders have little evidence to support them, so perhaps we should look to the modern teenage lifestyle to explain why so many members of our species worry about body weight – sometimes to the point of causing lasting physical harm.

Anxiety about failing to meet the cultural 'body ideal' may be one cause of eating disorders, but there are probably others. There is good evidence that eating disorders also result from poor development of self-image – they have been clearly linked to low self-esteem, excessive self-criticism and perfectionism. It has also been suggested that they are a way for teenagers to express their ability to control at least one aspect of their life. In the same way, eating disorders may allow them to express autonomy in the presence of overbearing parents. Such 'emotional eating' is now thought to be a widespread phenomenon, and many teenagers learn to eat (or not eat) because they are bored, frustrated, anxious or sad, or as a method of self-harm or punishment. Despite these psychological explanations, eating disorders may also have identifiable physical causes too – there are reports that they have a genetic basis, and variations in genes controlling brain metabolism and nerve cell activity have been implicated. Tying in with this are studies which show that teenagers who suffer from eating disorders often exhibit a variety of other cognitive abnormalities – in their perception of the world and their performance at arbitrary tests.

So, what with parental rejection, making and keeping friends, and competing with peers, there are a great many things that teenagers can anxiously misinterpret, and many social behaviours they can learn inappropriately. Things are tough for our compulsive-behaviour-learning juvenile primates, and probably even tougher now they are born into the abnormal environment of the modern world. Yet before we leave teenage anxiety behind, I should emphasize that we still do not know why some teenagers get so much more anxious than others. All teenagers go though troubling times, but only some react excessively to the good and the bad; only some tumble into excessive introspection and anxiety when things go wrong. Teenagers are simply very variable in their ability to establish relationships with other people, and only some succumb. Why do they vary so much?

There are many attempts underway to identify risk factors for anxiety disorders. As we have seen, genetic studies are promising. Also, brain imaging techniques have suggested altered responses of the amygdalae and prefrontal cortex to threat or emotion-provoking imagery – others have even claimed that the amygdalae are smaller in anxious teenagers. Hormone studies have suggested that the brain-hypothalamus-pituitary-adrenal system is more active in some individuals, and also that it behaves in a fundamentally different way in teenagers.

But all of these discoveries must still be seen in terms of answering the question of *why* teenagers vary so much in their ability to cope with stress. And this question may now be answered by our increasing understanding of the evolution of temperament. Studies in animals suggest that measurable characteristics such as aggression, sociability and boldness can be inherited just like physical attributes, and this means they can undergo natural selection. And in humans we suspect that evolution has acted to produce a population with a wide range of temperaments – an array of strategies for dealing with social situations. Some analyses have suggested that different parts of this human temperament range are more likely to suffer from certain problems – fear of failure, mental illness, cardiovascular disease, accidents and, of course, anxiety.

Something about human evolution has made us all different. Humans certainly look very different from each other, so perhaps it is no surprise that we are mentally, emotionally and socially different too. Celebrating diversity is all very well, but it is teenagers who face the awful task of working out where they fit into the sea of human social variation.

And what is love?

I apologize if you have found this part of the book rather depressing so far. I suppose it has been my concession to the widely held idea that adolescence is a universally negative and stressful experience. Although I do not agree with that idea, it is certainly true that teenagers have lots of issues to address, and that this may explain why they often become sad, confused or anxious, even to the point of mental illness. However, things can go well during adolescence too, and teenagers can feel happiness of an intensity unmatched in later life. You must remember that I am essentially optimistic and positive about adolescence. Also, there is one other phenomenon, as yet unmentioned, which can work in teenagers' favour. As a man with a beard said two thousand years ago, the thing that can save us all is love.

'Love' is not a word that sits easily in the world of science. Love seems too subjective, intangible and indefinable to be amenable to scientific study (although the same problem never stopped scientists studying 'consciousness'). Perhaps we think love is just too vague, or that it can be better explained in terms of drier concepts, such as reward, sexual attraction, mate choice or parental cooperation. Or maybe deep down we do not want love to be picked apart by science: we worry that it would lose its mystique. But romantic love – for that is the type that teenagers are most interested in – is a strong, resilient urge, and I doubt that understanding how it works will sour it.

To some extent romantic love can be dissected into its constituent parts, and we will start with one of the more clear-cut parts. Nature did not invent love in an act of charity to the human race. Instead, we think we evolved the subjective feeling of love to bring sexual partners together and keep them together. Long-term maintenance of sexual partnerships occurs in many vertebrate species, for which we use the term 'pair-bonding'. Whether pair-bonded animals experience 'love' in the way we do is, of course, unknown, but the social arrangement itself is widespread. Pair-bonding is not simply a drive for continual sexual activity because many pair-bonded species mate infrequently (although humans are unusual in this respect). Instead, it is thought that pair-bonding is a mating strategy that encourages parental cooperation to raise successful offspring. As a result, pair-bonded species tend to produce immature offspring that need a lot of care, and much of this care is lavished upon them by their father. Pair-bonding species are often social, and pair-bonding may be especially conducive to social development of offspring. So, at its root, romantic love can be seen as a mechanism that helps humans raise our slow-growing, socially blossoming children. This is why we do not fall in love before we become fertile: there is no need for romantic love until puberty.

So the 'why' of romantic love is the easy part, but the 'what' is more obscure. Before puberty, children experiment sexually and they also toy with the idea of romantic infatuation, but only in adolescence do sex and romantic love converge. Yet as soon as teenagers become aware of the two phenomena, they realize there is an uneasy inconsistency between them which society often does not want them to investigate. Love and sex are not the same, but they probably overlap more during the teenage years than in adulthood – many teenagers prefer to restrict their sexual activity to people for whom they feel love. Still, even during adolescence, teenagers can maintain long-term infatuations that never lead to a sexual union, and they can also enjoy 'casual' sex, sometimes with long-term non-romantic partners – they are learning the differences between sex and love.

This realization often comes sooner for boys than girls, and there may be cognitive reasons for this. Studies have suggested that teenage boys learn to get their 'fixes' of sex and love by interacting with their partners in different ways – using methods as simple as looking at their partner's body to derive sexual pleasure and then looking at their face to experience feelings of love. In fact, male sexual and romantic behaviour often continues in this alternating body/face manner throughout life, and this may explain men's sometimes alarming ability to separate love and sex. However, humans are complicated creatures, and girls also learn to enjoy and toy with the discrepancies between sex and love, albeit in a more subtle way. For example, people sometimes initiate romantic contact wishing to enter a loving mental communion, and at other times they wish to be used as a physical sexual target by their partner. And of course, they often want to do something in between those two extremes, or continually change the nature of the encounter as it progresses.

So teenagers face the daunting challenge of developing

their sense of romantic etiquette, and that is no mean feat – love entails a powerful mix of devotion, coercion, acceptance, shyness, pleasure, fear and humour, and that is when it is going well! But are there any fundamental differences between teenage love and adult love? Psychology gave the study of teenage romance a poor start because the early psychoanalysts had so little to say about adolescence – it was seen as a transitional phase rather than a life-stage in its own right, with its own distinctive features. Perhaps this was because teenage emotions can be so intense that it was difficult for psychoanalysts to get their adolescent patients to admit to them. In fact, intensity is probably the defining feature of adolescent romantic relationships, whether consummated or not (Romeo and Juliet were teenagers). There is a period of perhaps three years during adolescence when romantic attachments are often so intense that they are described as physically painful. After this period of 'infatuations', the drive to be with the targets of one's amorous desires is still strong, but it usually does not monopolize one's waking thoughts to such an extent. This waning of infatuation is a well-recognized psychological phenomenon, which as we will soon see, now has some hard biochemical evidence to support it.

Another unique feature of teenage romantic relationships is that they are, by their very nature, novel. You have little experience of love when you are a teenager, and it can feel delightfully or frighteningly unfamiliar. Romantic love is entirely outside a teenager's experience, the first time at least. As I suggested earlier, this may be because this is one form of social interaction for which platonic friendships do not prepare us. This explains why studies show little correlation between how secure and supported teenagers feel in their romantic relationships, and how they view their friendships. Maybe friendship and love are simply very different things, and this presumably explains the strong emotional jarring often reported when a previously platonic friendship metamorphoses into a romantic one. Surprisingly however, there is one prior relationship that may prepare us for romance, and that is our relationship with our parents: teenagers' feelings of security in matters romantic correlate well with how much they say they are supported by their parents. So this may be another reason for parents to try and maintain good relations with teenage children, even when there does not seem to be much reciprocation.

And of course, love is tough. It has difficult, painful aspects that can hit inexperienced, vulnerable teenagers hard. The first reason for this is that love 'consumes' us and 'drives us mad', or in more scientific terms it subverts our cognitive functions. Teenagers sleep less when they are in love, although they may wake more rested and feel more alert during the day. Also, as one might expect, they find it harder to concentrate. Some teenagers develop erroneous convictions that another person loves them – a state that in adults is considered abnormal: 'erotomania'. Indeed, teenage love has even been claimed to represent a state of disordered mood and thought only slightly removed from mental illness. As well as neglecting other aspects of life, the urge for romantic fulfilment can cause all sorts of problems, including unpremeditated infidelity and acquisition of sexually transmitted diseases. But of course, the thought-altering effects of love are also what make it pleasurable – it is after all a matter of letting yourself go, and falling helplessly into a new mental state. Anyway, what is considered acceptable is very much defined by social norms – after all, if an adult married couple are sexually and emotionally obsessed with each other, no one seems to worry.

A second inconvenient complication of love is jealousy. Romantic love almost always involves an element of protectiveness about one's partner, even if it is never articulated. However, in the racy, fluid teenage world, sexual jealousy often builds to a point where it causes conflict between partners. Teenagers are simply very attractive to each other, so most teenage relationships are continually beset by the predatory interest of others. This is worsened by the widely reported tendency of humans in romantic relationships to retain some interest in the attractiveness and availability of others. In fact, jealousy is such an established part of adolescent romantic life that many teenagers report that they worry if their partners are never jealous. Also, some express concern if no one else seems to be attracted to their partner. We humans are an exasperating bunch.

Finally, teenage romantic activities can have a direct effect on mental well-being. Just as the first flush of infatuation can be intensely felt, the end of an adolescent love affair can be a shattering experience. Lost love can trigger clinical anxiety and depression, probably because it so often leads to a period of intense introspection. Most of us find it very difficult to explain the end of a romantic relationship, even when we are the partner who has actively caused a split. In the absence of clear reasons for breaking up, many teenagers can only direct the blame inwards, assuming the relationship failed because of some intrinsic defect in themselves. And as we have seen, self-blame can destroy a teenager's fragile self-esteem – a well-trodden path to depression. I believe that many teenagers also respond by learning to tolerate subsequent relationships which, while superficially providing the framework of a long-term romantic pair-bond, are inherently destructive or abusive and serve only to perpetuate low expectations of how they deserve to be treated.

So if love is this tremendous productive-destructive mental force built into teenagers, what are the biological processes which generate it? Obviously love is a difficult thing to study in a laboratory, but modern brain imaging methods are giving us a little insight into this most elusive of phenomena. It is tempting to speculate that our brain 'generates love' using the same mechanisms by which it seeks out other rewards, such as food, drink, shelter, drugs and video games – the tegmentum–accumbens pathway we first encountered in Part Two. Although this pathway may be involved in sexual desire, the evidence that it produces love is less clear – perhaps love is not as closely linked to addiction as one might think. Brain imaging studies in which subjects were shown pictures of attractive people, asked to fill in questionnaires about passionate love, or asked about recent failed relationships, all suggest that love is 'constructed' by several brain regions. The tegmentum is fired up by attractiveness (and indeed, stalking behaviour may result from over-activity of the reward-seeking pathway), but thinking about love activates other brain regions – the caudate nucleus and 'fusiform' and 'angular' gyri (ridges) of the cortex. Love is, after all, a many splendoured thing, so it should come as no surprise that several different parts of the brain are needed to produce it.

Recently, remarkable advances have been made in the neurochemistry of love, charmingly enough because of studies on prairie voles. These grey rodents inhabit the vast grasslands of the North American interior and are a social species which exhibits strict pair-bonding and considerable paternal care of offspring. Pair-bonding behaviour in prairie voles has been found to be largely controlled by two very similar neurotransmitters: oxytocin and arginine vasopressin. The first of these chemicals encourages pair-bonding in both male and female voles, and the second drives vigilance and mate-guarding behaviour in male voles. However, these two chemicals are certainly not restricted to prairie voles – they are present in all vertebrates, albeit in different brain regions in different species. To pick three varied examples, they direct egg-laying in tortoises, sexual activity in salamanders and social behaviour in goldfish.

Some biologists have even gone as far as to call oxytocin and arginine vasopressin the 'hormones of love' in humans. We certainly secrete both of them: oxytocin causes uterine contractions during birth and ejection of breast milk during suckling, while arginine vasopressin, as it happens, makes us produce concentrated urine. But a variety of studies have demonstrated an additional role for these chemicals in many 'love-related' phenomena. Oxytocin sniffed into the nose has been shown to increase trust. Arginine vasopressin may be involved in inter-male aggression (just as in voles) and male sexual arousal. Also, a surge of oxytocin is released at orgasm in both sexes, lasting up to thirty minutes. Within the brain, these chemicals could promote a feeling of 'attachment' to others, and may create the emotional bonds that form between parents and children, as well as between lovers.

As we have seen previously, the transmitters dopamine and serotonin are probably involved in the mechanism's underlying mood, so it is no surprise that their levels also change when we fall in love – the former increasing, the latter decreasing. Some have suggested that this may alter the activity of the cerebral cortex, perhaps causing the cognitive alteration often described subjectively as 'losing one's senses'. Along with the oxytocin and arginine vasopressin data, this suggests that love involves a pervasive rebalancing of neurotransmitters in the brain. All this helps to draw two people together, establish them as intensely attractive in each other's eyes, suppress their inhibitions and alter their cognition and judgement. The multi-chemical nature of love also means that we should be cautious about how we play with people's brain chemistry. For example, the selective serotonin reuptake inhibitors commonly used to treat depression alter levels of not only serotonin, but also dopamine, oxytocin and arginine vasopressin. Are some of the effects of these drugs due to changes in patients' tendency to feel jealousy, aggression and love?

Last of all, it seems that a blood test for love has now been discovered. Nerve growth factor is a protein involved in the formation and maintenance of the nervous system. For some time it has been known to be important – its discoverers won a Nobel Prize in 1986 – but only recently has its amorous side been revealed. Levels of nerve growth factor in the blood increase when people fall in love, and rather sweetly the increase correlates with the reported intensity of their romantic feelings. This does not mean that increased amounts of nerve growth factor 'cause' the love, as love could just as easily be causing the increase in nerve growth factor. Strikingly, however, the increased levels of the chemical invariably decline after a year or two. This suggests that there is a cerebral cut-off which limits the initial surge of romance, just as the adolescent tendency for intense infatuation lasts only two or three years. It makes sense that intense romantic love should fade because its function is, after all, to encourage us to make babies. Once those babies are born, it would not make sense if their parents ignored them because of their intense infatuation for each other. Presumably, juvenile romantic obsession is replaced by a more mature and long-lasting bond between partners, whose cause is as yet undiscovered.

So what is love? Over the centuries there have been many attempts to answer that question: a feeling, an ambition, a commitment, an internal personal struggle, a social contract. Others have suggested that love is humans' way of coping with the realization of death: that only love makes it possible to temporarily forget the terrible fact of our own mortality. Science now suggests that love is a cerebral alteration which drives us to pair-bond and produce our own socially adept offspring. Indeed, in many ways making babies is the way we cheat death. We overcome the problem of dying by making more of ourselves.

And, for all sorts of reasons, teenage love is a thing apart. Adolescence is the time we first discover we all have an uncontrollable drive to seek the affections of a stranger. Unlike most drives, which can be satisfied by the acquisition of some goal, be it food, comfort or sex, the drive to love is uniquely unsatisfiable – it can only ever be partially sated by entering a relationship with the most complex thing in our experience: another human being. I think this is why love is such an unquenchable thirst – it is the only drive that cannot be calmed by the possession of its target. You cannot 'possess' another person, because they remain an autonomous, inde-pendent, unpredictable being. You want to lay claim to them, but they become less desirable the more you constrain them. Romantic relationships are often an emotional pendulum swinging between a warm togetherness which can become oppressive, and a refreshing separateness which can become lonely. Love cannot be satisfied because a loved one cannot be fully 'acquired'. If something is worth having, then it probably cannot be truly had.

5. Teenage Kicks
The ifs, whens and whys of sex

Let him kiss me with the kisses of his mouth: for thy love is better than wine. Because of the savour of thy good ointments thy name is as ointment poured forth, therefore do the virgins love thee.

The Song of Songs 1: 2-3

Teenage sex has a certain dramatic tension to it.
We all know it happens, but often we do not like to talk about it. Our gut reaction is to worry about it, yet many of us know from experience that it can be a rewarding, fulfilling part of growing up. We are sometimes so inconsistent as to want our sons and daughters to be sexually assured and responsible by the age of twenty, but deep in our hearts we would rather they magically arrived at that state without actually having sex.

People talk about sex far more than they used to – Western society's attitude to sex has been described as changing 'from constipation to diarrhoea'. Yet despite the sexual imagery that surrounds us, there remain some aspects of sex that lie on the boundary of taboo, and teenage sex is one of those. Teenage sex is neither as readily reprehensible as child sex, nor is it as instantly acceptable as adult sex. Once again adolescence – the stage in the human life-plan when everything collides – is playing with our ideas of right and wrong. Teenage sex is non-mature people wanting to experiment with something adult, intense and potentially hazardous, and sometimes wanting to do it with people older than themselves. This is why I described teenage sex as being on the boundary of taboo. In some contexts we are happy to discuss it but in others it remains off-limits. Recently a senior British police officer caused a media tempest by suggesting that sex with teenagers below the age of consent (sixteen in the UK) should not be a crime as long as the older partner's age did not exceed the younger's by more than a certain amount. The media response to this suggestion was furiously critical, especially considering that similar 'close in age' exceptions are in force in many countries around the world. Many teenagers have sex and they often do it with people a few years older than them, but this hardly seems a matter for police intervention.

I propose that negative attitudes to adolescent sex are damaging to teenagers. Making sex something furtive, criminal even, may give it a little extra tingle of excitement, but it hardly fosters a mature approach. A more positive view of teenage sex as a voluntary, consensual part of growing up would be far more helpful. But being positive about adolescent sex need not mean teenagers having more sex. Indeed, making sex more about open choices than hidden risks may mean teenagers do it *less*. Sex is not about some horrible biological drive that teenagers must get out of their system: it is about forming the most important relationships of our lives.

I have left sex until this last part for two reasons. First, from an evolutionary point of view, sex is all-important. Natural selection depends on the multiplication of individuals who can produce lots of thriving offspring. So sex should come last because it creates a dramatic crescendo of evolutionary importance. Second, human sex only makes sense in the context of everything else we do. Many books about teenagers concentrate on sex to the detriment of all the other things going on in teenage lives. Yet teenage sex makes no sense at all without thinking about bodily change, growing up, mental development, relationships, mental anguish and intoxicating substances. All these things blend together when we are teenagers, and as a result sex can become an expression of all our desires, hopes, fears and self-soothing. Our evolutionary drive to procreate has been hijacked by the human cerebral machine.

So the stakes are high where sex is concerned. Earlier in the book I suggested that many of the things teenagers do and many of the decisions they make do not necessarily have much effect on the rest of their lives. Teenage indiscretions are just that: formative errors at an age when it is good sometimes to err. Rather, I claimed it is the behaviours they learn, especially their responses to other people, that will live with them for ever. Well, sex is an exception. It is one time when teenagers' actions can irrevocably change their future. One small misjudgement and a child is created; one unprotected sexual experiment and future fertility is destroyed. Perhaps this is why teenage sex is so disquieting – it is the first immature dabbling with the most powerful force in our nature.

Why do teenagers have sex?

To find out whence this powerful force came, we must look into our past about as far as it is possible to go. Teenagers' sexual inheritance is the product of billions of years of evolution. Not only is sex itself an extremely ancient invention, but much of the extra biological paraphernalia that has come to surround it also evolved long before we were recognizably human. Teenagers have sex because that is the system with which evolution has equipped us, and to find out why, we need to do some primeval zoology.

The basic biological differences between males and females seem obvious enough. Males have testicles which make sperm (small, swimming 'germ' cells) and females have ovaries which make eggs (large, non-moving 'germ' cells). Yet these simple facts hide some real mysteries. For example, we do not know why sperm have to be so extremely small (just about the smallest cells in the body) and we do not know why eggs have to be so extremely large (just about the largest). However, we do have an inkling of why we use sex to make babies.

All life on earth is based on genetic information held in long molecules of deoxyribonucleic acid – DNA (or occasionally a related molecule called RNA). DNA is an incredibly long, ladder-shaped molecule which twists up to form its famous double helix shape. It is the rungs of the ladder which carry the information, as there are four different types of rung which can be inserted into the ladder in any order. Thus DNA is a digital code not unlike the binary code of computers, but in this case employing base-four arithmetic rather than base-two. And DNA has some other remarkable properties that make it the core of life on earth. First of all, the code can be used to make useful things, such as the proteins that do most of the varied and exciting things that living creatures can do. And second, the two sides of the DNA ladder can be wrenched apart, and each half used as a template to reconstruct a new ladder, carrying exactly the same code as the original. This is why cells can divide and why organisms can reproduce – each time, they are splitting and copying their DNA instruction manual.

So now we know what 'life' is, we can think about where sex came from. Many organisms are asexual: they simply split their DNA ladder and insert copies of it into their progeny. This is all very well, but it does have some problems. DNA is pretty robust stuff, but nothing is perfect. Every so often a toxic chemical or an incoming cosmic ray destroys part of the DNA ladder, and the organism has to cobble it back together again. However, this repair is not always perfect and the base-four genetic code may accidentally be altered during the repair. Usually these alterations mean that the code works less well and the organism is never quite the same again – a mutation has occurred. And if it reproduces asexually, that damage will be faithfully passed on to its offspring. This sort of genetic damage is a big problem for asexual creatures, and enormous numbers of them die due to the damaged DNA they inherit.

Sex is a way to cheat the system. Instead of interminably splitting their damaged DNA to make equally damaged offspring, sexual creatures take a brave risk. They package a randomly selected half of their genetic material into an egg or a sperm, and this then fuses with the sperm or egg of another individual. Because of this, the offspring of sexual parents are an incredibly varied bunch, each with a different combination of their parents' DNA. Some of them inherit the damaged stuff and suffer as a result, but others get all the good bits and thrive. Over the generations the unfortunates perish and the fortunates survive, effectively cleansing the population of damaged genes. So, by collaborating with sexual partners, we retain our vigour and stave off genetic degeneration.

There are other advantages to sex as well. Very rarely, DNA is damaged in a way that fortuitously makes it work better than before. A sexual organism who is this lucky tends to produce more progeny, and those progeny will inherit the same advantages and tend to produce more progeny of their own. As a result, advantageous mutations can spread throughout a sexual population very quickly, allowing it to thrive and adapt to new environments. Sex is all about change and survival, and this is why we do it. There are probably even more advantages to sex, but it might be better to refer you to my previous book, *A Visitor Within*, if you want to know more.

Once we accept that males make sperm and females make eggs, it becomes easier to understand some of the differences between men and women. First of all, sperm and eggs explain the existence of that strange thing – the penis. The origins of the penis lie far back in our mud-grubbing aquatic vertebrate past – after the acquisition of sex, but long before the human-centred evolutionary story we have followed through much of this book. Several hundred million years ago our ancestors were fish, and they did not have much time for penises. Like many modern fish, most of them simply squirted eggs and sperm out of their orifices, and the sperm had to swim through the water to find and fertilize the eggs.

When our ancestors clambered on to dry land a few hundred million years ago, this liberal sprinkling of sperm and eggs into the environment did not work any more, mainly because sperm die when exposed to dry air and hot sun. Also, if eggs are made tough enough to survive these harsh conditions, their shells become too thick for a sperm to fight its way through. Because of this problem, our reptile-like ancestors developed 'internal fertilization' in which males squirt their sperm directly into a female. This means the sperm are deposited in a warm, damp, conducive environment, where they get access to the egg before it has made its impenetrable shell. This was the start of that wonderful thing, copulation.

You do not have to have a penis to practice the subtle art of internal fertilization. Many animals simply bring their respective holes together and the male squirts his contribution into the female. This is what happens in most birds, for example, and this is why male birds do not walk about with a little penis flopping around between their legs (although one cute exception is that ducks and ganders do indeed have a little phallus tucked away in all those feathers). In contrast, we mammals developed a rather fine external penis, and it gives male mammals an unmatched sense of certainty that their sperm is actually going into their female acquaintances. Penises have evolved elsewhere in the animal kingdom, such as in insects, but it is mammals who represent the pinnacle of penis perfection – for example, a blue whale penis (or 'dork' as it is technically called) can be up to three metres long.

The evolution of the penis could not have occurred without a simultaneous innovation by females. If males are going to try out internal copulation, then females must be ready for it, so they evolved the vagina. A vagina is simply the lowest part of a female's reproductive system, specialized for receiving the male penis. In addition, it is physically resilient and non-sterile to cope with all that grubby coital action.

By this point in evolution, with penises and vaginas, we had acquired almost all the genitals we have today, but there was one more innovation on the way. Our ancestors' new-found system of internal fertilization gave them yet another possibility for making babies. If you lay your fertilized eggs on the ground then they are vulnerable to heat, cold, flood, desiccation and predators. This is a risky thing to do with your hoped-for babies. That is why so many of our closest relatives – some fish, amphibians, lizards and snakes, but not, for some reason, birds, crocodiles and turtles – have evolved pregnancy to solve the problem. Pregnancy allows females to carry their precious cargo of babies inside them until they are ready to be born, shell-less and live. And mammals have become real pregnancy experts – with the exceptions of the egg-laying platypus and echidna, we all do it. To support a pregnancy, our females now have a specialized section of their reproductive system to grow babies: the uterus. The uterus probably evolved from the sections of the old repro-ductive canal which once formed the white and shell of the egg.

So now we know where our genitals come from. Girls have ovaries to make their big eggs, a vagina for penises to go in and a uterus to grow babies. Boys have testicles to make their little sperm, and a penis to introduce them into girls. However, I must emphasize that all of this is based on circumstantial evidence. We have of course never directly observed a species evolving internal fertilization, penises, vaginas, uteri or pregnancy. However, when we look at the sweep of reproductive adaptations across a wide range of animals, we can easily identify groups that have developed internal fertilization, and within those we can find sub-groups with penises and vaginas, and also sub-groups with wombs and pregnancy. The process of evolution takes too long to be viewed directly – we can usually only infer its existence from its finished products.

One of the strange facts of life that we cannot explain so simply is why boys keep their testicles on the outside. This is where our circumstantial evidence lets us down. The female system seems much more sensible. A teenage girl's two ovaries are the only way she can make babies so she looks after them very carefully, tucking them into one of the most protected places in her body – nestling between her kidneys and uterus. Because of this it is extremely rare for girls to injure their ovaries, but the same cannot be said of teenage boys. Testicles are worryingly exposed to the world, protected only by a thin scrotal skin bag. Surely this is a risky way to arrange your anatomy?

To protect the testicles somewhat, boys can raise them. They hang from the abdominal wall by little hoist-like muscles called cremasters. These muscles contract when men ejaculate, when the weather is cold, or when someone kicks us down there. The cremasters even have their own readily testable reflex: gently slide a fingertip along an inner male thigh and the testicle on that side will lift a little. But the protection provided by this winching-up system is limited, and elevated testicles can feel uncomfortable after a while, as the many men with the common and harmless condition of 'retractile testicles' find when they go swimming or play football. And the story about sumo wrestlers sucking up their testicles before a bout is partly true – they do indeed massage them up into their lardy groins, but not all the way into their abdomens.

But why are those testicles on the outside in the first place? The sorts of zoologist who spend their time poking around underneath animals tell us that external testicles are a mammalian speciality. Fish, amphibians, reptiles and birds keep them tucked away, but most mammals wear them proudly on the outside. This is true of both the main groups of mammals: us 'placental' mammals who give birth to mature offspring, as well as the marsupials (indeed, the female marsupial's pouch is thought to be a modified form of the male scrotum). However, there are exceptions, of which dolphins, whales, seals and sea lions are the most obvious. Maybe the sea is too cold for external testicles, or perhaps they would slow their owners down by dragging in the water. This suggestion is supported by the fact that testicles are also internal in manatees, elephants and hyraxes. This collection of marine drifters, trunked giants and cat-sized scamperers may seem a strange assortment, but they are in fact thought to be a closely related family. Their ancestors probably went through an aquatic phase – one which gave elephants their snorkel-like trunk, and from which manatees never emerged – and this is presumably when their testicles retreated into the abdomen. However, the aquatic theory of testicle internalization is dealt a blow by the fact that anteaters have internal testicles and they are decidedly non-aquatic. And testicles are external in otters. And internal in sloths. And so on.

Evidence from humans has also been unhelpful in solving this external-testicle conundrum. Failure of a testicle to descend to its normal position is the commonest abnormality of sexual development in men; it is called 'cryptorchidism' ('orchid' is Greek for 'testicle', so think twice next time you visit the florist). The testicles should normally have descended into the scrotum by the first birthday, but sometimes they are left behind in the groin or inside the abdomen. We know that abdominal testicles are prone to developing tumours, and also that they produce little viable sperm, so this has led to the theory that men keep their testicles on the outside because they do not like heat. Indeed, human testicles do function best at lower temperatures – maybe 32°C instead of 37°C – but this is a poor argument. Just because human testicles now function better at lower temperatures does not mean that this was the original reason our ancestors squeezed them out of the abdomen. The fact that they are well adapted to their current external position should come as no surprise. Also, the ability of male elephants to make sperm from internal testicles shows that testicles can readily evolve to function at higher temperatures, an ability shown even more dramatically by the hummingbird's testicles which cope with daily temperature swings between 18 and 44°C.

As we near the end of this zoological quest we can see that the absolutely essential physical differences between men and women are quite small. To play their parts in making future generations, the two sexes need nothing more than a few discrepancies built into their genital plumbing. But we know that there is far more to sexual difference than that, and indeed many of the great works of human culture are dedicated to describing the wonderful additional differences between the two sexes. Why must boys be so unlike girls? Why does a young man's hand have to look so very different from a young woman's hand? The breadth of a youth's shoulders, the soft skin on a maiden's thigh – perhaps it is no coincidence that it is these 'extra' non-essential differences which we like so much about each other. Human eroticism is a complex, indirect thing. It is not just about plugging our reproductive organs together. Instead it is spread all around our bodies and seeps into our enormous minds.

Throughout this book we have seen that humans are unusual in the way that almost every bodily function has been subsumed into our brain; nowhere is this more true than sex. Most animals, including most mammals, have sex solely so they can produce offspring. Many species have a restricted 'breeding season' when they are sexually active, and this can mean that some individuals copulate only once or twice a year. Yet many primate species are exceptions to this rule because they use sex – vaginal and anal, heterosexual and homosexual – for a wide variety of social reasons, such as forming social bonds, expressing dominance or staking proprietary claims to each other. Members of some primate species copulate many times a day as a matter of course, yet few of these encounters generate baby primates. As the simian brain evolved ever more power, even sex became exploited as just another social tool.

Some anthropologists have tried to compile lists of the reasons why humans have sex, but there seems to be no limit to our ingenuity. People may copulate out of inquisitiveness, as a gesture of affection, as an act of mutual validation, as a comfort, as a shelter from grief, to experience contact, to reduce pain, as an athletic recreation, to derive material gain, to confirm an emotional union, to selfishly receive or selflessly give pleasure, to cure boredom, because they think they ought, or because they think it would be funny. Non-procreative sex looms large in the human constitution. After all what other species would be ridiculous enough to have sex during pregnancy?

So teenagers find themselves at the end of an immensely long story of sexual evolution. They carry all the reproductive baggage resulting from the original DNA-protecting innovation of sex, but they also find themselves as the most extreme manifestation of a more recent, monkeyish trend for using sex as a psychic and social tool. And each teenager must learn afresh that human sex may spring from their genitals, but it is most focused in their mind.

When are teenagers meant to have sex?

We do not know when teenagers are meant to have sex. For all we know, they may have evolved to undergo puberty at eleven and have their first child by thirteen, or they may have evolved to undergo puberty at eighteen and have their first child at twenty-one. Perhaps society's greatest problem with teenagers is that we simply do not know what they are meant to be doing. We do not know what is healthiest and we do not know what is best. We do not know if cultural norms of schooling and living with parents are distorting teenagers' natural biology, or if they support the evolved status quo of teen breeding, or if they are a messy compromise to protect teenagers from the unnaturalness of modern life. All we know for sure about teenage sex is that it varies a great deal between individuals, and it has changed over the course of human history.

Before teenagers can engage voluntarily in sexual intercourse, most must pass through puberty. In Part One I discussed the mechanics of puberty and how it involves a predictable sequence of biological changes. However, although that sequence is reliable, the time-trigger that sets it running is far less so. For such an important phenomenon, the timing of puberty is surprisingly variable. It is almost as if it evolved to be that way.

The most striking feature of the timing of puberty is the way it has shifted over recent centuries in developed Western countries. There is strong evidence that puberty has been occurring at younger and younger ages as the decades have elapsed. A frequently quoted piece of evidence for this is reports by seventeenth- and eighteenth-century choirmasters that choirboys' voices usually 'broke' around their eighteenth birthday – far later than occurs today. The clearest indicator of the hastening pace of puberty comes from medical records from Europe and the United States over the last century. Scientists debate how consistent the change has been between different countries, but most agree that puberty was occurring roughly three years earlier by the end of the twentieth century than it was at its beginning.

The rate of change in the timing of puberty over that century sounds even more spectacular when rephrased: puberty occurred *twelve days* earlier for *every year* that passed. This is an extremely rapid pace of change, and probably too rapid to be explained by evolution. A century is only four or five human generations and that is simply not enough for new genetic traits to take hold. Yes, genes have been identified which are strongly linked to the timing of puberty, and most of them are involved in hormone production or transport. And these genes are important because they probably explain much of the variation in the timing of puberty between individual teenagers. However, it is unlikely that their distribution in the human population could have changed much within one century. There must be other forces at work.

So we need to look beyond genetics to explain the steady decline in the age of puberty. As it happens, farmers have known for centuries that the timing of puberty in animals may be manipulated by changing their environment. Young female farm animals can be encouraged to undergo puberty by exposure to mature males, or by being housed with cycling females, or by feeding them up to 'breeding weight'. So it should come as no surprise that environmental changes can advance the onset of puberty in humans too.

The most popular theory is that improved nutrition has hastened human puberty over recent centuries. Four centuries ago most Europeans did not get enough to eat, whereas most of them now have too much – it is a truly dramatic change in the human experience. Evidence for this theory abounds in the present population: mildly overweight children start puberty earlier, whereas slightly lean ones start later. Frank malnourishment delays puberty markedly, and adolescent eating disorders can 'reverse' it, often switching off girls' reproductive cycles. Also, more girls now have their first period in winter, which is the time when they gain weight most quickly now that food is freely available year-round. Most striking of all is the hastening of puberty which occurs in girls whose families migrate from developing countries to developed ones during their childhood.

So the link between diet and timing of puberty seems very strong, although there is still much that we do not know. Although 'threshold weights' for puberty have been suggested – 47 kilograms in girls and 55 in boys – it must be emphasized that these are average values, and individuals often enter puberty at a completely different weight. It is now agreed that there is no single fixed weight that all teenagers must reach to start puberty, although everyone may well be preset with their own inbuilt threshold weight. Also, some have suggested that infant growth rate may be more important than late childhood growth – indeed, there may be a link between timing of puberty and the use of formula milk, which usually makes babies grow faster. And the causal relationship between weight and puberty is confusing anyway, because incipient puberty may cause weight gain even before any more obviously sexual changes take place. Despite all these uncertainties, from an evolutionary perspective, linking puberty to body weight seems eminently sensible. It means that individuals, especially girls, do not commit to the rigours of reproduction until they have mustered the frame, or the energy reserves, to cope. It is even possible that they are making a 'biological prediction' – that the food resources that supported their childhood growth will continue to be available to support their first attempts at breeding.

In the last few years, we may have discovered the mechanism by which human puberty is attuned to body weight. Human fat cells produce a hormone called leptin, and other body tissues probably use the amount of leptin in the blood as an indicator of total body fat content. For example, leptin is thought to control the appetite centres of the hypothalamus in the brain – and lab mice without leptin become hugely obese. Similarly, leptin may also control the activity of the hypothalamic gonadotrophin-releasing hormone (GnRH) cells which, in Part One, we saw control the start of puberty. And indeed, mice *sans* leptin do not undergo puberty. Most likely, leptin does not act directly on the GnRH cells – instead it probably affects them by changing the amounts of neuropeptide Y reaching them. As puberty approaches in humans, levels of leptin gradually rise and this may be essential for puberty to get started (although other factors are probably at work as well). Noticeably, once puberty starts, leptin levels follow different courses in the two sexes. In teenage girls, leptin levels continue to rise as they deposit womanly adipose curves, and leptin may continue to be important in permitting normal cycling. By contrast, leptin levels fall in boys because they often lose fat at this time, so boys' requirement for leptin may be less clear-cut. Yet whatever the details, leptin is certainly our best candidate for the brain's barometer for predicting when puberty should happen.

Speaking of prediction, there is another, more unexpected correlation, in this case between birth weight and puberty. Strangely, slow prenatal growth hastens puberty – exactly the opposite effect to that of slow postnatal growth. Yet the relationship is quite clear, with low birth weight causing puberty to occur up to ten months earlier. This apparently paradoxical effect is fascinating for two reasons. First, it implies that events in the womb can 'programme' the brain and reproductive system to behave differently ten years later when puberty starts – possibly this may occur through a rebalancing of the hormones which control metabolism, such as insulin. The second implication is that this mechanism evolved because in our past it was advantageous to breed earlier if we were born small. No one is sure why this might be, but it has been suggested that small babies are somehow 'making the best of a bad job'. Maybe they are taking their prenatal deprivation as a sign that the world out there is pretty tough, and that they may not live very long. And the sensible thing to do if you are expecting to die young is to cram in as much breeding as you can: by starting puberty early.

Factors other than genes and diet may also explain why the

timing of puberty varies so much between individuals, and why it has changed over the decades. For example, not only has nutrition improved, but health care has improved too, and it is probable that reduced childhood infection and parasite burden have supplemented the benefits of improved diet. Socio-economic status also seems to play a role, with higher status correlating with earlier puberty, although it is possible that this effect is partly due to better nutrition. Finally, there is an unexplained difference in puberty between northern and southern Europe, with Finns entering puberty a year later than Greeks. This could be due to genetic factors, or it might be an effect of day length and the passing of the seasons. If so, humans would not be the only species to have different patterns of reproduction depending on the latitude in which they find themselves – goats and cats certainly do.

A final factor controlling the timing of puberty is especially controversial: puberty in teenage girls may be hastened by stress. This is not accepted by all researchers, but there are data which seem to show that stress, and especially stressful family conditions, can exert just such an effect. In fact there are many examples of animals breeding earlier under stressful conditions, and sometimes even compromising their own growth and maturation to do so. This claimed reproductive response to stress may be another example of individuals predicting their future based on present conditions: maybe girls take social upheaval, deprivation and lack of available pair-bondable men as signs that the reproductive outlook is poor and that they are unlikely to live long. So is the most sensible response to breed as soon as possible, to try and produce at least some offspring, even if they do not live long enough to look after them? If this truly is a system built into our biology, then it suggests that human females must have experienced some pretty grim times in our evolutionary history. It implies that teenage girls were at real risk of dying prematurely – after all, in a long-lived species such as ours, a sensible response to a few years of non-fatal adversity would be to sit it out and breed when the good times return.

Now we know the factors which control the onset of puberty, including those that probably explain the rapid change in its timing over recent centuries. But are we any better placed to answer the question of when puberty is 'meant' to happen in humans? One reason we cannot answer this question with certainty is that we know virtually nothing about when puberty took place in our pre-agricultural ancestors. It has been suggested that puberty came early in those days – with menstruation starting between the ages of seven and twelve. However, the evidence for this is thin, being based mainly on extrapolating data from chimps to humans. It also assumes that agriculture had a disastrous effect on childhood health: allowing humans to have more children, but consigning them to a tightly packed, filth-ridden, undernourished village upbringing. This may be true – I discussed the possibility that agriculture shortened the human lifespan in Part One – but it is far from proven. Although the ancient hunter-gatherer life is what we evolved for, this does not mean we should idealize it – it could no doubt sometimes be nasty, brutish and short.

It has also been suggested that the shift to agriculture had profound effects on family life. The new settled lifestyle might have meant that children inherited their parents' land, so teenagers lived with their parents for longer. This is claimed to have had the advantage that they could use their teenage years to acquire from their parents the technological know-how required for farming. So did they delay puberty so they could extend the period over which they could cooperate? This may seem a reasonable suggestion, but I find it difficult to see how a need for technical hints and tips could *cause* later puberty. Another theory even suggests that delayed puberty evolved in settled human societies to prevent incest between parents and the teenagers now forced to live with them. Again, I find this hard to believe. The cognitive aversion to incest is so strong in humans that, in my view, delayed puberty would be an unnecessary precaution.

However little we know about our 'natural' pre-agricultural past, our current understanding of the timing of puberty does, I think, teach us one very important lesson. That lesson is that there is no 'correct' time for puberty. Puberty simply does not behave like part of the human life-plan that was ever meant to have a single, fixed, optimal time. Quite the opposite, it changes its timing at the whim of almost every factor you could think of – diet, weight, prenatal development, lighting, genes, social stress. Puberty is *meant* to be movable. This explains why it can vary so much between individual people with no apparent long-term effects. Even the one child in five thousand who experiences 'clinically' precocious puberty usually ends up sexually normal, physically and behaviourally, although he or she may experience a few adjustment problems along the way. Like learning to walk, puberty must happen, but when it happens is not set in stone. Because of this, our concerned quest to find out when puberty is meant to occur is doomed. Puberty is meant to happen when the time is right.

This has ramifications for the future of puberty. Many biologists have wondered if there is a lower age limit below which puberty cannot take place, or if it will continue to occur at an ever-decreasing age. One of the best indicators for the future is that the headlong fall in the age of puberty in developed countries seems to be slowing. A reasonable estimate might be down to three days' reduction each year, but some claim it has stopped altogether. We are not sure why the decline has slowed. Maybe diets cannot get any more conducive to puberty than they are now. Or perhaps hastening puberty simply follows a law of diminishing returns. Whatever the case, there does not yet seem to be an absolute lower age limit for human puberty, because some individuals still enter puberty long before the population average.

Of course, puberty is not the only prerequisite for the start of human sexual activity. To get nearer to an estimate of when teenagers are meant to start having sex, we need to think about why they either become eager to do it, or are coerced into doing it. Being a cognitively complex social species, the boundary between eagerness and coercion is not a clear one. Some teenagers desperately want to try sex even when their peers and family dissuade them; others' first sexual experience is as a rape victim. Many teenagers are somewhere between those two extremes – they have sex because they think everyone else is doing it, because their peers persuade them to try it, or their partner pressurizes them into it.

Around the world there is evidence that the age at first intercourse is not changing much, although a global increase in the age of marriage means that more premarital sex is taking place. In contrast, in the UK it is thought that the age of first intercourse decreased from sixteen to fourteen in girls between 1966 and 1996, and from fifteen to thirteen in boys. Less than 1 per cent of women now have their first sexual experience after marriage, compared to 40 per cent in 1950. The age discrepancy between boys and girls is confusing, as are reports that teenage boys claim to have had more sexual partners than girls at any given age. It is widely reported that most teenage heterosexual couples consist of a younger girl and an older boy, so the identity of the hordes of older girls with whom these younger male teenagers are having sex is unclear. It is of course tempting to suspect that boys over-report their number of sexual partners and under-estimate the age of their first intercourse, whereas girls may do the opposite.

Other studies have concentrated on teenagers' perceptions of their first sexual encounter. Boys tend to cite curiosity or even alcohol as a major spur to action, whereas girls are more likely to mention love as an incentive. This of course suggests that the intentions of the two partners in heterosexual teenage unions do not always coincide. A study in the United States asked a cohort of African-American girls about their attitudes to their first sexual experience. A startling 78 per cent of them felt they had been too young when they first had sex, and only 22 per cent thought they had timed it about right (which raises the unlikely possibility that no girls ever think they have left it too late).

Attitudes to sex are all-important because we brainy humans are not slaves to our hormones – we can 'ignore' puberty for as long as we like and start to have sex when we want. Considering this cognitive dimension of teenage sex, it is notable that teenagers with lower IQ scores tend to start having sex younger.

So, to conclude by returning to the question I asked at the beginning of this chapter: when are teenagers meant to have sex? It is no use taking our hunter-gatherer past as a benchmark of 'normal' human behaviour, because we have no idea when teenagers started puberty or sex back then. Sweaty teenage fumblings do not leave fossils. Anyway, puberty is so obviously a movable feast, if you will forgive the phrase, that the idea of a 'normal' time for it is meaningless. I would suggest that the time when humans are meant to start having sex is the time when they first want to. We have seen that there is a distinctive phase of infatuation and sexual experimentation during mid-adolescence which looks very much as if nature is telling teenagers to start having sex. And the end of this infatuation/experimentation phase looks strikingly like the time when teenagers are meant to redirect their attention towards the children thus generated. Whatever we may wish, I believe that teenage sex is the pivotal moment in the human sexual experience. How we deal with that is up to us.

Why do teenagers get sexually transmitted diseases?

More than half of sexually active under-sixteens are thought to have had unprotected sex. Along with pregnancy, sexually transmitted diseases are a major reason why teenagers are told to be careful with sex – to fear it almost – but it seems the warnings have little effect. A quarter of American adolescents may have been infected with an STD – indeed, five of the ten most commonly reported infectious diseases in the United States are sexually transmitted (chlamydia, gonorrhoea, HIV, syphilis and hepatitis B). Even worse, as many as half of all STD cases may go unreported, meaning not only that the truth is even worse than the published statistics, but also that many cases remain untreated, free to infect others.

The usual reaction to this rising tide of adolescent infection is, understandably, panic. Yet STDs are nothing new: they have been with us throughout recorded history, and probably a great deal longer. Also, they start to make more sense when they are viewed not as an unpredictable malignant scourge of contemporary youth, but as a product of millions of years of their, and our, evolution. STDs are caused by microbes which are constantly evolving by the same mechanisms as us, and they trace their origins just as far back as we do. They are a varied bunch – viruses, bacteria, protozoa and even the occasional louse – all of which just happen to have found a shared niche in human reproductive organs. But as we will see, there are some very special features of the spread of STDs – for one thing, they are extremely responsive to changes in human behaviour, which probably explains why the nature of the adolescent STD threat has changed so dramatically in recent years. Also, they have the potential ability to drive us to extinction.

It is not just humans who get STDs. They have been identified in other mammals, birds, reptiles, spiders, insects and even roundworms. This is almost reassuring, as it means we are not alone. It also means we have some animal models in which we can study STDs in a calm, dispassionate way. And as in humans, the infectious agents which cause animal STDs are not closely related to each other, but just happen to share a predilection for genitals.

One of the most unusual features of animal STDs is the arithmetic of how they travel around their host population. Most other infections spread at a rate which is mainly controlled by their 'density' in the environment. If members of a species are spread very thinly across the land, then most infections find it difficult to spread. A good example of this was influenza in pre-agricultural humans – we may have existed in such small groups, so widely scattered, that flu was never able to spread. Flu has now become a menace because we have clustered together in ever larger, now globally connected communities. This dependence on density has a good side to it – it often stops infections wiping out entire species because if a new virulent bug attacks, it usually kills enough individuals to reduce the population density to a level at which it can no longer spread.

But STDs are different. Instead of 'density', the rate at which they spread is more dependent on the *proportion* of the host species which is infected. Groups of animals can spread themselves thinly in the face of infection, but at some point they have to get together to mate. They simply must seek each other out and risk infection, thus losing any protection they derived from being widely dispersed in their environment. This is why STDs can wipe out entire species – we cannot escape them. And hunter-gatherer humans could not avoid STDs by staying in isolated tribal groups because that would have led to disastrous inbreeding. Instead, we believe our ancestors traded individuals between groups to prevent inbreeding, and trading early-teens was probably the best way to avoid trading STDs as well.

As you can see, STDs are where sex and risk become uncomfortably close. For an animal's survival, sex and its associated risk of infection raise stark choices. STDs often compromise fertility or even survival, so they have become the spectre lurking behind many species' sexual decisions. Indeed, it is thought that the presence of STDs can permanently alter the breeding patterns of an entire species. Depending on which individuals are most easily infected, and which suffer the worst effects of infection, host species may evolve to eschew non-procreative sex, or tend towards monogamy, polygamy, or its opposite, polyandry (stable sexual units containing one female and multiple males).

Every individual must weigh the pros and cons. For example, if you are a successful male, mating with many females offers a chance to scoop the jackpot in the game of natural selection. However, it also presents the risk of infecting yourself and your offspring with a devastating disease. In this context, there is good evidence that primates' defences against infection have been tailored to their sexual strategies – for example, some characteristics of the immune system correlate well with species' penchant for promiscuity. It is even possible that the modern human sexual system is actually a response to our STDs. After all, culturally and biologically imposed long-term monogamy is certainly a good way of avoiding infection. Maybe we have bugs to thank for marital bliss.

Yet it is not as if STDs are trying to hurt us. As far as we can tell, most of them are just evolving to spread efficiently. It is hardly in their interests to kill their host before they get a chance to spread; neither is it to their advantage to stop humans reproducing. Although they have not yet managed to shake off all their undesirable effects, they seem to be trying to get along with us. A good example of this is the early history of syphilis in Europe. Syphilis's European 'year zero' was around 1500 – the disease was either unknown before that time, or was extremely rare. It has been suggested that the bacterium was brought across the Atlantic from Haiti by Columbus' sailors, who later joined the army of Charles VIII of France, and spread the disease during the rapacious aftermath of the siege of Naples in 1495. Although some historians doubt this account, it is clear that syphilis appeared from *somewhere* around that time, but that it soon changed. There are good contemporary accounts which describe the severity of the disease decreasing as it spread across Europe during the following century. Strains of the bacterium which harmed their hosts less spread more easily and out-competed more virulent forms. Similar changes have been observed in some other STDs: they rarely kill, and often cause little immediate harm at all. They also develop the ability to evade their host's immune system so they can persist in the body for long periods – many STDs can last for years, hugely increasing their chances of infecting other victims.

The sudden appearance of syphilis demonstrates how human activity is crucial in deciding which STDs flourish and which disappear. Sexually transmitted diseases' fortunes are tightly bound up with the vicissitudes of human behaviour, and this is just as important for today's teenagers as it has been throughout our species' existence. Different STDs have come and gone as human lifestyles have changed, and epidemiologists are now piecing together the story of how human civilization has changed the fortunes of different infections.

By fifty thousand years ago, humans had spread to most parts of the world they inhabit now. As we have seen, they probably lived in scattered several-extended-family groups, protected from most infectious diseases by sheer geographical isolation. However, these groups had to interbreed, so STDs were still able to pass between them. Indeed, it has been claimed that one of the reasons why girls mature earlier than boys is so that teenage girls could be traded between groups at an early age, while still giving an indication of their future mental and physical attributes. Thus inter-group sexual mixing may have been strictly controlled, but we have no idea to what extent incest taboos and monogamy traditions prevented within-group promiscuity. Still, STDs were probably much rarer under these conditions, and some of them may not have existed at all.

The next great change occurred around ten thousand years ago, when some humans established larger settlements to allow them to focus on agriculture. We have already considered the possible effect of this change on human health as a whole, but it probably also affected STDs. In larger, more densely packed communities, there was more opportunity for STD transmission, and it is also likely that social customs changed in the new cramped living conditions. Maybe attitudes to adolescent sex changed because of increased childhood mortality and reduced life expectancy – any type of sex seems more attractive when your family is at risk of dying out. Also, the new settlements were not urban in the modern sense but more like rural villages, and this may have carried its own risks. The inhabitants of these villages were in constant contact with the wild environment because they presumably continued to gather wild plants and hunt wild animals despite the advent of agriculture. Thus they still regularly risked catching infections from wild animals, just as they had in the past. In the past those infections had fizzled out in the old isolated tribal communities, but now they could flourish in the new crowded villages. And we know to our cost that human STDs really can arise from contact with wild animals in this way – for that is almost certainly how we acquired HIV.

So human history rattled inexorably onwards, stirring its vat of infectious diseases. Two or three millennia ago, the major world civilizations had grown to a point at which they re-established contact with each other, either through trade or warfare. Now they could swap infections and this contact may have been responsible for the plagues of antiquity, such as the Black Death which swept across Europe from Central Asia. Global trade and global pandemics have two very different consequences, but both encourage STDs. First, times of economic prosperity often coincide with times of increased sexual liberty – maybe well-off people have more time on their hands and look more seductive. Moreover, medieval authors commented that pandemic disease often caused people to 'live life for the moment' – usually implying that this meant having more sex. Certainly, the half of the English population who survived the Black Death found their labour newly valued, their prosperity increasing, and a devastated country ripe for repopulation. Copulation must have seemed a valuable and enjoyable social duty.

Humans once more mixed their bubbling pot of sexual infection when the European powers spread their acquisitive grasp across the world during the age of colonial expansion. As I have mentioned, this may have started as early as Columbus, but it certainly led to the introduction of many diseases into new, naïve populations, often with devastating effects. It also sparked the process of global development that has continued to this day. Human infections can now flit around the world on jet aircraft. More people are travelling to foreign climes for sexual and non-sexual recreation. War – and its attendant legacy of rape – is ever-present. And in Africa, urban migration has meant that millions of people who trace their roots to areas where our closest primate relatives live (the most likely source of new infections) commute into densely packed cities where STDs are swapped, mixed and spread. Perhaps we have been fortunate that only one major STD has so far arisen by that route. It is now almost certain that HIV was first contracted from a chimpanzee near the Canaga River in south-eastern Cameroon around 1950. The human virus is closely related to the strain of simian immunodeficiency virus that infects chimps in that area, but notably does not kill them. Presumably one bite or one butchery cut was all it took for that single encroachment into the forest to change the course of human history.

So history shows us that the STDs we suffer are a product of our own behaviour. They are exquisitely sensitive to what we do and with whom we do it. Prevalence of any given STD depends on an array of interacting factors: numbers of people infected, how long infection lasts, how easy it is to transmit, how much damage it causes, how often people have sex, how many sexual partners they have, how often they change partners. So there is no reason to suppose that STDs have reached some sort of stable equilibrium. Quite the opposite, the rate of human social, environmental and sexual change is now faster than it has ever been, so we should not be surprised if STDs are in a state of flux.

We think that many of those changes in human behaviour are directly relevant to teenagers in developed countries. Teenagers are starting to have sex younger, and they may have sex with more people than in the past. Often their relationships are short-lived, which means they change partners often – one of the most important influences on STD acquisition. Thankfully, contraception is increasingly available, but hormonal contraception makes up a large part of that trend and it gives no protection against STDs. Condoms are by far the best defence but they are ineffective when misused and they can reduce the spontaneity and tactile sensation of sex – all important considerations for sexually impatient teenagers. Vaccines against chlamydia and papillomavirus will probably be available soon, but they risk giving teenagers a false sense of security – they will offer no protection against any other STDs. Finally, teenagers often assume that STDs are treatable when in fact many are not, and what treatments do exist are starting to fail – for example, gonorrhoea is gradually becoming resistant to antibiotics.

So where does all this leave the modern teenager?

Unfortunately we know even less about how STDs spread in teenagers than we do in adults. Always we face obstacles such as the symptomless nature of some infections, and the unwillingness of symptomatic patients to disclose their sexual history. It is thought that STDs in adult populations first gain momentum in relatively small, self-contained clusters of people who share sexual partners. Subsequently, the disease leaks out into the general population, where it spreads more slowly – the pattern of sexual affiliations changing from a 'tight tangle' to a more gradually branching pattern of spread. But we do not know if this 'two-phase' model of STD spread occurs in teenagers – of course they may follow the same pattern as adults, or their pattern may be more variable or chaotic. Also many teenagers have sex with people older than themselves, so they may be indistinguishably merged into the adult sexual network. In fact, sex between teenagers and adults is an extremely efficient way for STDs to spread: from older, infected individuals to younger initiates with many years of infecting left ahead of them. Worst of all, teenagers may actually be those early, densely interconnected, promiscuous groups that kindle new STD outbreaks.

Most worryingly of all, teenagers have the most to lose from STDs. They can be socially and sexually embarrassing to the point of causing clinical depression. They hurt and they look unsightly, and they may even establish a psychological revulsion to sex in teenage sufferers. Some may be treatable, such as gonorrhoea and syphilis. Others are not and may persist for life, such as herpes. Some cause few immediate symptoms but later cause infertility (such as chlamydia) or cancer (papillomavirus). Of course, HIV is often fatal. And because behaviour is changing in many developed countries, the balance of infections is also changing: the initially mild infections with long-term effects, such as chlamydia and papillomavirus, are now replacing the more acutely nasty bugs that predominated in the past.

But as with so many things in human life, teenagers' best defence is their cognitive ability to avoid infection. Infection rates correlate well with teenage ignorance of the importance of using condoms, and the relative risks of oral, vaginal and anal sex. Many studies show that school STD education has a very real beneficial effect. Also, contrary to what some teenagers might expect, condom use correlates well with self-esteem and emotional intimacy in romantic relationships – condoms do not mean mistrust. In addition, there is evidence that STD infection is reduced by some parental influences – especially when teenagers feel their lives are more 'supervised' by their parents. Of course love and desire will always try to overpower teenagers' decisions about contraception, but the evidence is considerable that well-advised teenagers in relaxed, happy relationships will often make time to pause at the height of amorous anticipation, and do the sensible thing.

So the good thing about STDs' dependence on teenage behaviour is that it means teenagers have the power to control them. Indeed, teenagers may be so important in the spread of STDs that they hold the key to reducing their impact on the entire human race. Yet the central evolutionary question remains. If over the millennia we have acquired this motley bunch of infections that threaten the very continuation of our species, why do our teenagers not seem evolved to avoid them? Why does every thirteen-year-old not feel driven to join with another thirteen-year-old in an irreversible act of chaste wedlock? That would certainly see the end of sexual infection, yet it does not happen. Human teenagers want to experiment and play and enjoy, even though it can be so dangerous. I suggest this sexual 'irresponsibility' is a product of our ancient past. Humans evolved in social groupings that were very different from how they are now. Back then, teenage sexual behaviour did not matter, because isolation and scarcity controlled sexually transmitted diseases for us. Now we have to control them ourselves.

Why is teenage pregnancy different?

The phrase 'teenage pregnancy' has a remarkable power. It is difficult to hear it and not feel some emotional reaction – pity, anger, worry or frustration. For an entirely natural phenomenon, it is remarkable what negative connotations it carries. Teenagers have been getting pregnant for thousands of years – indeed it probably used to happen more often than it does today. There is no doubt that teenagers are biologically able to have children, yet many modern societies expect them not to. Teenage pregnancy is seen as a sign of social failure which can damage the prospects of parent and child alike. Yet it has not always been like this. In many cultures, humans are celebrated as having come of age much younger than modern Western etiquette would like – at the first menstrual period, or at an arbitrary twelve or thirteen years old. And around the world many marriages took place and still take place in the early teens.

But what should we make of teenage pregnancy – this long-standing, spontaneous and usually successful phenomenon? How should it be modified and subjugated to contemporary aspirations for education, career and family?

Or does the fact that we evidently evolved to be able to do it mean we should accept it and support it? Teenage pregnancy strikes at the heart of the uneasy balance between our evolutionary heritage and our modern cultural systems, and as we will now see, it also involves some difficult biological compromises too. Put simply, a teenage girl's pregnancy is biologically unlike a pregnancy in an adult woman. It is not a perversion of human biology, but it is certainly different.

The incidence of teenage pregnancy varies enormously between countries – in some it is almost non-existent, whereas in others more than half of all women have become pregnant by the age of eighteen. In one year in the United States, it is thought that 5.3 per cent of girls between fifteen and nineteen become pregnant. The equivalent figures for other countries are: UK 2.0 per cent, Niger 23.3 per cent and Japan 0.2 per cent. Yet these figures are only an estimate because we suspect that as many as a third of teenage pregnancies end in abortion, and a ninth in stillbirth – rates far higher than those for adult pregnancies. We think rates of teenage pregnancy have declined over the last century in most developed countries, despite teenage sex becoming more frequent. Hence the decline is almost certainly due to increased use of contraception.

In developed countries there are clear statistical links between teenage pregnancy and an adverse environment. In the UK as many as half of teenage mothers are, by accepted measures, living in poverty. Teenage pregnancy also shows strong links to prior substance abuse, and in the USA over 10 per cent of pregnant teenagers are thought to use cocaine, a substance known to induce birth defects. On average, teenage mothers also score poorly on measures of self-esteem, commitment to education and educational achievement –

although the latter could be caused by pregnancy just as much as it might be its cause. Teenage pregnancy also correlates strongly with poor communication about sexual matters in the parental home, and pregnant teenagers are more likely to believe that avoiding contraception is an act of love and commitment. Finally, pregnancy is more common in teenage girls brought up by a single parent, and more common in children themselves born to teenage mothers – a sign that it may be 'transmitted' down the generations.

Much less research has been carried out on the fathers of babies conceived by teenage mothers. This may reflect not only their elusive nature, but also societal assumptions that women bear the responsibility of pregnancy, and thus the responsibility for avoiding it. What data have been published do, however, show a similar story to that in girls – linking siring a teenage pregnancy to poor educational attainment, low income, drug use and trouble with the law. Most alarmingly of all, some studies suggest that between 10 and 20 per cent of all teenage pregnancies in developed countries are conceived as the result of rape. Others have suggested this problem may be even worse, with up to 60 per cent of teenage pregnancies more vaguely reported as 'preceded by unwanted sexual experiences'. Whatever one may think about the perceived difference between that phrase and rape, the figures give a depressing insight into the activities and attitudes of some teenagers.

Teenage pregnancies are more likely to be unintended than pregnancies in adult women, but this should not blind us to the fact that many are planned, or at least wished-for. Many teenagers see pregnancy as a way of achieving independence from their family, usually by leaving home and getting married – and of course this is often exactly what happens.

Furthermore, teenagers who wish to get pregnant often make strikingly mature changes to their lifestyle in anticipation of conception. For example, they reduce their intake of recreational drugs to a level statistically lower than it was before; a level also lower than that of their non-pregnant peers. They may also improve their diet, deliberately forsaking the characteristically adolescent pattern of 'browsing' and snacking. Intriguingly, many pregnant teenage girls report that they used to worry about their fertility – suggesting that they welcomed pregnancy because they feared their reproductive life might be short, and that an early start would be wise. But even in these more calculating groups of teenage parents, there are still strong correlations with poor education and little communication about sex. Most striking of all is an association between the intentions of boys to make girls pregnant, and their own mothers' poor educational achievements.

So before we look at the place of teenage pregnancy in the human life-plan, and the risks it may pose, we must realize that teenage pregnancy is not universally unwanted, unwelcome and unsupported. But it is also clear that so many adverse socio-economic factors encourage teenage pregnancy that it will be difficult to work out which risks arise from teenage pregnancy itself, and which are caused by the adverse factors which lead to those pregnancies. After all, poverty, social upheaval and substance abuse can all adversely affect the outcome of pregnancy, even in adult women. So is it actually teenage mothers' age that puts them at risk?

To some extent, youth does seem to be a problem. Teenage mothers are at increased risk of many problems, some of which may stem from their age and others from their circumstances. They are more likely to suffer from anaemia, which could be due to a combination of poor diet and a normal biological adaptation to teenage pregnancy (anaemia makes blood flow more easily through the vessels in the placenta). Teenage mothers are also more likely to suffer from pre-eclampsia, a strange syndrome in which maternal blood pressure rises and the placenta may degenerate. The high blood pressure may compromise the fetus, or it can cause swelling of the mother's feet, hands or face, liver problems, a sensation of lights flickering in front of the eyes, or seizures – in fact, pre-eclampsia is the leading cause of maternal death in some developed countries.

Things do not get much better as birth approaches. Teenage mothers are more likely to enter labour prematurely; birth is more likely to become obstructed; they are more likely to die during delivery – up to five times more likely in some developing countries. Should they opt for abortion, they are also more likely to suffer complications because they often avoid the publicity of the medical mainstream by seeking illegal terminations. Throughout the whole process of pregnancy and early motherhood they are more than 50 per cent more likely to suffer depression, and they are also more likely to be victims of domestic violence. A superficial statistical glance also suggests that the outlook for the children of teenage mothers is bleak – they are more likely to be neglected, to be physically abused, to become ill, to die of cot-death, to die before school age, to fare poorly at school and to become teenage parents themselves. Teenage mothers have also been reported to touch, look at and smile at their children less often than older mothers.

Although the evidence looks bleak, there is still much debate about how many of these problems are due to youth, and how many to disadvantage. Individually, every item on this list of problems could be argued to result from either cause. However, notable variations have been reported in the risks faced by teenage mothers. For example, many of the claimed risks of teenage pregnancy appear to be lower in the UK than they are in the USA. Of course, there could be genetic differences between the two populations, but it has also been strongly argued that the disparity is due to a greater level of social, economic and medical support for teenage mothers in the UK. And this raises the uncomfortable question of whether we could nullify teenage mothers' burden of risk by giving them the opportunities available to older mothers. Could teenage pregnancy be more of an economic problem than a medical one?

However, there is one effect of teenage pregnancy that may be entirely biological – indelibly engraved into the biology of the human race, indeed – and that is the size of babies. On average, teenage mothers have smaller babies than older women, and this does not seem to be entirely explained by their socio-economic woes. Low birth weight is important because it is associated with infant disease and mortality, and there is no reason to think that this is not also true of teenage pregnancy. It seems obvious that teenage girls should produce smaller babies – after all, they are smaller than adult women and they may not have accumulated as many bodily reserves to support their pregnancy. And yet studies in humans and animals suggest that the relationship between a young mother and her fetus is complex – the result of aeons of evolution under changing stressful conditions. A mother who is herself still growing is an unusual creature.

What few data we have from human teenage mothers suggest that something strange is going on. I have already mentioned that teenage girls have more erratic eating habits and less ability to select a good diet than older women, and this could certainly have an effect – after all, menstruating teenage girls have dietary needs as great as those of adult women. However, detailed studies of pregnant teenagers also show an unsettling degree of competition between immature mother and unborn child. In the last third of pregnancy, mothers who are still themselves growing (this is assessed by measuring whether the height of their knees above the ground is increasing, because pregnancy distorts the shape and stance of the upper body) do something apparently selfish. Despite the fact that their baby may be small, they continue to deposit body fat like any other growing teenager would. The response of an older mother to a poorly growing baby would be to use her own metabolic reserves to correct her child's growth retardation, but teenage mothers seem unable to do this. Unlike mature women's pregnancies in which the fetus has first call on most resources, growing mothers are in competition with their growing babies.

In an attempt to discount social and economic factors, the focus of young-mother research has now turned, strangely enough, to sheep. Studying sheep allows us to do all the experiments we are not allowed to do in teenage girls. We can allow young ewes to be mated at any time after puberty, and we can manipulate their diet before, during and after pregnancy. Yet far from simplifying our view of teenage pregnancy, these studies have shown that a complex set of checks and balances has evolved to control division of resources between young mothers and their offspring. For example, if an immature ewe (in other words, still herself growing) is underfed throughout pregnancy to stop her putting on weight, she responds by making less glucose available for transfer across the placenta to her fetus. As a result, her lamb is born smaller. However, if a young ewe is underfed before pregnancy and again during mid-pregnancy, her lamb will also be small, but in this case its reduced growth is due to the fact that it has a smaller placenta. In other words, there is a time window during which the growth and blood supply of the placenta is dependent on maternal nutrition – and if the placenta has been stunted by the end of this critical phase, it cannot catch up later. Finally, and most unexpectedly of all, if an immature ewe is *overfed* throughout pregnancy, she will herself gain weight but produce a smaller lamb (with a smaller placenta), often prematurely.

These confusing results show that the interactions between an immature mother and her fetus are more complex than those in her later pregnancies. In the natural course of events many animals and people do, of course, become pregnant before they themselves have finished growing. So we must assume that all this complex interplay has been written into our genetic instructions over the course of evolution. And the priorities of the growing baby are simple: it wishes to reach a good, healthy weight before birth to give it the best chance of surviving in the world outside (although it does not want to grow so big that it cannot get out). However, a teenage mother is evolutionarily torn. Her aim is to produce as many successful offspring as she can, but this child is only the first of them. Yes, she wants it to succeed, but she also wants to give all her future children the best chance to succeed. Thus it does not make sense for her to shut down her own growth and development just for the sake of this one, first child. Her body must divide its efforts between this baby and her future chances of high social status, unrestricted mate choice and good fertility. Really, the unborn child is not competing with its mother: it is competing with its future siblings.

This convoluted jostling for resources during teenage pregnancy may also have much longer-term effects. We have seen that teenage pregnancies often lead to smaller babies. Yet in the previous chapter I also mentioned that children born small tend to start their own puberty earlier. So if teenage pregnancy causes small babies, and small babies cause early puberty, does this mean there is a vicious circle built into human biology allowing us to 'pass on' early puberty to our children by dint of starving them in the womb?

Strangely, this bizarre, non-genetic, trans-generational method of controlling the timing of our first pregnancy might even make sense. Perhaps undernourished human mothers are using nutritional deprivation to warn their unborn children that life is going to be hard, so they should hurry up and breed as soon as possible. And as a result, that message is then conveyed, in turn, to their grandchildren. But this vicious circle need not be inescapable. For a start, some species may not experience it at all. Young mother mice do have smaller pups, but those pups undergo puberty later rather than sooner, so pregnant mice do not seem to nutritionally 'warn' their pups. Also, other influences might wrest human females out of the vicious circle connecting early puberty and small babies. For example, we saw previously that slow growth during childhood can delay puberty, and thus nullify the effects of low birth weight.

All these uncomfortable compromises and conflicting influences give the distinct impression that a woman's first pregnancy is *meant* to be controlled by her environment, past and present. And surely this makes more sense than an arbitrary and immovable time for her first conception. Girls could become pregnant as soon as they are fertile, but this would compromise their own physical and mental development. Alternatively, they could wait until they are fully mature (whatever that is) to have babies, but this would waste years of potential baby-producing opportunity. Instead, there is a happy medium to be found, where the disadvantages of immature breeding are balanced by the advantages of getting started with motherhood. Ten thousand years ago, that happy medium may have been around thirteen years of age, but things are different in the modern world. Despite earlier puberty, women now take longer to become socially, cognitively and technically mature mainly because they have to function in a complex, demanding, career-oriented world. Quite simply, there is more to learn, so they take longer to learn it. And because of this, it makes sense for them to start having children later.

So teenage pregnancy is not just a matter of biology: it must also take its place in our modern social, medical and economic world. We do not discourage teenage pregnancy because it is biologically abnormal, but because it does not fit our current view of the position of teenagers in society. As a species we have the unique ability to plan our own future, and by developing social codes to discourage teenage pregnancy we are doing just that. After all, our great brain has taken control of every other part of our lives, so why not let it decide whether we still need teenage pregnancy?

Why are teenagers meant to have sex?

Although we probably evolved to produce off-spring in our teens, our success as individuals is now so dependent on education and career that teenage parenthood suddenly seems undesirable. Deep down, teenagers want to make babies, but society warns them not to. But if the demands to delay pregnancy are now so great, where does this leave teenage sex? As we approach the end of this book, I propose that teenage romantic and sexual relationships, while preferably not procreative, still play an important role in the process of growing up. Becoming a sexually assured adult takes practice and learning. The practice and learning do not have to take place during adolescence, but our evolutionary heritage ensures that they usually do.

Perhaps the most important thing most of us learn as teenagers is our sexual orientation. This can mean learning minor sexual preferences, or something as crucial as discovering the sex to which we are attracted. I believe that current evidence shows that we are already destined to be heterosexual or homosexual by the time we enter puberty, but that does not mean teenagers have nothing to learn. Because homosexuality is less common than heterosexuality, and also because it is often frowned upon, many homosexuals enter puberty assuming that they will be heterosexual. For example, surveys suggest that many experiment with heterosexual relationships, with varying degrees of fulfilment, before they finally decide they prefer same-sex relationships. Heterosexuals do have homosexual dalliances although this is less common, presumably because heterosexuality is society's 'default' expectation.

Even if a teenager is 'destined' to be homosexual, he or she may not realize it for some time. That realization can be traumatic, often turning their previous assumptions about their life upside down. Adolescence can be socially challenging at the best of times, and many homosexual teenagers conceal their sexual orientation because of embarrassment or fear. If other teenagers discover that one of their peers is homosexual they often do not know how to react – so much of adolescent social life centres around establishing male and female heterosexual dominance hierarchies, that when a homosexual teenager 'comes out' other teenagers may not know where that person fits in the social scheme. Add to this the immature assumption made by many teenagers that all homosexuals indiscriminately lust after every member of their own sex, and you can see why gay teenagers can have a rough time. Whether the cause is others' ignorance, hostility or just plain bemusement, there is considerable evidence that adolescence is harder for homosexuals. Homosexual teenagers are more likely to become depressed, to be victims of violence, or to become homeless. It has been claimed that as many as 10 per cent attempt suicide. Because of this, parental support can be essential at this time, since there may not be much support coming from elsewhere.

Although searching for a 'cause' of homosexuality is a controversial quest (some claim it implies that homosexuality is a defect or disease), the fact remains that homosexuality is a strikingly unusual feature of human evolution. First of all, life-long homosexuality is rare in other species, although not unknown, and it usually occurs in only a tiny fraction of the population. Also, homosexuality has a dramatic negative effect on an individual's chances of passing on their genes – which is the criterion by which natural selection acts. Despite much research, we still know very little about why this reproductively counterproductive trait is so common in our species, nor why it occurs in some individuals but not others. I have discussed some of the possible causes of homosexuality in previous books, but the topic is a minefield of claim and counter-claim.

One thing is clear: there is little evidence that social factors or upbringing have much effect on sexual orientation. So what other influences could be at work? In Part Two we saw that there could be differences between heterosexuals and homosexuals in the shape or size of certain brain regions. Also, there may be discrepancies in finger dimensions, or growth of the long limb bones, and these have been claimed to reflect differences in hormone secretion during childhood. Scientists have looked even earlier in life for clues, but a genetic basis for homosexuality has not yet been clearly demonstrated (although the 'gay gene' idea sporadically seizes the attention of the media). Theories based on other early factors, such as the effect of a pregnant woman's immune system on her developing baby boy's brain, are slightly more convincing because they could explain statistical evidence that boys with several older brothers are more likely to be homosexual (the immune system 'learns' from previous exposure to foreign things – in this case 'male molecules' in a pregnant woman). Some have suggested more sociological explanations for the commonness of homosexuality, such as that it may be an exaggerated form of a human cerebral tendency to develop same-sex social bonds, or reduce aggression. The scientific jury is still out on this heated debate but many now believe that our sexual orientation is indeed decided long before puberty. But whatever the truth, it is still teenagers who must deal with its implications.

Another aspect of sex that teenagers must learn, or at least hone, is sexual attraction. Some models of evolutionary reproductive theory suggest that sexual attraction is all very simple – males seek young, faithful, attractive, fertile mates, and females seek older, taller, dominant mates who behave a bit like themselves. However, the human brain seems to have made the whole issue more complicated than that. Sexual or romantic attraction is evident in children, many of whom spontaneously express their attraction to 'handsome men' or 'pretty ladies'. But adolescence is different because it allows us to put our romantic ideas into practice – it lets us experiment with real sexual decisions. And to encourage this, some evolutionary biologists believe that humans evolved a dedicated adolescent period of romantic and sexual experimentation. Teenagers can select mates on the basis of some criterion or other, and see how the relationship works out. Although the average teenager's statistical sample size may be small, they can investigate whether the most attractive mate is necessarily the best recipe for long-term happiness, or see if they become sexually bored if they chose a plainer mate who is nicer to them, for example. Thus, teenage sex is the time when teenagers can modify their untested childish desires in the light of experience. They can even learn to select different mates for different purposes: older teenagers have been shown to prefer different potential mates depending on whether they are intending to establish a long committed relationship, or just have a one-night stand.

There are a few different characteristics that render people sexually attractive to others, but we do not know why we use any of them as a cue for desire. To add to this uncertainty, we do not know which of our ideas of attractiveness are innate, and which are moulded by society. For example, visual attractiveness is extremely important, and probably paramount when people first meet. And later on in relationships people still report that they consider their partner's attractiveness very important. Some studies have suggested that people are more likely to marry people who are (by independent assessors) classed at a similar level of attractiveness to themselves – so much so that 'looks' may be more consistently similar between married couples than any other characteristic. Most of us are suckers for beauty, but from the evolutionary perspective it is not clear why. Looks are, at best, a very indirect indicator of health or future success, so why are we so bewitched by them? Are they really telling us anything useful or are we all being fooled? Some neuroscientists have even claimed that our perceptions of beauty are nothing more than a quirky by-product of the way our brains process information about other people's faces and bodies. And presumably if everybody's brain is wired this way, beautiful people *will* do well in life, because everyone will be nice to them.

Although beauty, famously, is in the eye of the beholder, psychologists and neuroscientists have made some intriguing observations about what makes a beautiful face. The first criterion of beauty, surprisingly, is 'averageness'. Although people may express preferences for certain prominent features, in general they like their sexual partners to conform closely to the facial 'norm'. Of course, we must bear in mind that as a species, humans are unusually variable in physical appearance. Yet we seem to be very good at seeing through this variation and agreeing which of our disparate faces are 'quirky' and which ones just plain 'ugly'. Maybe a face which 'falls within the normal range' is an indicator of healthy genes and development – crucial for a potential future co-parent. Of course, the importance of averageness in all this human variation is complicated by the fact that humans enjoy variety, and many of them will deliberately seek out sexual partners who look somewhat different from their past paramours. Indeed, I think many of us value this form of visual experimentation, and sometimes find it slightly amusing when a friend shows a tendency to become romantically attached to a string of partners who all look strangely alike.

A second element of subjective beauty is facial symmetry. Having two matching sides to a face is unexpectedly important in assessments of beauty, a finding based on computer-generated images of symmetrical and asymmetrical versions of the same faces. Once again, symmetry may be a good indicator that a person's own embryonic development proceeded successfully, implying that they carry no nasty genetic surprises to pass on to their children. But as with averageness, we seem to be able to tolerate, even appreciate, a little deviation from the ideal. No one has a perfectly symmetrical face, and slight mouth or eye asymmetries can presumably be overlooked, even valued. For example, do people choose markedly asymmetrical hairstyles because perfectly symmetrical faces are slightly boring? The assessment of facial symmetry is deeply ingrained in our brain circuits, and there is even evidence that it may be affected by reproductive hormones. For example, women are better at assessing facial symmetry at certain phases of their menstrual cycle, although for some reason this does not mean they actually vary in their preference for symmetry.

A third important component of facial attractiveness is sexual dimorphism, or looking distinctively masculine or feminine. As we have seen, children are already dimorphic by the time they enter puberty, and sexual maturation increases the differences between them. Boys' faces change more than girls' faces, and many characteristics of the 'classic' feminine face are actually similar to those of children. Girls, in contrast, usually prefer the massive shape of the male head, with its prominent brow and jutting jaw. Also, teenage boys have more expressive faces than girls, or at least they make more dramatic expressions, and this may explain why wrinkles caused by a life of facial contortion are seen as more attractive in men than women. Sexually dimorphic features are certainly part of the human blueprint, but we do not know whether they evolved to allow the two sexes to succeed in their different hunter-gatherer roles, or whether instead sexual selection has been at work – small visual attractiveness cues used by one sex becoming progressively exaggerated in the other sex. Whatever the reason for human sexual dimorphism, its attractiveness depends on the perspective of its beholder. For example, women find more 'masculine' men attractive at times when they have a higher opinion of their own attractiveness. Also, for some reason individuals who become sexually active earlier in adolescence tend to prefer partners who are more sexually dimorphic – more 'typically' masculine or feminine.

The last and most controversial aspect of visual beauty is

body shape. We all have ideas of what constitutes a sexually attractive body, but people differ in their concepts of an ideal shape. One only needs to go into a newsagent's and study the shape of women on the covers of magazines produced for women and magazines produced for men to see a discrepancy (do not spend *too* long doing this). One parameter of female body shape which has been suggested as attractive to men is the ratio between hip and waist measurements, the implication being that narrowing in the middle and swelling out at the bottom is the quintessentially feminine shape, regardless of absolute measurements. This shape has even been given its own name, 'gynoid', and several studies have investigated how preferences for the gynoid vary between males of different races. There is some logic to the gynoid theory, as this shape may indicate that women are able to lay down nutrient reserves for childbearing – in particular the fats required to build large baby brains can be stockpiled in the buttocks. However, I wonder if men may simply use this shape as a measure of sexual dimorphism, because very few men are gynoid.

Body mass index (BMI) has been suggested as a better indicator of female physical attractiveness than the gynoid, on the grounds that it is a better indicator of fertility and health. Indeed, studies in the USA have shown that men do currently tend to select women of average or slightly less-than-average BMI as their ideal shape, but I have doubts about BMI as a valuable cue in itself. There are tremendous variations in preferred female BMI between cultures, and there are also recorded changes in preferred BMI in western societies over the course of history – the 'ideal' level was high at the start of the twentieth century, reached a nadir mid-century and has been increasing since. This suggests to me that preferences for female BMI are culturally imposed rather than built into the male brain, and that at most, BMI is only used as a general indication of 'averageness'. I also suspect that men may admit to preferences for female BMI that conform to cultural ideals, rather than their own desires.

Looking at sexual attraction from the opposite view, there have been surprisingly few studies of what women find attractive in the male body, perhaps because boys and men suffer less body image problems. What data do exist suggest that height is an important factor, although the 'ideal' height for a man may be a relative thing. Women seem to seek partners who are a certain amount taller than their own height, rather than all aiming for the same absolute ideal.

So teenagers must find a balance between three influences as they learn to develop their sense of visual sexual attraction. First, they probably have inbuilt preferences for what they like to look at, and no doubt those are important. Second, they may assimilate cultural ideals of attractiveness – for example, teenagers today are more likely to find people of different races attractive than a century ago, or concerns about scarcity or obesity may make overweight partners seem more or less attractive. And third, teenagers get their chance to learn first-hand from their sexual encounters – they can find out for themselves how it feels to have a certain type of face look at them amorously, or investigate how different-looking bodies actually feel when they touch them. Most of all, they can develop a sense of what is important to them, as well as what they are likely to get – studies show that attractive people are more picky about their partners' looks.

If learning to analyse looks was not hard enough, teenagers must also learn to assess the cognitive abilities and foibles of potential partners. Once looks have drawn an adolescent couple together, there often starts a long period of flirting, as the respective parties mentally circle each other, testing each other's intellectual and emotional reactions. This protracted and rather enjoyable phase could serve more than one function. For example, it has been claimed that teenagers often seek partners with similar character traits to themselves. Initially, they may do this to validate their own view of the world, but as time goes on, it can mean that couples mutually encourage each other's strange idiosyncrasies. This phenomenon is charmingly called 'behaviour contagion' and can be thoroughly irritating to all their single friends (and may also be why many married couples can seem a bit cranky).

Another possibility is that teenagers flirt to allow them to assess their prospective partner's cognitive abilities. They may be looking for someone similar in mental stature to them, or someone either more or less intelligent, and there are studies which show people doing all of these things for their own personal reasons. One particularly iconoclastic theory suggests that humans developed the skills of conversation, music, humour and art as means of impressing suitors with their intellectual acumen. And if women do most of the choosing, could this explain why most professional artists, musicians and comedians are men? Many women have admitted to falling in love because their man could make them laugh, or because of the way he looked with an electric guitar. Whatever the truth, I think it would be wonderful if 'high culture' evolved simply to tempt other people into bed.

As well as physical appearance and mental affinity, there is a third factor at work in sexual attraction, and it may seem worryingly primal: smell. For decades we have known that mice select their mates on the basis of their smell, and we now think the same may be true of humans. And for murine romantic assignations at least, studies have shown that there is an undeniable logic to how they sniff out their chosen partner.

The odours which female mice use to select their mate are linked to a special set of genes known as the Major Histo-compatibility Complex, or MHC. The MHC has been studied in great detail because it plays an important role in the immune system. The most unusual feature of the MHC is that its several component genes vary tremendously between different members of the human (or mouse) population. Unlike most genes, there are hundreds of different variants of each of the genes in the MHC, and we all inherit a random set of these from each of our parents. An individual's MHC genes are a very personal thing, and you are unlikely to share them with people outside your own family. If you select a random person, the chances are that you will share few, if any, MHC genes with them. This is why indiscriminate (in other words, not tested for MHC similarity) organ transplants do not work – because the recipient's immune system realizes that the donated organ's MHC is foreign and rejects it.

However, the transplant surgeon's problem is the romantic mouse's solution. Because the MHC is usually very different in unrelated mice, female mice can tell whether a male mouse is related to them simply by sniffing the MHC-related chemicals they exude. When they want to mate, they seek out MHC-different partners and in doing so they ensure that their pups will be vigorous little things, untainted by inbreeding. Then, once they are pregnant they seek out MHC-*similar* mice, presumably their own kin, with whom to nest.

So is there any evidence that humans select their mates on the basis of their MHC genes? For some time this was thought unlikely because humans were claimed to lack a vomeronasal organ – the tiny odour-detecting tunnel on the floor of the nasal cavity which detects most pheromones. Human embryos have a vomeronasal organ but we thought it withered as the rest of us grows. But new studies have shown that not only does the organ exist in adult humans, but it even responds to pheromones by activating many areas of the brain. Most strikingly, the brain's response patterns show reliable differences between men and women, suggesting that the organ may indeed be involved in reproduction, just as it is in most other mammals.

However, showing a link between smell and human adolescent mate choice has been more difficult, largely because it is unethical to shut human teenagers in an enclosed space and see who responds sexually to whose MHC smells. However, we do have a similar experimental set-up and it is called 'university': many early studies of human mate choice involved students sniffing clothes which other students had worn. When the subjects' MHC types were determined by the same molecular techniques used to tissue-type organ donors, a pattern similar to that seen in mice appeared. Teenage girls really do seem to find the smell of MHC-dissimilar boys more attractive. Furthermore, the boys whose smell they found most attractive often had similar MHC genes to their own current sexual partners.

These early findings are now being extended by studies which suggest that unconscious odour selection may play an alarmingly important role in human sexual behaviour. One study showed that women who are more MHC-similar to their partners are also more likely to have affairs. Another suggested that recent changes in the timing of puberty have been caused by new patterns of working. According to this theory, fathers now spend more of their time at home, whereas mothers spend less time there, and this has changed the odour milieu in which many teenagers now live – and this smelly change drives the brain to start puberty earlier. Whatever the validity of these claims, it is disconcerting to think that some of the most important choices of our lives might be made subconsciously on the basis of smell. Yet perhaps it is not surprising: many people report that the smell of their lover is one of the most enjoyable aspects of sex. Indeed I have occasionally studied the role of smell in romance by canvassing the opinion of my teenage students on this matter – by asking them whether they would rather date an otherwise attractive person who *looks* slightly unusual, or someone who *smells* slightly unusual. The revolted faces elicited by this question confirm that smell is central to sexual attraction.

So adolescence is a time to learn sexual preferences based on a heady cocktail of appearance, cognition and smell. Our understanding of human mate choice is still at an early stage, but already amazing abilities are coming to light – for example, it has been claimed that women can assess men's hormone concentrations, and even how much they like caring for children simply by looking at their faces. Also, some old assumptions seem to have been confirmed – recent studies suggest that teenagers do indeed use their different-sex parent as a model of what is attractive, provided that parent has been emotionally supportive to them in the past. All in all, adolescent lust is now emerging as a very complex thing indeed – a process of marshalling all the different ways of wanting and needing, and distilling them down into an individualized repertoire of desire.

Yet sex is more than wanting and needing, it is also about doing. At some stage in our lives we must learn the physical skills of sex, and often we work them out when we are teenagers. What little verbal advice we receive is no substitute for real 'hands on' trial and error. And because the human brain monopolizes sex in human beings, there is a great deal for young humans to learn. Many animals simply have to recognize the crude signs of receptivity in the opposite sex, hook up their genitals and the deed is done. Human sex is, by comparison, a mental minefield of teasing, feigned shyness, humour and reciprocation.

As we saw back in Part One, one of the unusual features of humans is that women do not show clear-cut episodes of 'heat' when they are receptive and fertile. This has led to the suggestion that women's fertility is deliberately hidden from not only themselves, but also any men who happen to be loitering nearby. Indeed, surveys of modern-day hunter-gatherers suggest that although they realize that sex causes pregnancy, they often have erroneous beliefs about when in the cycle women are most likely to conceive. Therefore fertility is concealed in humans, and presumably it is even hidden from the females of our chatty species because they would probably not be able to keep it a secret from their favourite men. Admittedly women's ability to discern facial, bodily and odour cues does change over the course of a cycle, as does their gait. Also, there is evidence that women are more likely to 'dress to impress' around the time of ovulation. However, the fact remains that human ovulation is quite a well-kept secret.

Presumably the cryptic nature of women's fertility evolved because procreation is only one of the functions of sex in our species. Maintaining the pair-bond is crucially important, and it is probably why humans have sex at all stages of the cycle. Yet hidden fertility makes instigating sex a potentially embarrassing prospect. Two young flirting humans know they can have sex any time, but they also know that one of them might not want it at all. Knowing when to make your move, either at the start of a relationship or later on, is a matter of subtle sexual etiquette. Suggesting sex carries the risk of rejection, and this can be extremely humiliating. Usually it is boys who suffer this rejection, and I wonder if this is why boys often have an element of resilient self-confidence built into them – so they can shrug off this repeated sexual rejection. However, girls do not always seem that well prepared to act as sexual moderators – studies suggest that many girls do not feel able to assert control over when and how they have sex, and this inability often persists into adulthood. For all teenagers, instigating and consenting to sex is especially daunting: they often already have problems with self-esteem, they are inexperienced in the social niceties of suggesting sexual liaisons, and they are frequently unconfident about their abilities to perform the act itself.

Copulation itself is also something that does not come naturally to teenagers – they have to learn how to have sex. This learning can go through several stages, often starting with frank incredulity that anyone would ever want to have sex with them at all, or fear that they will never learn to 'perform' adequately. Masturbation is often the next step, and of course the primate hand is well adapted for this (although I have searched, I have never found anyone who has actually suggested that the primate hand evolved expressly to promote masturbation). When a teenage couple first get together, various forms of sexual contact often precede coitus itself – in one study 30 per cent of teenage virgins reported experience of mutual masturbation, 10 per cent of oral sex and 1 per cent of anal sex. Then, once teenagers have started to have sex, there follows a process of learning by experimentation that lasts many years.

Although it is rarely reported, adolescence is probably the time when we suffer most sexual dysfunction. Teenage sexual dysfunction is important because it is perceived differently by its sufferers: unlike adults who become frustrated when their sexual expectations are not met, teenagers often panic because they do not know what their expectations should actually be. They also often assume the problem reflects a fundamental failing in themselves. However, the manifestations of teenage sexual dysfunction are reassuringly similar to those in adults: by far the commonest forms of sexual dysfunction in teenagers are premature ejaculation in boys and lack of orgasm in girls. Both of these problems are often psychological in origin and usually improve after frequent sexual intercourse within a stable, relaxed relationship – but teenagers often do not have that luxury. Thus teenage sexual problems can cause repeated relationship failure, which means there is never enough time with any one partner for them to abate. After a while, this cycle of perceived failure may make some teenagers avoid sex altogether – often well into adulthood. Finally, and unfortunately, there is also a sinister side to teenage sexual dysfunction – teenagers are four times more likely to be victims of sexual assault; a fifth of all arrests for sexual offences in the USA are of teenagers less than eighteen years old; a fifth of boys and a quarter of girls report having used some form of violence during a date.

But among all this negativity, we must remember that sex can be one of the most pleasurable and rewarding parts of life, and this is just as true for teenagers as it is for adults. Although the positive aspects of teenage sex cannot be measured or explained as easily as the negative aspects, they are still there, expressed every day in entwined young couples experiencing some of the most profound happiness they will ever feel. Teenagers grow up so fast in so many ways, and they are learning all the time. At an age when all aspects of their lives, past and future, are colliding in a central adolescent crossroads of pleasure and pain, their new-found ability to give and receive such fulfilment can for a little while rescue them from the teenage tumult, and take their breath away.

Conclusion
The Long Game

At the start of Part One, I made a list of some things that make humans an unusual species.

Locomotion	Brain	Reproduction	Life-plan
Bipedal walking	Increased cognitive abilities	Menstruation	Longevity
		No period of 'heat'	Paternal provision of food/resources
	Language	Sex for non-procreative reasons	Long post-reproduction survival
		Menopause	
			Prolonged period of dependence by offspring

In the rest of the book we saw how teenagers mature physically, mentally, emotionally and sexually, and on the way we saw that most of the distinctive features of our species have their roots in the teenage years. Of course it is not surprising that our reproductive idiosyncrasies should appear around puberty – instead it is the teenage sculpting of our all-important brain that impresses. Put together, it is the unusually protracted and profound nature of the physical *and* cerebral change that gives human adolescence its unique flavour.

This is why the teenager is not just a modern cultural invention. It is a biological phenomenon unique in the animal kingdom. Human adolescence is a constellation of carefully timed events – the coordinated sequence of pubertal change, often staggered between the sexes so that girls develop faster; the catalogue of phased cerebral development which draws the human mind into new realms of analysis, abstraction and creativity; the flurry of social change forcing a reanalysis of the self, detachment from parents and affiliation with friends; the excitement of romantic and sexual experimentation. The central feature of human adolescence is that all these phenomena occur contemporaneously over a remarkably long period of time: a decade or more. The only thing that has changed much recently is that puberty now occurs earlier while at the same time teenagers are told to avoid pregnancy. If anything, this tension between hastening fertility and delaying conception only enhances the already unique flux of adolescence. In most other ways this part of the human life-plan has stayed the same. All these things are what human teenagers evolved to do.

Not satisfied with being unique, teenagers are also the most important part of human life. Evolution occurs because successful animals survive and breed. Because of this, the times in our lives when we acquire skills and breed are the most crucial – they are the times when natural selection acts on us. And for humans, that time is when we are teenagers – or at least it used to be, before we dissuaded teenagers from having babies. So in the past, natural selection acted on the human race mainly according to the success or failure of teenagers. We are not the product of evolving adults, but evolving teenagers.

There is good reason to think that the human life-plan is built around the centrepiece of adolescence. For example, evolutionary theory makes some intriguing predictions about species in which one sex benefits most from making additional investment in breeding early in life. The nature of reproduction in most mammals means that it is males who have the most to gain or lose from reproductive success or failure, and the same is probably true of humans. However, because they dedicate so many of their adolescent resources to finding and impressing sexual partners when young, evolutionary theory predicts that boys will suffer a later evolutionary payoff – they should die younger. Of course, that is exactly what men do: they gamble young and pick up the tab later. Adolescence dictates the whole of life.

A dramatic example of the central importance of adolescence is how it has created human longevity. In the last few million years humans have become the primate *de luxe*. Our cognitive and social abilities have become increasingly complex and ever more dominant over the rest of our biology. Because of this, humans take an extremely long time to develop. A single young human requires an incredibly long period of parental investment. So once a human has produced some children in their youth, they are then committed to a further two decades of nurturing those children. Even after that, the nature of human society means we can continue to contribute, by supporting the development of our grandchildren. The needs of teenagers probably even explain why women undergo menopause: to redirect their energies away from producing more babies to caring for the children they already have.

Adolescence is the reason why we live so long, long, long. Human longevity has evolved because we need to bring up our intensively supported, slowly developing offspring. This claim is supported by the fact that a similar thing seems to have happened during the evolution of a few other intelligent, long-lived, slow-growing mammalian species: elephants and some whales (intriguingly, certain whales are the only non-human species thought to undergo something akin to menopause). One can almost imagine this trend spiralling out of control during human evolution – teenagers honing their brains to be yet more intelligent, but having to live ever longer to transmit their huge accumulated wisdom to their own offspring. Human life is a long-term, high-investment, knowledge economy, and it is teenagers who made it that way. This is why adolescence is not an irritating transitional phase, but is literally pivotal in the human life-plan: it is the fulcrum about which the rest of our life turns.

Once we accept that adolescents are the most important people, it is tempting to suggest that the rest of us are an irrelevance. We know that natural selection acts less and less as we pass further beyond reproductive age, but does this mean we have no function beyond twenty-five? Should we go as far as to claim that it is teenagers who are living and the rest of us are just dying? Is a life no more than three acts in which we grow, breed and are spent? I would refute that suggestion by claiming that it is actually teenagers who save adults from meaningless redundancy. After all, adults have a very important function, and that is to support children and teenagers – quite simply, this is what adults are *for*. If teenagers did not need support we could probably die at thirty. So natural selection does act on adults a little bit, but only because they have to support teenagers – it is teenagers who give adults their reason for existence.

Even in the modern world, when the human race may not actually be evolving much any more, still the teenagers hold sway. I wonder how much of our irritation with teenagers comes from the undeniable fact that we know they will one day replace us. Soon they will be the adults who set the codes and ethics and laws, and we will be pushed aside. Their day will come and ours will be gone. Not only that, but teenagers also mock the rest of us by being the most creative humans in existence. So many of the greatest sparks of inspiration, invention and creation find their origins in the capricious teenage mind; so many geniuses cite their teenage years as the source of their drive. This is why teenagers are always destined to change the world into something that becomes increasingly alien to their elders.

So this is why the teenage years are the difficult years: it is because they are the *important* years. Teenagers deserve adults' support in their uniquely human mental quest because they are simply more important than everyone else. Every different aspect of our lives collides when we are teenagers, but this is not because childhood and adulthood just happen to exhibit an unfortunate tendency to overlap. Teenage life is full of everything humans do because teenage life is what matters to the human race. Maybe this is why being a teenager is such an intense experience.

Being a teenager is not an embarrassing side-effect of being human. Instead, teenagers are what make us human. Adolescence is the key: all human life is here.

Acknowledgements

I would like to thank Aitken Alexander Associates for permission to reprint the extract from The Magus by John Fowles in the epigraph to Part Four.

It was a great help to have late drafts of this book picked over by the combined critical power of my friends Angie Tavernor and Jill de Laat. I would like to thank Dr Barry Bogin, who sent me some articles that pushed me in some interesting directions. I would also like to thank my agent Peter Tallack and my editor Laura Barber for their support throughout this project. And thank you to everyone else who has helped me along the way: my family, my friends, my colleagues, my distorted teenage memories, Steve Reich, and Johann Sebastian Bach.

About the author

Evolved as a teenager on the savannahs of 1980s Essex, David Bainbridge is the Clinical Veterinary Anatomist at Cambridge University, and a fellow of St Catharine's College. He trained as a veterinary surgeon and has carried out research at the Institute of Zoology at Regent's Park, the Royal Veterinary College, and Cornell, Sydney and Oxford

Universities. His previous popular science books cover topics including pregnancy (*Making Babies*, 2001, published in the UK as *A Visitor Within*, 2000), genes and sexuality (*The X in Sex*, 2003), and the brain (*Beyond the Zonules of Zinn*, 2008). He lives in Suffolk with his wife and their children, all three of whom are edging inexorably towards adolescence.

Bibliography

Further information available at www.davidbainbridge.org

Akil, M., Pierri, J.N., Whitehead, R.E., Edgar, C.L., Mohila, C., Sampson, A.R. and Lewis, D.A. (1999). Lamina-specific alterations in the dopamine innervation of the prefrontal cortex in schizophrenic subjects. *American Journal of Psychiatry* 156, 1580–9.

Alloy, L.B. and Abramson, L.Y. (2007). The adolescent surge in depression and emergence of gender differences. In (Romer, D. and Walker, E.F. eds.) *Adolescent Psychopathology and the Developing Brain.* Oxford: Oxford University Press.

Anhalt, K. and Morris, T.L. (1998). Developmental and adjustment issues of gay, lesbian, and bisexual adolescents: a review of the empirical literature. *Clinical Child and Family Psychology Review* 1, 215–30.

Apter, D. (2003). The role of leptin in female adolescence. *Annals of the New York Academy of Science* 997, 64–76.

Ara, K., Hama, M., Akiba, S., Koike, K., Okisaka, K., Hagura, T., Kamiya, T. and Tomita, F. (2006). Foot odor due to microbial metabolism and its control. *Canadian*

Journal of Microbiology 52, 357–64.

Armelagos, G.J., Brown, P.J. and Turner, B. (2005). Evolutionary, historical and political economic perspectives on health and disease. *Social Science & Medicine* 61, 755–65.

Aron, A., Fisher, H., Mashek, D.J., Strong, G., Li, H. and Brown, L.L. (2005). Reward, motivation, and emotion systems associated with early-stage intense romantic love. *Journal of Neurophysiology* 94, 327–37.

Badanich, K.A., Adler, K.J. and Kirstein, C.L. (2006). Adolescents differ from adults in cocaine conditioned place preference and cocaine-induced dopamine in the nucleus accumbens septi. *European Journal of Pharmacology* 21, 95–106.

Bainbridge, D.R.J. (2000). *A Visitor Within: The Science of Pregnancy.* London: Weidenfeld and Nicolson.

Bainbridge, D.R.J. (2003). *The X in Sex: How the X Chromosome Controls our Lives.* Cambridge, MA: Harvard University Press.

Bainbridge, D.R.J. (2008). *Beyond the Zonules of Zinn: A Fantastic Journey Through Your Brain.* Cambridge, MA: Harvard University Press.

Baron-Cohen, S. (2003), *The Essential Difference: Men, women and the extreme male brain.* London: Allen Lane.

Barth, J.H. and Clark, S. (2003). Acne and hirsuties in teenagers. *Best Practice and Research Clinical Obstetrics and Gynaecology* 17, 131–48.

Ben-Dor, D.H., Laufer, N., Apter, A., Frisch, A. and Weizman, A. (2002). Heritability, genetics and association findings in anorexia nervosa. *Israel Journal of Psychiatry and Related Sciences* 39, 262–70.

Bereczkei, T., Gyuris, P. and Weisfeld, G.E. (2004). Sexual

imprinting in human mate choice. *Proceedings of the Royal Society: Biological Sciences* 271, 1129–34.

Beuten, J., Ma, J.Z., Payne, T.J., Dupont, R.T., Crews, K.M., Somes, G., Williams, N.J., Elston, R.C. and Li, M.D. (2005). Single- and multilocus allelic variants within the GABA(B) receptor subunit 2 (GABAB2) gene are significantly associated with nicotine dependence. *American Journal of Human Genetics* 76, 859–64.

Bimonte, H.A., Fitch, R.H. and Denenberg, V.H. (2000). Neonatal estrogen blockade prevents normal callosal responsiveness to estradiol in adulthood. *Brain Research, Developmental Brain Research* 122, 149–55.

Berenbaum, S.A. (1999). Effects of early androgens on sex-typed activities and interests in adolescents with congenital adrenal hyperplasia. *Hormones and Behaviour* 35, 102–10.

Blakemore, S.J. and Choudhury, S.A. (2006). Development of the adolescent brain: implications for executive function and social cognition. *Journal of Child Psychology and Psychiatry* 47, 296–312.

Bloom, D.F. (2004). Is acne really a disease?: a theory of acne as an evolutionarily significant, high-order psychoneuroimmune interaction timed to cortical development with a crucial role in mate choice. *Medical Hypotheses* 62, 462–9.

Bogin, B. (1999). Evolutionary perspective on human growth. *Annual Review of Anthropology* 28, 109–53.

Bogin, B. (2003). The human pattern of growth and development in palaeontological perspective. In Thompson, J.L., Krovitz, G.E. and Nelson, A.J. eds. *Patterns of Growth and Development in the Genus Homo.* Cambridge: Cambridge University Press.

Bogin, B. (2006). Language and life history: a new perspective on the development and evolution of human language. *Behavioural and Brain Sciences* 29, 259–325.

Boots, M. and Knell, R.J. (2002). The evolution of risky behaviour in the presence of a sexually transmitted disease. *Proceedings of the Royal Society: Biological Sciences* 269, 585–9.

Bourgeois, J-P., Goldman-Rakic, P.S. and Rakic, P. (1994). Synaptogenesis in the pre-frontal cortex of rhesus monkeys. *Cerebral Cortex* 4, 78–96.

Brand, S., Luethi, M., von Planta, A., Hatzinger, M. and Holsboer-Trachsler, E. (2007). Romantic love, hypomania, and sleep pattern in adolescents. *Journal of Adolescent Health* 41, 69–76.

Brody, S. (1945). *Bioenergetics and growth.* New York City: Reinhold.

Burger, J. and Gochfeld, M. (1985). A hypothesis on the role of pheromones on age of menarche. *Medical Hypotheses* 17, 39–46.

Burns, J.K. (2006). Psychosis: a costly by-product of social brain evolution in *Homo sapiens. Progress in Neuropsychopharmacology and Biological Psychiatry* 30, 797–814.

Buss, D.M (1999), *Evolutionary Psychology: The New Science of the Mind.* Needham Heights: Allyn & Bacon.

Byrd-Bredbenner, C., Murray, J. and Schlussel, Y.R. (2005). Temporal changes in anthropometric measurements of idealized females and young women in general. *Women and Health* 41, 13–30.

Caldwell, J.C., Caldwell, P., Caldwell, B.K. and Pieris, I. (1998). The construction of adolescence in a changing world: implications for sexuality, reproduction, and marriage. *Studies in Family Planning* 29, 137–53.

Campbell, B. (2006). Adrenarche and the evolution of human life history. *American Journal of Human Biology*, 18, 569–89.

Campbell, B.C. and Udry, J.R. (1994). Implications of hormonal influences on sexual behavior for demographic models of reproduction. *Annals of the New York Academy of Science* 709, 117–27.

Cardinal, R.N. and Everitt, B.J. (2004). Neural and psychological mechanisms underlying appetitive learning: links to drug addiction. *Current Opinion in Neurobiology* 14, 156–62.

Carpenter-Hyland, E.P. and Chandler, L.J. (2007). Adaptive plasticity of NMDA receptors and dendritic spines: implications for enhanced vulnerability of the adolescent brain to alcohol addiction. *Pharmacology Biochemistry and Behavior* 86, 200–8.

Carskadon, M.A., Acebo, C. and Jenni, O.G. (2004). Regulation of adolescent sleep: implications for behavior. *Annals of the New York Academy of Science* 1021, 276–91.

Carter, C.S., DeVries, A.C., Taymans, S.E., Roberts, R.L., Williams, J.R. and Getz, L.L. (1997). Peptides, steroids, and pair bonding. *Annals of the New York Academy of Sciences* 807, 260–72.

Caspari, R., Lee, S.H. (2006). Is human longevity a consequence of cultural change or modern biology? *American Journal of Physical Anthropology* 129, 512–17.

Caspi, A., Sugden, K., Moffitt, T.E., Taylor, A., Craig, I.W., Harrington, H., McClay, J., Mill, J., Martin, J., Braithwaite, A. and Poulton, R. (2003). Influence of life stress on depression: moderation by a polymorphism in the 5-HTT gene. *Science* 301, 386–9.

Catlow, B.J. and Kirstein, C.L. (2007). Cocaine during

adolescence enhances dopamine in response to a natural reinforcer. *Neurotoxicology and Teratology* 29, 59–65.

Chugani, H.T., Phelps, M.E. and Mazziotta, J.C. (1987). Positron emission tomography study of human brain functional development. *Annals of Neurology* 22, 487–97.

Chemes, H.E. (2001). Infancy is not a quiescent period of testicular development. *International Journal of Andrology* 24, 2–7.

Clarkson, J. and Herbison, A.E. (2006). Development of GABA and glutamate signalling at the GnRH neuron in relation to puberty. *Molecular and Cellular Endocrinology* 254-255, 32–8.

Coall, D.A. and Chisholm, J.S. (2003). Evolutionary perspectives on pregnancy: maternal age at menarche and infant birth weight. *Social Science & Medicine* 57, 1771–81.

Cornwell, R.E., Law Smith, M.J., Boothroyd, L.G., Moore, F.R., Davis, H.P., Stirrat, M., Tiddeman, B. and Perrett, D.I. (2006). *Philosophical Transactions of the Royal Society of London B Biological Sciences* 361, 2143–54.

Cotton, S., Mills, L., Succop, P.A., Biro, F.M. and Rosenthal, S.L. (2004). Adolescent girls perceptions of the timing of their sexual initiation: 'too young' or 'just right'? *Journal of Adolescent Health* 34, 453–8.

Cox, G. (1995). De virginibus puerisque: the function of the human foreskin considered from an evolutionary perspective. *Medical Hypotheses* 45, 617–21.

Cunningham, M.G., Bhattacharyya, S. and Benes, F.M. (2002). Amygdalo-cortical sprouting continues into early adulthood: implications for the development of normal and abnormal function during adolescence. *Journal of Comparative Neurology* 453, 116–30.

Cyranowski, J.M., Frank, E., Young, E. and Shear, M.K.

(2000). Adolescent onset of the gender difference in lifetime rates of major depression: a theoretical model. *Archives of General Psychiatry* 57, 21–7.

Dalley, J.W., Fryer, T.D., Brichard, L., Robinson, E.S., Theobald, D.E., Lääne, K., Peña, Y., Murphy, E.R., Shah, Y., Probst, K., Abakumova, I., Aigbirhio, F.I., Richards, H.K., Hong, Y., Baron, J.C., Everitt, B.J. and Robbins, T.W. (2007). Nucleus accumbens D2/3 receptors predict trait impulsivity and cocaine reinforcement. *Science* 317, 1033–5.

Darroch, J.E. (2001). Adolescent pregnancy trends and demographics. *Current Women's Health Reports* 1, 102–10.

Davey, C.G., Yücel, M. and Allen, N.B. (2008). The emergence of depression in adolescence: Development of the prefrontal cortex and the representation of reward. *Neuroscience & Biobehavioral Reviews* 32, 1–19.

Debiec, J. (2007). From affiliative behaviors to romantic feelings: a role of nanopeptides. *FEBS Lett* 581, 2580–6.

Dean, C., Leakey, M.G., Reid, D., Schrenk, F., Schwartz, G.T., Stringer, C. and Walker, A. (2001). Growth processes in teeth distinguish *Homo erectus* and earlier hominids. *Nature* 414, 628–31.

Degenhardt, L. and Hall, W.A. (2006). Is cannabis use a contributory cause of psychosis? *Canadian Journal of Psychiatry* 51, 556–65.

Dehaene, S., Molko, N., Cohen, L. and Wilson, A.J. (2004). Arithmetic and the brain. *Current Opinion in Neurobiology* 14, 218–24.

Di Chiaraa, G. and Bassareoa, V. (2007). Reward system and addiction: what dopamine does and doesn't do. *Current Opinion in Pharmacology* 7, 69–76.

Doremus, T.L., Brunell, S.C., Rajendran, P. and Spear, L.P.

(2005). Factors influencing elevated ethanol consumption in adolescent relative to adult rats. *Alcoholism: Clinical and Experimental Research* 29, 1796–1808.

Dorus, S., Vallender, E.J., Evans, P.D., Anderson, J.R., Gilbert, S.L., Mahowald, M., Wyckoff, G.J., Malcom, C.M. and Lahn, B.T. (2004). Accelerated evolution of nervous system genes in the origin of *Homo sapiens*. *Cell* 119, 1027–40.

Dunbar, R.I. and Shultz, S. (2007). Evolution in the social brain. *Science* 317, 1344–7.

Dunkel, L. (2006). Use of aromatase inhibitors to increase final height. *Molecular and Cellular Endocrinology* 254-255, 207–16.

Ebling, F.J. (1987). The biology of hair. *Dermatology Clinics* 5, 467–81.

Einarsson, J.I., Sangi-Haghpeykar, H. and Gardner, M.O. (2003). Sperm exposure and development of preeclampsia. *Americal Journal of Obstetrics and Gynaecology* 188, 1241–3.

Eisenberg, N., Zhou, Q., Spinrad, T.L., Valiente, C., Fabes, R.A. and Liew, J. (2005). Relations among positive parenting, children's effortful control, and externalizing problems: a three-wave longitudinal study. *Child Development* 76, 1055–71.

Elliot, A.J. and Thrash, T.M. (2004). The intergenerational transmission of fear of failure. *Personality and Social Psychology Bulletin* 30, 957–71.

Emanuele, E., Politi, P., Bianchi, M., Minoretti, P., Bertona, M. and Geroldi, D. (2006). Raised plasma nerve growth factor levels associated with early-stage romantic love. *Psychoneuroendocrinology* 31, 288–94.

Enoch, M.A. (2006). Genetic and environmental influences on the development of alcoholism: resilience vs. risk.

Annals of the New York Academy of Science 1094, 193–301.

Esenyel, M., Walsh, K., Walden, J.G. and Gitter A. (2003). Kinetics of high-heeled gait. *Journal of the American Podiatric Medical Association* 93, 27–32.

Essex, M.J., Klein, M.H., Cho E. and Kalin, N.H. (2002). Maternal stress beginning in infancy may sensitize children to later stress exposure: effects on cortisol and behavior. *Biol Psychiatry* 52(8), 15 Oct 2002, 776–84.

Fales, C.L., Barch, D.M., Rundle, M.M., Mintun, M.A., Snyder, A.Z., Cohen, J.D., Mathews, J. and Sheline, Y.I. (2008). Altered Emotional Interference Processing in Affective and Cognitive-Control Brain Circuitry in Major Depression. *Biological Psychiatry*, 63, 377–84.

Feldmann, J., Middleman, A.B. (2002). Adolescent sexuality and sexual behavior. *Current Opinion in Obstetrics & Gynecology* 14, 489–93.

Fernandez-Fernandez, R., Martini, A.C., Navarro, V.M., Castellano, J.M., Dieguez, C., Aguilar, E., Pinilla, L. and Tena-Sempere, M. (2006). Novel signals for the integration of energy balance and reproduction. *Molecular and Cellular Endocrinology* 254-255, 127–32.

Fessler, D.M. (2002). Dimorphic foraging behaviors and the evolution of hominid hunting. *Rivista di Biologia* 95, 429–53.

Field, T. (2002). Violence and touch deprivation in adolescents. *Adolescence* 37, 735–49.

Finkelstein, J.W., Susman, E.J., Chinchilli, V.M., Kunselman, S.J., D'Arcangelo, M.R., Schwab, J., Demers, L.M., Liben, L.S., Lookingbill, G. and Kulin, H.E. (1997). Estrogen or testosterone increases self-reported aggressive behaviors in hypogonadal adolescents. *Journal of*

Clinical Endocrinology and Metabolism 82, 2433–8.

Fisher, H.E., Aron, A. and Brown, L.L. (2006). Romantic love: a mammalian brain system for mate choice. *Philosophical Transactions of the Royal Society of London B Biological Sciences* 361, 2173–86.

Fisher, H.E., Aron, A. and Brown, L.L. (2005). Romantic love: an fMRI study of a neural mechanism for mate choice. *Comparative Neurology* 493, 58–62.

Fisher, S.E. and Marcus, G.F. (2006). The eloquent ape: genes, brains and the evolution of language. *Nature Reviews, Genetics* 7, 9–20.

Flensmark, J. (2004). Is there an association between the use of heeled footwear and schizophrenia. *Medical Hypotheses* 63, 740–7.

Floresco, S.B. and Magyar, O. (2006). Mesocortical dopamine modulation of executive functions: beyond working memory. *Psychopharmacology* 188, 567–85.

Florian, V., Mikulincer, M. and Hirschberger, G. (2002). The anxiety-buffering function of close relationships: evidence that relationship commitment acts as a terror management mechanism. *Journal of Personality and Social Psychology* 32, 527–42.

Foster, D.L, Jackson, L.M. and Padmanabhan, V. (2006). Programming of GnRH feedback controls timing puberty and adult reproductive function. *Molecular and Cellular Endocrinology* 254-255, 109–19.

Fraley, R.C., Brumbaugh, C.C. and Marks, M.J. (2005). The evolution and function of adult attachment: a comparative and phylogenetic analysis. *Journal of Personality and Social Psychology* 89, 731–46.

Frisch, R.E. (2002), *Female Fertility and the Body Fat Connection*. Chicago: University of Chicago Press.

Frith, U. (2001). Mind blindness and the brain in autism. *Neuron* 32, 969–79.

Gamba, M. and Pralong, F.P. (2006). Control of GnRH neuronal activity by metabolic factors: the role of leptin and insulin. *Molecular and Cellular Endocrinology* 254-255, 133–9.

Garcia-Falgueras, A., Junque, C., Giménez, M., Caldú, X., Segovia, S. and Guillamon, A. (2006). Sex differences in the human olfactory system. *Brain Research* 1116, 103–11.

Garver-Apgar, C.E., Gangestad, S.W., Thornhill, R., Miller, R.D. and Olp, J.J. (2006). Major histocompatibility complex alleles, sexual responsivity, and unfaithfulness in romantic couples. *Psychological Science* 17, 830–5.

Gatward, N. (2007). Anorexia nervosa: an evolutionary puzzle. *European Eating Disorders Review* 15, 1–12.

Gavrilov, L.A., Gavrilova, N.S. (2002). Evolutionary Theories of Aging and Longevity. *The Scientific World* 2, 339–56.

Geller, D.A. (2006). Obsessive-compulsive and spectrum disorders in children and adolescents. *Psychiatric Clinics of North America* 29, 353–70.

Giedd, J.N., Castellanos, F.X., Rajapakse, J.C., Vaituzis, A.C., Rapoport, J.L. (1997). Sexual dimorphism of the developing human brain. *Progress in Neuropsychopharmacology and Biological Psychiatry* 21, 1185–1201.

Giedd, J.N., Clasen, L.S., Lenroot, R., Greenstein, D., Wallace, G.L., Ordaz, S., Molloy, E.A., Blumenthal, J.D., Tossell, J.W., Stayer, C., Samango-Sprouse, C.A., Shen, D., Davatzikos, C., Merke, D. and Chrousos, G.P. (2006). Puberty-related influences on brain development. *Molecular and Cellular Endocrinology* 254-255, 154–62.

Gilbert, P., Allan, S., Brough, S., Melley, S. and Miles, J.N. (2002). Relationship of anhedonia and anxiety to social rank, defeat and entrapment. *Journal of Affective Disorders* 71, 141–51.

Gluckman, P.D. and Hanson, M.A. (2006). Changing times: the evolution of puberty. *Molecular and Cellular Endocrinology* 254-255, 26–31.

Gluckman, P.D. and Hanson, M.A. (2006). Evolution, development and timing of puberty. *Trends in Endocrinology and Metabolism* 17, 7–12.

Gogtay, N., Giedd, J.N., Lusk, L., Hayashi, K.M., Greenstein, D., Vaituzis, A.C., Nugent, T.F., Herman, D.H., Clasen, L.S., Toga, A.W., Rapoport, J.L. and Thompson, P.M. (2004). Dynamic mapping of human cortical development during childhood through early adulthood. *Proceedings of the National Academy of Sciences USA* 101, 8174–9.

Goldberg, D. (1994). A bio-social model for common mental disorders. *Acta Psychiatrica Scandinavica supplement* 385, 66–70.

Gonzalez, F.J. and Nebert, D.W. (1990). Evolution of the P450 gene superfamily: animal-plant 'warfare', molecular drive and human genetic differences in drug oxidation *Trends in Genetics* 6, 182–6.

Grant, V.W. (1976), *Falling in Love: the psychology of the romantic emotion.* New York: Springer.

Green, A.R., Mechan, A.O., Elliott, J.M., O'Shea, E. and Colado, M.I. (2003). The pharmacology and clinical pharmacology of 3,4-methylenedioxymethamphetamine (MDMA, 'ecstasy'). *Pharmacological Reviews* 55, 463–508.

Guindalini, C. and others (2006). A dopamine transporter gene functional variant associated with cocaine abuse in a Brazilian sample. *Proceedings of the National Academy of Sciences USA* 103, 4552–7.

Gur, R.C. (2005). Brain maturation and its relevance to

understanding criminal culpability of juveniles. *Current Psychiatry Reports* 7, 292–6.

Gurven, M., Kaplan, H. and Gutierrez, M.A. (2006). How long does it take to become a proficient hunter? Implications for the evolution of extended development and long life span. *Journal of Human Evolution* 51, 454–70.

Hall, W.D. (2006). Cannabis use and the mental health of young people. *Australian and New Zealand Journal of Psychiatry* 40, 105–13.

Hall, W.D. and Lynskey, M. (2005). Is cannabis a gateway drug? Testing hypotheses about the relationship between cannabis use and the use of other illicit drugs. *Drug and Alcohol Review* 24, 39–48.

Halpern, C.T., Udry, J.R., Campbell, B. and Suchindran, C.A. (1993). Testosterone and pubertal development as predictors of sexual activity: a panel analysis of adolescent males. *Psychosomatic Medicine* 55, 436–47.

Halpern, C.T., Joyner, K., Udry, J.R. and Suchindran, C. (2000). Smart teens don't have sex (or kiss much either). *Journal of Adolescent Health* 26, 213–25.

Halpern, C.T., Udry, J.R. and Suchindran, C. (1997). Testosterone predicts initiation of coitus in adolescent females. *Psychosomatic Medicine* 59, 161–171.

Harrop, C. and Trower, P. (2001). Why does schizophrenia develop at late adolescence?. *Clinical Psychology Review* 21, 241–65.

Higuchi, S., Matsushita, S., Masaki, T., Yokoyama, A., Kimura, M., Suzuki, G. and Mochizuki, H. (2004). Influence of genetic variations of ethanol-metabolizing enzymes on phenotypes of alcohol-related disorders. *Annals of the New York Academy of Science* 1025, 472–80.

Hill, R.S. and Walsh, C.A. (2005). Molecular insights into

human brain evolution. *Nature* 437, 64–7.

Hofman, M.A., Fliers, E., Goudsmit, E. and Swaab, D.F. (1988). Morphometric analysis of the suprachiasmatic and paraventricular nuclei in the human brain: sex differences and age-dependent changes. *Journal of Anatomy* 160, 127–43.

Holmes, K.K., Bell, T.A. and Berger, R.E. (1984). Epidemiology of sexually transmitted diseases. *Urologic Clinics of North America* 11, 3–13.

Horn, M., Collingro, A., Schmitz-Esser, S., Beier, C.L., Purkhold, U., Fartmann, B., Brandt, P., Nyakatura, G.J., Droege, M., Frishman, D., Rattei, T., Mewes, H.W. and Wagner, M. (2004). Illuminating the evolutionary history of chlamydiae. *Science* 304, 728–30.

Huffman, M.A. (2003). Animal self-medication and ethnomedicine: exploration and exploitation of the medicinal properties of plants. *Proceedings of the Nutrition Society* 62, 371–81.

Hughes, I.A. and Kumana, M.A. (2006). A wider perspective on puberty. *Molecular and Cellular Endocrinology* 254-255, 1–7.

Hull, E.M., Muschamp, J.W. and Sato, S. (2004). Dopamine and serotonin: influences on male sexual behavior. *Physiology and Behavior* 83, 291–307.

Huttenlocher, P.R. and Dabholkar, A.S. (1997). Regional differences in synaptogenesis in human cerebral cortex. *Journal of Comparative Neurology* 387, 167–78.

Hyde, J.S., Fennema, E. and Lamon, S.J. (1990). Gender differences in mathematics performance: a meta-analysis. *Psychological Bulletin* 107, 139–55.

Insel, T.R. (2003). Is social attachment an addictive disorder? *Physiology & Behavior* 79, 351–7.

Insel, T.R. and Hulihan, T.J. (1995). A gender-specific mechanism for pair bonding: oxytocin and partner preference formation in monogamous voles. *Behavioral Neuroscience* 109, 782–9.

Irwin, C.E. and Millstein, S.G. (1992). Correlates and predictors of risk-taking behavior during adolescence. In Lipsitt, L.P. and Mitnick, L.L. eds. *Self-regulatory behavior and risk-taking: causes and consequences.* Norwood, NJ: Ablex.

Isbell, L.A. (2006). Snakes as agents of evolutionary change in primate brains. *Journal of Human Evolution* 51, 1–35.

Izenwasser, S. (2005). Differential effects of psychoactive drugs in adolescents and adults. *Critical Reviews in Neurobiology* 17, 51–67.

James, A.C., James, S., Smith, D.M. and Javaloyes, A. (2004). Cerebellar, prefrontal cortex, and thalamic volumes over two time points in adolescent-onset schizophrenia. *American Journal of Psychiatry* 161, 1023–9.

Johansson, T. and Ritzén, E.M. (2005). Very long-term follow-up of girls with early and late menarche. *Endocrine Development* 8, 126–36.

Kanazawa, S. A. (2007). Beautiful parents have more daughters: a further implication of the generalized Trivers-Willard hypothesis (gTWH). *Journal of Theoretical Biology* 244, 133–40.

Kaplan, H., Hill, K., Lancaster, J. and Hurtado, A.M. (2000). A theory of human life history evolution. *Evolutionary Anthropology* 9, 156–85.

Keller, M.C. and Miller, G. (2006). Resolving the paradox of common, harmful, heritable mental disorders: which evolutionary genetic models work best? *Behavioral and Brain Sciences* 29, 385–404.

Keller, M.C. and Nesse, R.M. (2006). The evolutionary significance of depressive symptoms: different adverse situations lead to different depressive symptom patterns. *Personality and Social Psychology* 91, 316–30.

Kelley, B.M. and Rowan, J.D. (2004). Long-term, low-level adolescent nicotine exposure produces dose-dependent changes in cocaine sensitivity and reward in adult mice. *International Journal of Developmental Neuroscience* 22, 339–48.

Keshavan, M.S. and Hogarty, G.E. (1999). Brain maturational processes and delayed onset in schizophrenia. *Developmental Psychopathology* 11, 525–43.

Kessler, R.C., Amminger, G.P., Aguilar-Gaxiola, S., Alonso, J., Lee, S. and Ustün, T.B. (2007). Age of onset of mental disorders: a review of recent literature. *Current Opinion in Psychiatry* 20, 359–64.

Kessler, R.C., Berglund, P., Demler, O., Jin, R., Merikangas, K.R. and Walters, E.E. (2005). Lifetime prevalence and age-of-onset distributions of DSM-IV disorders in the National Comorbidity Survey Replication. *Archives of General Psychiatry* 62, 593–602.

Keverne, E.B. (2004). Understanding well-being in the evolutionary context of brain development. *Philosophical Transactions of the Royal Society of London B Biological Sciences* 359, 1349–58.

Kiess, W., Meidert, A., Dressendörfer, R.A., Schriever, K., Kessler, U., König, A., Schwarz, H.P. and Strasburger, C.J. (1995). Salivary cortisol levels throughout childhood and adolescence: relation with age, pubertal stage, and weight. *Pediatric Research* 37, 502–6.

Killgore, W.D., Oki, M. and Yurgelun-Todd, D.A. (2001). Sex-specific developmental changes in amygdala responses to affective faces. *Neuroreport* 12, 427–33.

Knell, R.J. (2004). Syphilis in renaissance Europe: rapid evolution of an introduced sexually transmitted disease? *Proceedings of the Royal Society: Biological Sciences* 271, supplement 4, s174–6.

Koelman, C.A., Coumans, A.B., Nijman, H.W., Doxiadis, I.I., Dekker, G.A. and Claas, F.H. (2000). Correlation between oral sex and a low incidence of preeclampsia: a role for soluble HLA in seminal fluid? *Journal of Reproductive Immunology* 46, 155–66.

Korte, S.M., Koolhaas, J.M., Wingfield, J.C. and McEwen, B.S. (2005). The Darwinian concept of stress: benefits of allostasis and costs of allostatic load and the trade-offs in health and disease. *Neuroscience & Biobehavioral Reviews* 29, 3–38.

Kreek, M.J., Nielsen, D.A., Butelman, E.R. and LaForge, K.S. (2005). Genetic influences on impulsivity, risk taking, stress responsivity and vulnerability to drug abuse and addiction. *Nature Neuroscience* 8, 1450–7.

Kroger, J. (1989), *Identity in Adolescence: The Balance Between Self and Other*. London: Routledge.

Kudwa, A.E., Bodo, C., Gustafsson, J.A. and Rissman, E.F. (2005). A previously uncharacterized role for estrogen receptor beta: defeminization of male brain and behavior. *Proceedings of the National Academy of Sciences USA* 102, 4608–12.

Lai, S., Lai, H., Page, J.B. and McCoy, C.B. (2000). The association between cigarette smoking and drug abuse in the United States. *Journal of Addictive Diseases* 19, 11–24.

Lane, R.C., Hull, J.W. and Foehrenbach, L.M. (1991). The addiction to negativity. *Psychoanalytical Review* 78, 391–410.

Lang, U.E., Sander, T., Lohoff, F.W., Hellweg, R., Bajbouj, M., Winterer, G. and Gallinat, J. (2007). Association of the met66 allele of brain-derived neurotrophic factor (BDNF) with smoking. *Psychopharmacology* 190, 433–9.

Larke, A. and Crews, D.E. (2006). Parental investment, late reproduction and increased reserve capacity are associated with longevity in humans. *Journal of Physical Anthropology* 25, 119–31.

Larsen, C.S. (2000). *Skeletons in Our Closet: Revealing the Past Through Bioarchaeology.* Princeton, NJ: Princeton University Press.

LaVelle, R.G. (1995). Natural selection and developmental sexual variation in the human pelvis. *American Journal of Physical Anthropology* 98, 59–72.

LeBlanc, S.A. and Barnes, E. (1974). On the adaptive significance of the female breast. *The American Naturalist* 108, 577–8.

Leigh, S.R. (1996). Evolution of human growth spurts. *American Journal of Physical Anthropology* 101, 455–74.

Leigh, S.R. (2005). Brain growth, life history and cognition in primate and human evolution. *American Journal of Perinatology* 62, 139–64.

Leigh, S.R. and Park, P.B. (1998). Evolution of human growth prolongation. *American Journal of Physical Anthropology* 107, 331–50.

Levine, S.B. (2005). What is love anyway? *Journal of Sex & Marital Therapy* 31, 143–51.

Lewis, D.A. and González-Burgos, G. (2008). Neuroplasticity of Neocortical Circuits in Schizophrenia. *Neuropsychopharmacology* 33, 141–65.

Little, A.C., Jones, B.C. and Burriss, R.P. (2007). Preferences for masculinity in male bodies change across the menstrual cycle. *Hormones and Behavior* 51, 633–9.

Locke, J.L. and Bogin, B. (2006). Language and life history: a new perspective on the development and evolution of human language. *Behavioral and Brain Science* 29, 259–325.

Lockhart, A.B., Thrall, P.H. and Antonovics, J. (1996). Sexually transmitted diseases in animals: ecological and evolutionary implications. *Biological Reviews of the Cambridge Philosophical Society* 71, 415–71.

Lovejoy, C.O. (2005). The natural history of human gait and posture: part I. Spine and pelvis. *Gait and Posture* 21, 95–112.

Luna, B., Garver, K.E., Urban, T.A., Lazar, N.A. and Sweeney, J.A. (2004). Maturation of cognitive processes from late childhood to adulthood. *Child Development* 75, 1357–72.

Maccoby, E.E. (1991). Different reproductive strategies in males and females. *Child Development* 62, 676–81.

Maggini, C., Lundgren, E. and Leuci, E. (2006). Jealous love and morbid jealousy. *Acta Biomedica* 77, 137–46.

Malamitsi-Puchner, A. and Boutsikou, T. (2006). Adolescent pregnancy and perinatal outcome. *Pediatric Endocrinology Reviews* 3, supplement 1, 170–1.

Makinson, C. (1985). The health consequences of teenage fertility. *Family Planning Perspectives* 17, 132–9.

Manzanares, J., Ortiz, S., Oliva, J.M., Pérez-Rial, S. and Palomo, T. (2005). Interactions between cannabinoid and opioid receptor systems in the mediation of ethanol effects. *Alcohol and Alcoholism* 40, 25–34.

Marlowe, F.W. (2004). Is human ovulation concealed? Evidence from conception beliefs in a hunter-gatherer society. *Archives of Sexual Behavior* 33, 427–33.

Martin, J.T. and Nguyen, D.H. (2004). Anthropometric analysis of homosexuals and heterosexuals: implications for early hormone exposure. *Hormones and Behavior* 45, 31–9.

Masterson, J. (1972), *Treatment of the borderline adolescent*. New York: Wiley.

Mayr, E. (2002). *What Evolution Is*. New York: Basic Books.

Mazur, A. and Booth, A. (1998). Testosterone and dominance in men. *Behavioral and Brain Sciences* 21, 353–63.

McEwen, B.S. (1999). Permanence of brain sex differences and structural plasticity of the adult brain. *Proceedings of the National Academy of Sciences USA* 96, 7128–30.

McGivern, R.F., Andersen, J., Byrd, D., Mutter, K.L. and Reilly, J. (2002). Cognitive efficiency on a match to sample task decreases at the onset of puberty in children. *Brain and Cognition* 50, 73–89.

McMichael, A.J. (2004). Environmental and social influences on emerging infectious diseases: past, present and future. *Philosophical Transactions of the Royal Society of London B Biological Sciences* 359, 1049–58.

Meinhardt, U.J. and Ho, K.K. (2006). Modulation of growth hormone by sex steroids. *Clinical Endocrinology* 65, 413–22.

Meloy, J.R. and Fisher, H. (2005). Some thoughts on the neurobiology of stalking. *Journal of Forensic Science* 50, 1472–80.

Mendoza, Antonio (2002). *Teenage Rampage: The Worldwide Youth Crime Phenomenon*. London: Virgin.

Menon, V. and Levitin, D.J. (2005). The rewards of music listening: response and physiological connectivity of the mesolimbic system. *Neuroimage* 28, 175–84.

Meyer, C., Jung, C., Kohl, T., Poenicke, A., Poppe, A. and Alt, K.W. (2002). Syphilis 2001 – a palaeopathological reappraisal. *Homo* 53, 39–58.

Michaud, P.A., Suris, J.C. and Deppen, A. (2006). Gender-related psychological and behavioural correlates of pubertal timing in a national sample of Swiss adolescents. *Mol Cell Endocrinol.* 254-255, 25 Jul 2006, 172–8.

Michener, W., Rozin, P., Freeman, E. and Gale, L. (1999). The role of low progesterone and tension as triggers of perimenstrual chocolate and sweets craving: some negative experimental evidence. *Physiology & Behavior* 67, 417–20.

Milham, M.P., Nugent, A.C., Drevets, W.C., Dickstein, D.P., Leibenluft, E., Ernst, M., Charney, D. and Pine, D.S. (2005). Selective reduction in amygdala volume in pediatric anxiety disorders: a voxel-based morphometry investigation. *Biological Psychiatry* 57, 961–6.

Miller, G. (2000). Sexual selection for indicators of intelligence. *Novartis Foundation Symposium* 233, 260–70.

Miller, N.S., Mahler, J.C. and Gold, M.S. (1991). Suicide risk associated with drug and alcohol dependence. *Journal of Addictive Diseases* 10, 49–61.

Mithen, S. (2007). Did farming arise from a misapplication of social intelligence? *Philosophical Transactions of the Royal Society of London B Biological Sciences* 362, 702–18.

Mittal, V.A., Tessner, K.D. and Walker, E.F. (2007). Elevated social Internet use and schizotypal personality disorder in adolescents. *Schizophrenia Research* 94, 50–7.

Molez, J.F. (2006). A comparative study of the emergence of the AIDS and syphilis pandemics (in French). *Santé* 16, 215–53.

Monti-Bloch, L., Jennings-White, C., Dolberg, D.S. and Berliner, D.L. (2000). Have dual survival systems created the human mind? *Psychoneuroendocrinology* 63, 178–201.

Moller, L. (2000). The human vomeronasal system. *Psychiatry* 63, 178–201.

Morrison, M.A., Smith, D.E., Wilford, B.B., Ehrlich, P. and Seymour, R.B. (1993). At war in the fields of play: current perspectives on the nature and treatment of adolescent chemical dependency. *Journal of Psychoactive Drugs* 25, 321–30.

Muscarella, F., Cevallos, A.M., Siler-Knogl, A. and Peterson, L.M. (2005). The alliance theory of homosexual behavior and the perception of social status and reproductive opportunities. *Neuro Endocrinology Letters* 26, 771–4.

Myers, D.P. and Andersen, A.R. (1991). Adolescent addiction. Assessment and identification. *Journal of Pediatric Health Care* 5, 86–93.

Nebert, D.W. and Dieter, M.Z. (2000). The evolution of drug metabolism. *Pharmacology* 61, 124–35.

Nesse, R.M. and Berridge, K.C. (1997). Psychoactive drug use in evolutionary perspective. *Science* 278, 63–6.

Neumann, C.S. and Walker, E.F. (2003). Neuromotor functioning in adolescents with schizotypal personality disorder: associations with symptoms and neurocognition. *Schizophrenia Bulletin* 29, 285–98.

Nunn, C.L., Gittleman, J.L. and Antonovics, J. (2000). Promiscuity and the primate immune system. *Science* 290, 1168–70.

O'Brien, C.P. (2007). Brain development as a vulnerability factor in the etiology of substance abuse and addicton. In Romer, D. and Walker, E.F. eds. *Adolescent Psychopathology and the Developing Brain.* Oxford: Oxford University Press.

O'Brien, E.M. and Mindell, J.A. (2005). Sleep and risk-taking behavior in adolescents. *Behavioral Sleep Medicine* 3, 113–33.

Ochsner, K.N. (2004). Current directions in social cognitive neuroscience. *Current Opinion in Neurobiology* 14, 254–8.

Oinonen, K.A. and Mazmanian, D. (2007). Facial symmetry detection ability changes across the menstrual cycle. *Biological Psychology* 75, 136–45.

Ong, K.K., Ahmed, M.L. and Dunger, D.B. (2006). Lessons from large population studies on timing and tempo of puberty (secular trends and relation to body size): the European trend. *Molecular and Cellular Endocrinology* 254-255, 8–12.

Paul, T., Zijdenbos, A., Worsley, K., Collins, D.L., Blumenthal, J., Giedd, J.N., Rapoport, J.L. and Evans, A.C. (1999). Structural maturation of neural pathways in children and adolescents: in vivo study. *Science* 283, 1908–11.

Pawlowski, B. and Grabarczyk, M. (2003). Center of body mass and the evolution of female body shape. *American Journal of Human Biology* 15, 144–50.

Penn, D.J. and Smith, K.R. (2007). Differential fitness costs of reproduction between the sexes. *Proceedings of the National Academy of Sciences USA* 104, 553–8.

Porter, M.W. (2001). Why do we have apocrine and sebaceous glands? *Journal of the Royal Society of Medicine* 94, 236–7.

Provost, M.P., Quinsey, V.L. and Troje, N.F. (2007). Differences in Gait Across the Menstrual Cycle and Their Attractiveness to Men. *Archives of Sexual Behavior* 37, 598–604.

Quinlivan, J.A. (2004). Teenagers who plan parenthood. *Sexual Health* 1, 201–8.

Rapoport, S.I. (1999). How did the human brain evolve? A proposal based on new evidence from *in vivo* brain imaging during attention and ideation. *Brain Research Bulletin* 50, 149–65.

Réale, D., Reader, S.M., Sol, D., McDougall, P.T. and Dingemanse, N.J. (2007). Integrating animal temperament within ecology and evolution. *Biological Reviews of the Cambridge Philosophical Society* 82, 291–318.

Rhodes, G. (2006). The evolutionary psychology of facial beauty. *Annual Review of Psychology* 57, 199–226.

Rhodes, G., Chan, J., Zebrowitz, L.A. and Simmons, L.W. (2003). Does sexual dimorphism in human faces signal health? *Proceedings of the Royal Society: Biological Sciences* 270, supplement 1, s93–5.

Rikowski, A. and Grammer, K. (1999). Human body odour, symmetry and attractiveness. *Proceedings of the Royal Society: Biological Sciences* 266, 869–74.

Ritchey, P.N., Reid, G.S. and Hasse, L.A. (2001). The relative influence of smoking on drinking and drinking on smoking among high school students in a rural tobacco-growing county. *Journal of Adolescent Health* 29, 386–94.

Robinson, L. (1892). On a possible obsolete function of the axillary and pubic hair tufts in man. *Journal of Anatomy and Physiology* 26, 254–7.

Rosenfeld, R.G. (2004). Gender differences in height: an evolutionary perspective. *Journal of Pediatric Endocrinology and Metabolism* 17, supplement 4, 1267–71.

Rosenfeld, R.G. and Nicodemus, B.C. (2003). The transition from adolescence to adult life: physiology of the 'transition phase' and its evolutionary basis. *Hormone Research* 60, supplement 1, 74–7.

Ryder, J.J., Webberley, K.M., Boots, M. and Knell, R.J. (2005). Measuring the transmission dynamics of a sexually transmitted disease. *Proceedings of the National Academy of Sciences USA* 102, 15140–3.

Savin-Williams, R.C. and Cohen, K.M. (2004). Homoerotic development during childhood and adolescence. *Child and Adolescent Psychiatric Clinics of North America* 13, 529–49.

Scherf, K.S., Sweeney, J.A. and Luna, B. (2006). Brain basis of developmental change in visuospatial working memory. *Journal of Cognitive Neuroscience* 18, 1045–58.

Schlegel, A. (1995). Cross-cultural approach to adolescence. *Ethos* 23, 15–32.

Scholl, T.O., Hediger, M.L., Schall, J.I., Khoo, C.S. and Fischer, R.L. (1994). Maternal growth during pregnancy and the competition for nutrients. *American Journal of Clinical Nutrition* 60, 183–8.

Schneider, J.E. (2006). Metabolic and hormonal control of the desire for food and sex: implications for obesity and eating disorders. *Hormones and Behavior* 50, 562–71.

Schultz, W. (2004). Neural coding of basic reward terms of animal learning theory, game theory, microeconomics and behavioural ecology. *Current Opinion in Neurobiology* 14, 139–47.

Schuster, M.A., Bell, R.M. and Kanouse, D.E. (1996). The sexual practices of adolescent virgins: genital sexual activities of high school students who have never had vaginal intercourse. *American Journal of Public Health* 86, 1570–6.

Seeman, E. (2001). Sexual dimorphism in skeletal size, density and strength. *Journal of Clinical Endocrinology and Metabolism* 86, 4576–84.

Segalowitz, S.J. and Davies, P.L. (2004). Charting the maturation of the frontal lobe: an electrophysiological strategy. *Brain and Cognition* 55, 116–33.

Sharp, F.R. and Hendren, R.L. (2007). Psychosis: atypical limbic epilepsy versus limbic hyperexcitability with onset at puberty? *Epilepsy & Behavior* 10, 515–20.

Shilling, P.D., Kuczenski, R., Segal, D.S., Barrett, T.B. and Kelsoe, J.R. (2006). Differential regulation of immediate-early gene expression in the prefrontal cortex of rats with a high vs low behavioral response to methamphetamine. *Neuropsychopharmacology* 31, 2359–67.

Silverman, I., Choi, J., Mackewn, A., Fisher, M., Moro, J. and Olshansky, E. (2000). Evolved mechanisms underlying wayfinding. Further studies on the hunter-gatherer theory of spatial sex differences. *Evolution and Human Behavior* 21, 201–13.

Skegg, K. (2005). Self-harm. *Lancet* 366, 1471–83.

Slotkin, T.A. (2002). Nicotine and the adolescent brain: insights from an animal model. *Neurotoxicology and Teratology* 24, 369–84.

Smith, A.M., Kelly, R.B. and Chen, W.J. (2002). Chronic continuous nicotine exposure during periadolescence does not increase ethanol intake during adulthood in rats. *Alcoholism: Clinical and Experimental Research* 26, 976–9.

Snowdon, C.T., Ziegler, T.E., Schultz-Darken, N.J. and Ferris, C.F. (2006). Social odours, sexual arousal and pairbonding in primates. *Philosophical Transactions of the Royal Society of London B Biological Sciences* 361, 2079–89.

Sowell, E.R., Peterson, B.S., Kan, E., Woods, R.P., Yoshii, J., Bansal, R., Xu, D., Zhu, H., Thompson, P.M. and Toga, A.W. (2007). Links Sex Differences in Cortical Thickness Mapped in 176 Healthy Individuals between 7 and 87 Years of Age. *Cerebral Cortex* 17, 1550–60.

Sowell, E.R., Peterson, B.S., Thompson, P.M., Welcome, S.E., Henkenius, A.L. and Toga, A.W. (2003). Mapping cortical change across the human life span. *Nature Neuroscience* 6, 309–15.

Sowell, E.R., Thompson, P.M., Holmes, C.J., Batth, R., Jernigan, T.L. and Toga, A.W. (2002). Localizing age related changes in brain structure between childhood and adolescence. *Neuroimage* 9, 587–97.

Sowell, E.R., Thompson, P.M. and Toga, A.W. (2007). Mapping adolescent brain maturation using structural magnetic resonance imaging. In Romer, D. and Walker, E.F. eds. *Adolescent Psychopathology and the Developing Brain*. Oxford: Oxford University Press.

Spear, L.P. (2000). The adolescent brain and age-related behavioral manifestations. *Neuroscience & Biobehavioral Reviews* 24, 417–63.

Spear (2007). The developing brain and adolescent-typical behaviour patterns: an evolutionary approach. In Romer, D. and Walker, E.F. eds. *Adolescent Psychopathology and the Developing Brain*. Oxford: Oxford University Press.

Sperry, R. (1982). Some effects of disconnecting the cerebral hemispheres. *Science* 217, 1223–6.

Sullivan, R.J. and Hagen, E.H. (2002). Psychotropic substance-seeking: evolutionary pathology or adaptation? *Addiction* 97, 389–400.

Swaab, D.F., Gooren, L.J. and Hofman, M.A. (1995). Brain research, gender and sexual orientation. *Journal of Homosexuality* 28, 283–301.

Takahashi, H., Matsuura, M., Yahata, N., Koeda, M., Suhara, T. and Okubo, Y. (2006). Men and women show distinct brain activations during imagery of sexual and emotional infidelity. *Neuroimage* 32, 1299–1307.

Terasawa, E. and Fernandez, D.L. (2001). Neurobiological mechanisms of the onset of puberty in primates. *Endocrine Reviews* 22, 111–51.

Thomas, K.M., Drevets, W.C., Dahl, R.E., Ryan, N.D.,

Birmaher, B., Eccard, C.H., Axelson, D., Whalen, P.J. and Casey, B.J. (2001). Amygdala response to fearful faces in anxious and depressed children. *Archives of General Psychiatry* 58, 1057–63.

Thompson, P.M., Giedd, J.N., Woods, R.P., MacDonald, D., Evans, A.C. and Toga, A.W. (2000). Growth patterns in the developing brain detected by using continuum mechanical tensor maps. *Nature* 404, 190–3.

Todd, R.D. and Botteron, K.N. (2001). Family, genetic, and imaging studies of early-onset depression. *Child and Adolescent Psychiatric Clinics of North America* 10, 375–90.

Tosevski, J. and Tosevski, D.L. (2006). Concealed female external genitals: possible morpho-psychological clue to unique emotional and congnitive evolutionary matrix of man. *Medical Science Monitor* 12, 11–19.

Tucker, D.M. and Moller, L. (2007). The metamorphosis: individuation of the adolescent brain. In Romer, D. and Walker, E.F. eds. *Adolescent Psychopathology and the Developing Brain*. Oxford: Oxford University Press.

Upadhyaya, H.P., Deas, D., Brady, K.T. and Kruesi, M.A. (2002). Cigarette smoking and psychiatric comorbidity in children and adolescents. *Journal of the American Academy of Child and Adolescent Psychiatry* 41, 1294–1305.

Uvnäs-Moberg, K., Bjökstrand, E., Hillegaart, V. and Ahlenius, S. (1999). Oxytocin as a possible mediator of SSRI-induced antidepressant effects. *Psychopharmacology* 142, 95–101.

Wallace, J.M., Luther, J.S., Milne, J.S., Aitken, R.P., Redmer, D.A., Reynolds, L.P. and Hay, W.W. Jr (2006). Nutritional modulation of adolescent pregnancy outcome – a review. *Placenta* 27, supplement A, s61-28.

Wallen, K. (2001). Sex and context: hormones and primate

sexual motivation. *Hormones and Behavior* 40, 339–57.

Wallen, K. and Zehr, J.L. (2004). Hormones and History: the evolution and development of primate female sexuality. *Journal of Sex Research* 41, 101–2.

Wang, M.H. and vom Saal, F.S. (2000). Maternal age and traits in offspring. *Nature* 407, 469–70.

Ward, H. (2007). Prevention strategies for sexually transmitted infections: importance of sexual network structure and epidemic phase. *Sexually Transmitted Infections* 83, supplement 1, 143–9.

Weisfeld, G.E. (1999), *Evolutionary Principles of Human Adolescence*. New York: Basic Books.

Weisfeld, G.E. (2006). Uniqueness of human childhood and adolescence? *Behavioural and Brain Sciences* 29, 298–300.

Weisfeld, G.E., Czilli, T., Phillips, K.A., Gall, J.A. and Lichtman, C.M. (2003). Possible olfaction-based mechanisms in human kin recognition and inbreeding avoidance. *Journal of Experimental Child Psychology* 85, 279–95.

Weisfeld, G.E. and Woodward, L. (2004). Current evolutionary perspectives on adolescent romantic relations and sexuality. *Journal of the American Academy for Child and Adolescent Psychiatry* 43, 11–19.

Wellings, K., Collumbien, M., Slaymaker, E., Singh, S., Hodges, Z., Patel, D. and Bajos, N. (2006). Sexual behaviour in context: a global perspective. *Lancet* 368, 1706–28.

Wellings, K. and Field, B. (1996). Sexual behaviour in young people. *Baillière's Clinical Obstetrics and Gynaecology* 10, 139–60.

Wellings, K., Wadsworth, J., Johnson, A., Field, J. and Macdowall, W. (1999). Teenage fertility and life chances. *Reviews of Reproduction* 4, 184–90.

White, A., Bae, J., Truesdale, M., Ahmad, S., Wilson, W. and Swartzwelder, H.S. (2002). Chronic intermittent alcohol exposure during adolescence prevents normal developmental changes in sensitivity to alcohol-induced motor impairments. *Alcoholism: Clinical and Experimental Research* 26, 960–8.

Whitlock, K.E., Illing, N., Brideau, N.J., Smith, K.M. and Twomey, S.A. (2006). Development of GnRH cells: setting the stage for puberty. *Molecular and Cellular Endocrinology* 254-255, 39–50.

Wiers, R.W., Bartholow, B.D., van den Wildenberg, E., Thush, C., Engels, R.C., Sher, K.J., Grenard, J., Ames, S.L. and Stacy, A.W. (2007). Automatic and controlled processes and the development of addictive behaviors in adolescents: a review and a model. *Pharmacology Biochemistry and Behavior* 86, 263–83.

Worret, W.I. (2002). Screening for depression in adult acne vulgaris patients: tools for the dermatologist. *Journal of Cosmetic Dermatology* 1, 202–7.

Yacubian, J., Sommer, T., Schroeder, K., Gläscher, J., Kalisch, R., Leuenberger, B., Braus, D.F. and Büchel, C. (2007). Gene-gene interaction associated with neural reward sensitivity. *Proceedings of the National Academy of Sciences USA* 104, 8125–30.

Yuferov, V., Fussell, D., LaForge, K.S., Nielsen, D.A., Gordon, D., Ho, A., Leal, S.M., Ott, J. and Kreek, M.J. (2004). Redefinition of the human kappa opioid receptor gene (OPRK1) structure and association of haplotypes with opiate addiction. *Pharmacogenetics* 14, 793–804.

Yun, A.J., Bazar, K.A. and Lee, P.Y. (2004). Pineal attrition, loss of cognitive plasticity, and onset of puberty during the teen years: is it a modern maladaptation exposed by evolutionary displacement? *Medical Hypotheses* 63, 939–50.

Yurgelun-Todd, D.A., Killgore, W.D. and Cintron, C.B. (2003). Cognitive correlates of medial temporal lobe development across adolescence: a magnetic resonance imaging study. *Perceptual & Motor Skills* 96, 3–17.

Zehr, J.L., Maestripieri, D. and Wallen, K. (1998). Estradiol increases female sexual initiation independent of male responsiveness in rhesus monkeys. *Hormones and Behavior* 33, 95–103.

Zeki, S. (2007). The neurobiology of love. *FEBS Letters* 581, 2575–9.

Zhang, P.W., Ishiguro, H., Ohtsuki, T., Hess, J., Carillo, F., Walther, D., Onaivi, E.S., Arinami, T. and Uhl, G.R. (2004). Human cannabinoid receptor 1: 5' exons, candidate regulatory regions, polymorphisms, haplotypes and association with polysubstance abuse. *Molecular Psychiatry* 9, 916–31.

Index

creativity, 135, 152, 211–12, 310
crime, 126–7, 175
cryptorchidism, 254

decision-making, 136
depression
    and anxiety, 196, 217
    causes, 176, 193–6, 208
    clinical, 194, 196–8, 201–2
    drugs that help and their side
        effects, 202–3, 241
    and love, 238
    reasons for teenage, 198–203
    and teenage pregnancy, 283
    thought processes of, 196–8
desire see sexual attractiveness
DHEA
    (dehydroepiandrosterone), 38
diaries, 9–10, 13
DNA, 86, 247–9
dolphins, 79, 253
dominance, 127, 228
dopamine
    and drugs, 155, 159–62
    and learning, 132, 133–6
    and love, 240–1
    overview of effects, 119
    and risk-taking, 119–21
    and schizophrenia, 213, 214
drugs
    addiction process, 153, 159–63
    addictiveness of different
        types, 171
    adverse effects and dangers,
        170–7, 182
    animals and psychotic drugs,
        150–1
    contemporary availability, 153
    craving, 157–8

cross-drug tolerance, 179
    dependency, 157
    effects on the brain, 154–6
    frequency of use of different
        types, 171
    history of use, 150–2
    origins, 146–50
    positive effects, 152, 181
    progression from 'soft' to
        'hard', 177–81
    reasons for contemporary
        increase in addiction, 152–3
    reasons for need for increasing
        doses, 162
    teenage reaction to, 167–9
    teenage use, 163–82
    to help depression, 202–3, 241
    tolerance, 157
    toxicity of different types, 171
    triggers to drug use, 164–7
    unreliability of advice to
        teenagers, 2, 143
    variations in sensitivity to,
        179–81
    see also addiction
ducks, 250
dyslexia, 140

eating disorders, 57, 174, 196,
    230–1, 259
eccrine sweat glands, 47–8
ecstasy (MDMA), 148, 155, 172–3
education
    general, 129–30, 141
    sex, 277
    see also learning
eggs, 247
elephants, 253, 254, 309
embryos, 82

genes
   and age of onset of puberty,
      258
   and the brain, 86–7
   and drug susceptibility, 180–1
   and eating disorders, 231
   and homosexuality, 291
   and pheromones, 299–300
   and schizophrenia, 212–13
   see also DNA
genitals, 249–54
girls and women
   abilities to assess suitability of
      mates, 301
   age at first intercourse, 265–6
   age of onset of puberty, 38–9,
      262–3
   age of reproductive maturity,
      62–4
   and anger and aggression,
      124–8
   athletic abilities, 57
   attitudes to first intercourse,
      266
   body and facial hair, 47
   body shape, 55–61
   body shapes preferred by
      males, 296–7
   brains and minds, 89–96, 100,
      104, 140
   carrying styles, 58
   chromosomes and sex
      allocation, 31
   and cognition, 140–1
   and communicating, 141
   competitiveness, 229
   and control over sex, 303
   and depression, 199–200
   faces and voices, 61

fat stores, 57–8
and fear, 124
and friendship, 226–7
genitals, 251
height and growth, 64–72,
   66
importance of physical
   attractiveness, 229–31
and jealousy, 125
and language, 140–1
leptin levels, 261
limb shape and size, 58–9
longevity, 308
and love, 235
MHC genes and propensity
   for affairs, 300
and movement and walking,
   57, 59–60
neonatal reproductive activity,
   37
puberty stages, 41–2
pubic hair, 43–4, 45–6
reasons for early maturity, 71,
   272
reasons for not going into
   heat, 302
rejection of parents, 221–2
and reproduction, 17
risks of teenage pregnancy,
   282–8
sexual behaviour, 96–100, 235
sexual dysfunction, 304
strength and muscle, 57
types of male preferred by,
   295, 297, 298
and weight gain, 58
glandular fever, 198
globus pallidus, 94, 95
glutamate, 34, 214